Place, Space and the
New Labour
Internationalisms

Edited by
Peter Waterman
and
Jane Wills

First published as a special issue of *Antipode* Vol.33, No. 3, 2001

Blackwell Publishers Ltd
108 Cowley Road
Oxford OX4 1JF
UK

Blackwell Publishers Inc.
350 Main Street
Malden, Massachusetts 02148
USA

British Library Cataloguing in Publication Data
A CIP catalogue record for this book is available from the British Library.

Library of Congress Cataloging-in-Publication Data has been applied for

ISBN: 0-631-22983-3

Typeset in Great Britain by Advance Typesetting Ltd, Oxon.
Printed in Great Britain by MPG Books Ltd, Bodmin, Cornwall

This book is printed on acid-free paper.

PLACE, SPACE AND
INTERNATI

About the cover

La Solidaridad Obrera No Tiene Fronteras (Labour Solidarity Has No Frontiers) is one of a series of five murals produced by US labour movement artist, Mike Alewitz. Entitled *The Worker in the New World Order*, this was produced for the International Federation of Chemical, Energy, Mine and General Workers Unions (ICEM). The series can be found at http://www.icem.org/ gallery/ gallery.html.

Apart from the influences of the Mexican tradition of left (and internationalist) murals, this one makes evident reference to the drawing by British socialist artist Walter Crane, *Labour's Mayday*, which was "dedicated to the workers of the world", and produced for the International Socialist and Trades Union Congress, 1896. More of Crane's work can be found on the website of the International Institute of Social History, Amsterdam, at http://www.iisg.nl/exhibitions/art/indexcrane.html.

The Editors

Contents

Antipode

Edited by
Jamie Peck and Jane Wills

For 30 years *Antipode* has been the place to publish radical scholarship in geography. The journal attracts the best and most provocative of radical geographical theory and research, particularly that which contributes to politics and practice. *Antipode* has an ecumenical approach to radical geography. It aims to challenge dominant and orthodox views of the world through debate, scholarship and politically-committed research, creating new spaces and envisioning new futures.

Antipode welcomes the infusion of new ideas and the shaking up of old positions, without being committed to just one view of radical analysis or politics. The editors are especially seeking papers that address questions of radical political economy, emerging forms of political protest, radical social theory, and practical strategies for achieving progressive change. In addition to publishing academic papers, *Antipode* has space to publish short polemical interventions and longer, more reflective, explorations of radical geography in particular fields or locations.

Visit the *Antipode* home page for up-to-date contents listings, editorial information, submission guidelines, and ordering information:

www.blackwellpublishers.co.uk/journals/anti

ISSN: 0066-4812, VOLUME 34 (2002), 5 ISSUES PER YEAR

108 Cowley Road, Oxford OX4 1JF, UK
350 Main Street, Malden, MA 02148, USA

1
Place, Space and the New Labour Internationalisms: Beyond the Fragments?

Peter Waterman and Jane Wills

[I]nternationalism ought to consist, not only in listening attentively to an internationalist discourse, but in contributing to it on our own account. We are not truly present in any conversation if we are only silent auditors ... Internationalism should not be like a net-work of television stations, each beaming national programmes to passive viewers in alien lands. It should be a concourse, an exchange. (Thompson 1978:iv)

The solution ... needs more than just ad hoc contact between the different movements. Neither is the merging of the movements any solution; there are good reasons for each movement preserving its autonomy, controlling its own organisation. For women, blacks, trade unionists, gays, youth and national minorities have specific interests which may sometimes be antagonistic to each other both now and probably in a socialist society. The solution lies in bringing together all those involved in the different movements and campaigns who agree on a wider programme of socialist change, based on demands of the different movements in the context of organising for social ownership and popular political power. (Rowbotham, Segal and Wainwright 1979:5–6)

A network ... is a set of interconnected nodes—and has no centre ... [D]ominant activities in our societies are made of networks: global financial markets; production and consumption organised around the network enterprise ... global/local media connected in the electronic hypertext ... the network state, made of supranational, national, regional and local institutions lining up to exert joint influence on global flows of wealth and information ... I would also add that, increasingly, counterdomination operates through networks as well, as in the case of the environmental movement, or of countercultural movements, or human rights organisations, linking up the local and the global through the Internet. Because networks are extremely efficient organisations, they eliminate, through competition, alternative structures, so their logic expands. (Castells 2000:110)

In the wake of antiglobalisation protests in Seattle, Washington, Davos, Prague and Porto Alegre (not to speak of such localised anti-global protests as those in Cochabamba in Bolivia, in India and both inside and outside French outlets of McDonalds), increasing numbers of people are taking part in dialogues about the theory and practice of internationalism. There is renewed energy to find alternatives to neo-liberal globalisation, and it is becoming more widely acknowledged that labour/union internationalism is central to the struggle. Yet, as presently constituted, trade unions appear ill suited to the coalition politics and alliance-building so critical to contemporary countercultural protest.

The present collection of arguments about labour internationalism provides both a critique of the prevailing order of things in the labour movement and a contribution to discussion about alternatives to such. In the post-Seattle period, at a time in which international unions, labour-oriented NGOs and related social movements are coming together to discuss common international strategies in the light of globalisation, we hope this collection will be seen as both an original and a timely publication.

Classically, labour internationalism has been thought of, or fought for, in terms of a homogeneous working class—seen as the universal emancipatory subject. This internationalism has been mostly discussed in terms of political economy, whether of the left or the centre. As the development of capitalism was accompanied by a state-defined nationalism, political economy often followed this course, contrasting the international nature of capitalism with the national nature of the state. Within this tradition, trade union internationalism came to mean the interrelation of national trade union bodies, whether this combination was to serve reformist, revolutionary, practical or moral goals. The labour internationalism of the national/industrial capitalist period eventually declined into institutionally defined trade union forms, mirroring the ritualistic procedures of interstate and interorganisational politics.

In the meantime, what in the 1970s and 1980s was called "the internationalisation of production" has transmogrified into something much more general, called "neoliberalism" or "globalisation", *"mondialisation"* or other names, each with disputed meanings. Whatever name we give to this process, however, there is increasing agreement on both the political and theoretical left that it is undermining or transforming the state-defined nation, industrial relations, the welfare or collectivist state, the trade union, the "homogeneous" working class and such formalised union internationalism as remains. It has also, of course, undermined traditional ways of viewing and understanding the world. As the intellectual and activist left splintered into different bodies of thought and action, reflected in the growth of academic feminism, social geography, cultural studies and environmentalism, worldviews have also been crafted that look beyond nation-states. Radical geography has itself given particular attention to the differing roles of gender, race, sexuality, labour and environmentalism in the production of place, space and scale inter/nationally (see Blunt and Wills 2000; Harvey 1996; Herod 1998, 2001; Massey 1994; McDowell 1999; Peck 1996).

Yet the question of whether we are finally moving "beyond the fragments" remains open. Scholars are still searching for ways in which complexity, difference and multideterminacy can be combined with a universalism relevant to the transformation of the contemporary world (Fraser 2000; Harvey 2000; McDowell 2000; Smith 2000). Radical thinkers and activists are still grappling with the challenges posed in the UK by Sheila Rowbotham, Lynne Segal and Hilary Wainwright (1979). In her introductory remarks to *Beyond the Fragments* (1979), Wainwright highlighted two problems to be faced in uniting a variety of political agents in the struggle for social change. The first was the need to find common cause while meeting the needs of all oppressed groups; the second was to unify popular protest from the community with that of workers in the workplace. She also used the word "socialism"—a word with a marginal presence, even today, in both the minds of intellectuals and the mouths of labour activists internationally.

In this collection, authors explore the ways in which labour can find both itself and its allies in international struggle to transform the present order of things. The politics of coalition and alliance are evidently and increasingly critical to the future of trade unionism and labour internationalism. Indeed, the relevant places/spaces of such new internationalisms must also surpass physical cartography to include those of cyberspace and utopia. Our contributors include internationally minded and labour-oriented academics alongside theoretically minded internationalist labour activists. This facilitates a critique of dominant, and even alternative, labour internationalisms alongside constructive proposals for the future—Gramsci's pessimism of the intellect combined with his optimism of the will. The contributions here are radical in that they look for the roots of the contemporary conjuncture while remaining engaged in struggle as it unfolds on the ground. Each grapples, in its own way, with the challenges faced by those seeking to reinvent the labour movement in order to meet the needs of working people worldwide.

In the first part of the collection, five authors outline some of the developments that are taking place as trade unions seek to respond to the challenges of globalisation. One attempts to provide a general orientation to labour internationalism. Others cover the creation of a new network of trade unions in the South (the Southern Initiative on Globalisation and Trade Union Rights, SIGTUR); the reconfiguration of trade union internationalism in Latin America (through reforms to the Organización Regional Interamericana de Trabajadores, ORIT); new international strategies developed by South African trade unions (taking the case of the South African Municipal Workers Union, SAMWU); and the different sociogeographic protest strategies that can be taken in the face of globalisation (illustrated by disputes at Ravenswood Aluminium Corporation and General Motors, US).

In the second part of the collection, contributors consider different aspects of contemporary labour internationalism at a variety of spatial scales. The section opens with the thorny issue of workers' rights being instituted in international trade, a matter hotly disputed amongst both labour and feminist activists. The next contribution puts flesh on the bones of this argument by addressing the opportunities that have arisen for cross-border mobilisation around violations of labour standards in the North American Free Trade Agreement (NAFTA) region. Echoing such debate about NAFTA, the following two essays consider the possibilities for international labour solidarity across and beyond Europe. The first sets the scene, outlining the implications of the single market for industrial relations and social standards; the second addresses the particular role of European Works Councils.

Contributors to the remainder of the collection raise long-neglected questions for labour organising at an international scale: the development of ethical trading initiatives; the growth of informal work; the particular kind of solidarity relevant to women workers in a Mexican city; and the necessity and possibilities of fostering "internationalism in one country" (the case of solidarity with immigrants in Florida, US). Each points to exciting new possibilities for building alliances and reviving labour/trade union internationalism. But the fragments are still here: the challenge—to the unions, to internationalist activists, to committed academics—remains.

Readers and reviewers will come to their own conclusions about whether this whole is more than the sum of its parts. We would like to believe that the collection reflects the spirit of Seattle, the growing feeling that there is an alternative, and that the institutions and ideology of neoliberal globalisation can be confronted. But what about the relationship between this global alternative and *socialism*? During the last international wave of radicalism, in the 1970s, socialism was the name of that alternative—even if 1968 was simultaneously a sign and cause of its fragmentation. In one of the most original of the contemporary books about the movement against "globalisation from above", however, alternatives are proposed to the processes of globalisation, rather than to capitalism itself (Brecher, Costello and Smith 2000). Socialism is still, to a considerable extent, a utopia that dare not speak its name, and our collection is no exception. It would be safe to say that most of our contributors *are* socialists, many of them from a recognisably Marxist tradition, yet we continue to avoid the ideology and utopia that inspired the internationalist waves of the 19th and 20th centuries. When, as a result of Seattle, even the dominant media inform us that we (or, rather, they) are confronted by an "anticapitalist" movement, is it not time to give this negative name a positive face? Perhaps, like Brecher, Costello and Smith, we believe it is possible to be a socialist internationalist without waving a red flag or singing the Internationale? Perhaps we feel that we should first nurture the seeds of a many-splendoured internationalism rather than overfertilising it with an excess of socialism? Or—to switch metaphors—that we need to take socialism on a long march, through the international social movements against globalisation, before arriving at a new Yenan? Ourselves people of different international Marxist traditions, of different generations and genders, we are happy to leave these questions hanging in the air for our readers to respond to—or for another international/ist collection to address.

Our attention is, however, firmly addressed to the contemporary theory and practice of labour and trade union internationalism. The past problems and present possibility of such come out of the quotations at the beginning of this introduction. Edward Thompson, last of the Old Testament prophets of the old internationalist left, was a lone voice crying in the wilderness of a national industrial capitalism. Then, as the quotation shows, networks were still hyphenated, but Thompson insisted even then that internationalism must be "a concourse, an exchange". Today Manuel Castells, theorist of a globalised capitalism, insists just as energetically on the centrality of the network (unhyphenated): it is the means of articulation not only for the forces of domination but also for what he calls countercultural, and we would call emancipatory, movements. Both the Castells of 2000 and the Thompson of 1978 are some way ahead of international labour realities. Indeed, an evaluation of the International Confederation of Free Trade Unions (ICFTU) campaign to get international labour standards under the jurisdiction of the World Trade Organisation reveals precisely the extent to which the most powerful national and international trade union organisations have been engaged in "beaming", in Thompsonian terms, a preconceived Northern programme to "passive viewers in alien lands" (Anner 2001).

As Castells suggests, the challenge for the new labour internationalisms is to recognise the ways in which capitalism is being transformed from a set of organisations into a collection of networks. Institutionalised labour internationalism is thus challenged, not only by such capitalist networking, but also by that of the anticapitalist movement worldwide—and by the increasing incidence of international labour networking! We predict that the new internationalist labour networking will transform the old international labour institutions. This collection is, finally then, dedicated to furthering this process.

Acknowledgements

We are very grateful to Ros Whitehead for superb editorial assistance in compiling this collection, and for making an onerous task a very enjoyable one. Alana Dave, Rebecca Johns and Carla Lipsig-Mummé took part in the early stages of this endeavour and we thank them for their enthusiastic response. We are sorry that the tight deadlines precluded their involvement in the final production. We would like to thank all those who took part in refereeing the contributions for this collection, and for doing so much to improve the quality and incisiveness of the text you read now. Last, but not least, this project has provided a wonderful opportunity to bring together a number of activists and scholars from different places and different generations. In talking to each other across traditional divides of age, location and occupation, we have identified a shared passion for the politics of international solidarity. It is in this spirit that the collection was conceived and produced, and it is our hope that you will read it with this vision in mind.

References

Anner M (2001) Evaluation Report: ICFTU Campaign for Core Labour Standards in the WTO. Oslo: The Norwegian Confederation of Trade Unions (LO-Norway)

Blunt A and Wills J (2000) *Dissident Geographies: An Introduction to Radical Ideas and Practice*. Harlow: Prentice Hall

Brecher J, Costello T and Smith B (2000) *Globalisation from Below: The Power of Solidarity*. Boston: South End Press

Castells M (2000) Globalisation and identity in the network society: A rejoinder to Calhoun, Lyon and Touraine. *Prometheus: Firing the Mind* 4:109–123

Fraser N (2000) Rethinking recognition. *New Left Review* 3:107–120

Harvey D (1996) *Justice, Nature and the Geography of Difference*. Oxford: Blackwell

Harvey D (2000) *Spaces of Hope*. Edinburgh: Edinburgh University Press

Herod A (ed)(1998) *Organising the Landscape*. Minneapolis: University of Minnesota Press

Herod A (2001) *Labour Geography: Workers and the Landscape of Capitalism*. London: Guilford

McDowell L (1999) *Gender, Identity and Place: Understanding Feminist Geographies*. Cambridge, UK: Polity Press

McDowell L (2000) Economy, culture, difference and justice. In I Cook, D Crouch, S Naylor and J R Ryan (eds) *Cultural Turns/Geographical Turns: Perspectives on Cultural Geography* (pp 182–195). Harlow: Prentice Hall

Massey, D. (1994) *Space, place and gender*. Cambridge, UK: Polity Press

Peck J (1996) *Work-Place: The Social Regulation of Labor Markets*. London: Guilford

Rowbothom S, Segal L and Wainwright H. (1979) *Beyond the Fragments: Feminism and the Making of Socialism*. London: Merlin Press

Smith D (2000) *Moral Geographies: Ethics in a World of Difference*. Edinburgh: Edinburgh University Press

Thompson E P (1978) *The Poverty of Theory and Other Essays*. London: Merlin Press

2

Trade Union Internationalism in the Age of Seattle

Peter Waterman

It is widely recognised within and around the labour movement that labour (as wage work, as class identity, in the trade union form, as a partner in industrial relations, as a radical-democratic social movement, as a part of civil society) is in profound crisis. Even more is this the case for labour as an international movement at a time in which the old international capitalist order is being challenged by the new capitalist disorder. Recovery requires a critique of traditional labour internationalism, reconceptualisation, new kinds of analysis and a new dialogue and dialectic between interested parties. Presented here in turn are the following: (1) a critique of the union internationalism of the national/industrial/colonial era; (2) a reconceptualisation of unionism and labour internationalism appropriate to a globalised/networked/informatised capitalist era; (3) the millennial dialogue on labour and globalisation; and (4) the role of communication, culture and the new information and communication technology. The conclusion stresses the centrality of networking, communication and dialogue to the creation of a new labour internationalism. An extended resource list on international unionism is attached.

Union Internationals and the National/Industrial/Colonial Era[1]

There have been and still are various types of "international" union organisation, such as: a marginal social-Christian one, now known as the World Confederation of Labour (WCL); autonomous regional ones, such as the Organisation of African Trade Union Unity; and even the US American Federation of Labor-Congress of Industrial Organisations (AFL-CIO), operating for decades as if it were a parallel and competing international, complete with its own regional institutions and operations. I will be unable to give the space deserved to such organisations as (1) the World Federation of Trade Unions (WFTU), which represents the Communist tradition of union inter-nationalism (Carew 2000; Silverman 2000), and which was in ideological/political competition with the International Confederation of Free Trade Unions (ICFTU) during the Cold War era; and (2) the industry-based International Trade Secretariats (ITSs), which represent a precursor to the literally inter/national (ie inter-state) type represented by the ICFTU (Fimmen 1924; Reinalda 1997). (Today, the ITSs also claim to represent a relevant alternative to the confederations of national unions, although they share a number of the structural limitations of those organisations.) The question remains of whether nationally or industrially based internationals or something rather different are most appropriate for a new *union*, *labour* or *general* internationalism in the era of globalisation. I hope this question can be adequately raised by considering the ICFTU alone.

The ICFTU is an organisation with 100 years of tradition behind it. It is backed by the overwhelming majority of Northern national unions; it won the trade union cold war. It has recruited to its ranks the major new radical national unions of the South, it claims 155 million members and it looks set to eventually gain those of China.[2] So why is it today in question, and even *self*-questioning? It is, I think, because this international confederation continues to express the national/industrial/colonial (NIC) capitalism that gave it birth and shape. The ICFTU is an international confederation of national(ist) union federations; themselves historically representing the male industrial worker in large-scale capitalist or state enterprise, seeking from employers and governments recognition, protection and representation within individual state-nations and a world of such. This tradition is one of competition/collaboration with Taylorism (the mass-production assembly line), Fordism (workers paid enough to become mass consumers of their own mass products), Keynesianism (social redistribution and welfare from growth) and state-nationalism (workers defined as national citizens in distinction from, competition with and even war against others).

Since the 1919 creation, under considerable labour movement pressure, of the International Labour Organisation (ILO), the ideology, institutions and procedures of "social partnership" have become hegemonic. The ICFTU internalised the tripartism of the ILO.[3] To tripartism there was added during the Cold War the ideology of "free" trade unionism, tending to identify the ICFTU with the "free world", led by the USA.[4] As colonialism (with which the ICFTU was complicit) collapsed, to this in turn there was added the ideology of "development" toward some implicit Swedish social utopia or Californian cornucopia. The international organisation was built on the model of the era, a nation-state-based and formally representative-democratic body addressed primarily to competition/collaboration with other union internationals and lobbying of inter-state organs. The internationalism this produced was a "national internationalism"

—the winning of social-democratic rights and standards within the liberal-democratic state-nation and the gaining of such state-nations for those workers previously denied them (apartheid South Africa, communist Poland).

On the ICFTU's 50th anniversary, a special issue of its journal *Trade Union World* (1999) presented itself in terms of "How the ICFTU Has Influenced Global Developments Year after Year". Van der Linden's (2000) impressive recent history of the ICFTU, which shares this institutional-evolutionary perspective, nonetheless reveals many problematic aspects of its half century. These include intimate—even symbiotic—relations with states, capital, empires and blocs, and even with their intelligence agencies. Equally revealed, and equally problematic, is the extent to which ICFTU policy has been determined by its major Northern national member organisations, and by the internecine (if customarily concealed) conflicts between its leading unions and officers. Indeed, one comes away from this book with the impression that the ICFTU is not so much the major tradition and leading force within the international labour movement as an international office or pressure group, relating to other national and inter-state and employers' organisations, quite separately from what might be going on amongst workers on the shop floor.

This feeling is reinforced by the conclusion to the 1972–1990s chapter of the book, which quotes one prominent Northern national leader's words to its 1975 Congress: "I do not know how many people in your own country are deeply aware and conscious of the existence of the ICFTU, but I suspect in my country it is very few ..." (van der Linden 2000:516). The author of this book-length chapter, Rebecca Gumbrell-McCormick (2000:517), concedes the point and recognises other limitations, but she asserts that "many workers in Africa, Chile or other trouble spots, where their colleagues have been arrested or killed, and others rescued through the intervention of the ICFTU or its affiliates, may well be aware of it, whether or not they know its name". Even if this is true, it still suggests a body more akin to the International Committee of the Red Cross than an international SMO (social movement organisation—a useful Americanism).

Nonetheless, one must avoid either demonising or dismissing the ICFTU. If workers had wanted a different ICFTU (or a different international union body), they would have organised to achieve one. The ICFTU could and possibly should be seen as operating a dependent, defensive and self-limiting operation, within and under NIC capitalism and despite the competition of communist unionism from the East and of radical-nationalist/populist unionism in the South.

The ongoing search for alternatives for or to the ICFTU is marked by global concerns and challenges. One major challenge has to do with the role of a literally inter*national* confederation in times of globalisation. The ICFTU is an institution formally subordinate to national(ist) unions, and—in terms of the politics of power and money that have dominated the ICFTU historically—to its richest and most powerful members. It is at the peak of a pyramidal structure several removes—and gatekeepers—away from any flesh-and-blood workers.[5] It is also an institution heavily incorporated into a traditional world of inter-state institutions, with much of its energy addressed to lobbying these. The second major challenge, to my mind, is the virtual *invisibility* of the ICFTU. Here is an organisation with 155 million members and rising that has no presence at all in the global media or culture, whether dominant, popular or alternative.

The ICFTU is changing. Both the extent and limits to this change were revealed at its Millennial Congress in 2000 Durban, South Africa (see South African Labour Bulletin 2000). Reflecting on it shortly afterwards, ICFTU General Secretary Bill Jordan said: "[I]n periods of revolutionary change, and we are in one now, we must be able to think and act outside the straight-jacket of our traditions ... The trade union movement, once again, needs new ideas for the needs of new workers, new occupations, new forms of work organisation, new employment relationships" (Jordan 2000). The Congress decided on a "millennial review" of the organisation to confront such challenges. However, we have no evidence that this review will be carried out in front of even the member unions, far less with the participation of the members of its members; or after consultation with the radical-democratic and internationalist public that the ICFTU is currently courting.

I think that the ICFTU and ITSs will inevitably add new elements to the old model of international trade unionism. Stuck with a communist and inter/nationalist tradition it can neither positively claim nor positively surpass, the WFTU is likely to remain simply as a warning of what happens if a labour organisation cannot come to terms with a past tradition, recognise the demands of the day and shape itself to meet the future. As for the rest of international unionism, if it is not to remain a prisoner of its past, seeking a return to some golden age of partnership between Labour, State and Capital (now on a world scale and allowing room for selected NGOs?), it is surely going to need an understanding of labour internationalism appropriate to our globalised capitalist disorder.[6]

Conceiving a New Labour Internationalism
There is increasing talk by academics and unionists alike of some kind of international or global "social movement unionism" (Ashwin 2000; Bezuidenhout 1999; Moody 1997). There is, however, a strange reluctance to conceptualise this (Munck 2000 is a partial exception). In the hope of provoking a critical response, I therefore want to present here three interrelated pieces of conceptualisation relevant to the matter.

A New Social Unionism[7]
By "new social unionism", I mean one surpassing existing models of "economic", "political" or "political-economic" unionism by addressing itself to all forms of work, by taking on sociocultural forms and by addressing itself to civil society. Such a union model would be one that would, amongst other things, be:

- Struggling within and around waged work, not simply for better wages and conditions but for increased worker and union control over the labour process, investments, new technology, relocation, subcontracting, training and education policies. Such strategies and struggles should be carried out in dialogue and common action with affected communities and interests so as to avoid conflicts (with, eg, environmentalists or women) and to positively increase the appeal of the demands
- Struggling against hierarchical, authoritarian and technocratic working methods and relations, for socially-useful and environmentally-friendly products, for a reduction in the hours of work, for the distribution of that which is available and necessary, for the sharing of domestic work and for an increase in free time for cultural self-development and self-realisation
- Intimately related to the movements of other nonunionised or nonunionisable working classes or categories (petty-commodity sector, homeworkers, peasants, housewives, technicians and professionals)
- Intimately related to other non- or multiclass democratic movements (base movements of churches, women's, residents', ecological, human rights and peace movements, etc) in the effort to create a powerful and diverse civil society
- Intimately related to other (potential) allies as an autonomous, equal and democratic partner, neither claiming to be nor subordinating itself to a "vanguard" or "sovereign" organisation or power

- Taking up the new social issues within society at large, as they arise for workers specifically and as they express themselves within the union itself (struggle against authoritarianism, majoritarianism, bureaucracy, sexism, racism and so on)
- Favouring shop floor democracy and encouraging direct horizontal relations both between workers and between the workers and other popular/democratic social forces
- Active on the terrain of education, culture and communication, stimulating worker and popular culture, supporting initiatives for democracy and pluralism both inside and outside the dominant institutions or media, locally, nationally and globally
- Open to networking both within and between organisations, understanding the value of informal, horizontal, flexible coalitions, alliances and interest groups to stimulate organisational democracy, pluralism and innovation.

Over the years, various writers have identified "social movement unionism" with (1) particular national organisations, (2) left or militant union tendencies and (3) the South.[8] I believe that this represents an analytical, theoretical and strategic error. *Analytically*, it tends to identify as "social movement unions" those involved in various kinds of *labour-popular* alliance, primarily during (semi)insurrectionary movements against military/right-authoritarian regimes. *Theoretically*, it tends to reduce a conceptual category to an analytical one, thus preventing its critical application to the evidence offered. *Strategically*, it tends to make social movement unionism a characteristic of one world area, at a time in which globalisation is homogenising/ diversifying the world in ways that both require and make possible the search for universal (not universalistic) alternatives.

A New Labour Internationalism
Insofar as this addresses itself to the problems of a globalised national industrial (GNI) capitalism (of which inter-state relations are but one part), a new labour internationalism would have to see itself as part of a general global solidarity movement, from which it must learn and to which it must contribute. A new kind of labour internationalism implies, amongst other things:

- Moving from the international relations of union or other officials towards face-to-face relations of concerned labouring people at the shop floor, community or grassroots level

- Surpassing dependence on the centralised, bureaucratic and rigid model of the pyramidal international organisation by stimulating the self-empowering, decentralised, horizontal, democratic and flexible model of the international information network
- Moving from an "aid model" (one-way flows of money and material from the "rich, powerful, free" unions, workers or others), to a "solidarity model" (two-way or multidirectional flows of political support, information and ideas)
- Moving from verbal declarations, appeals and conferences to political activity, creative work, visits or direct financial contributions (which will continue to be necessary) by the working people concerned
- Basing international solidarity on the expressed daily needs, values and capacities of ordinary working people, not simply on those of their representatives
- Recognising that, whilst labour is not the privileged bearer of internationalism, it is essential to it, and therefore linking up with other democratic internationalisms, so as to reinforce wage-labour struggles and surpass a workerist internationalism
- Overcoming ideological, political and financial dependency in international solidarity work by financing internationalist activities from worker or publicly collected funds and carrying out independent research activities and policy formulation
- Replacing the political/financial coercion, the private collusion and the public silences of the traditional internationalisms with a frank, friendly, constructive and public discourse of equals made available to interested workers
- Recognising that there is no single site or level of international struggle and that, whilst the shop floor, grassroots and community may be the base of struggle, the traditional formal terrains can be used and can also be influenced
- Recognising that the development of a new internationalism requires contributions from and discussion with labour movements in the West, East and South as well as within and between other sociogeographic regions

Elements of such an understanding can be found within both international union pronouncements and practice. It is, I think, becoming the common sense amongst left labour internationalists (see, for example, Lambert in this collection). Some still seem to consider labour or even union internationalism as the one that leads, or ought to lead, the new wave of struggles against neoliberal globalisation (Open World Conference 2000a). However, others are beginning to go beyond ideal types to spell out global labour/popular and democratic alternatives to "globalisation-from-above" in both programmatic and relational terms (Brecher, Costello and Smith 2000).

One last specification is necessary to distinguish between the concepts of "internationalism", "labour internationalism" and "union internationalism". Within social movement discourse, internationalism is customarily associated with 19th century labour, with socialism and Marxism. It *may* be projected backwards to include the ancient religious universalisms or the liberal cosmopolitanism of the Enlightenment. And it *should* be extended, in both the 19th and 20th century, to include women's/feminist, pacifist, anticolonial and human rights forms. Insofar as it is limited to these two centuries and to what has customarily been thought of as a "world of nation states", we need a new term for the era of globalisation. Some talk of *transnationalism*. I prefer *global solidarity*, insofar as it is addressed to globalisation, its discontents and alternatives. *Labour internationalism* refers to a wide range of past and present labour-related ideas, strategies and practices, including those of co-operatives, labour and socialist parties, socialist intellectuals, culture, the media and even sport. As for *union internationalism*, this is restricted to the primary form of worker self-articulation during the NIC era. Trade union internationalism has so displaced or dominated labour internationalism during the later 20th century that it is commonly conflated with the latter. Yet it is precisely *union* internationalism that is most profoundly in crisis, and in question, under our GNI capitalism.

I will now consider, in the light of the above, the ways in which international labour/labour internationalism is either coming or failing to come to terms with globalisation and the new global solidarity movements. Once again, the traditional international union institution will remain at the centre of the analysis, as will the question of forms and procedures.

International Labour's Millennial Dialogue

"International Labour's Millennial Dialogue" is my name for something that exists empirically and that I wish to further programmatically. In 1999–2000, we saw increasing numbers of union, labour, socialist and academic dialogues on labour and globalisation. These have been obviously stimulated by the coincidence of the millennium with what we have to call a "globalisation crisis". The latter means not only the crisis of labour but also that of the neoliberal globalisation project as such. Amongst the conferences held, we must note first the major international initiative of the ICFTU and ILO in the form of an open, bilingual, electronic Conference on Organised Labour in the Century (COL21; see Resources section at the end of this chapter) in 1999–2000. Second, I am aware of nine or ten international labour events on neoliberalism/globalisation, most of which occurred in the period between 1999 and 2000. These have been customarily organised either beneath, at the periphery of, across or outside the traditional international union structures.

COL21: The Dialogue of Which Millennium?

Despite its electronic form, its international accessibility and its apparent openness, COL21 was a dialogue largely imprisoned by the history of its two sponsors and their joint interest in preserving or restoring their past centrality to the world of international labour relations. With one exception (that of left labour specialist Richard Hyman [1999]) the launching statements of the institutional sponsors and invitees were cast within the traditional discourses of "industrial relations", "social partnership" and "development". Other keywords, such as "international solidarity", "ICFTU" and "ILO"—surely all central to the future of organised labour—hardly came under discussion, far less challenge. My rule-of-thumb analysis of COL21, at an early moment, suggested that those participating were mostly the usual on-line suspects: white, Anglo-Saxon and male. (With the partial exception of the Chilean Director General of the ILO, Juan Somavia, all of the initial agenda-setters fitted this profile as well!). Most of the background papers commissioned by the ILO were restricted to unions-and-globalisation-in-my-country. Whilst conference contributors provided much information on the site and occasionally took critical positions, there was little or no engagement with the opening statements, nor were participants in significant dialogue with each other. When the Spanish-language site was first launched, most of the messages were those of greeting. If this particular site later became livelier, this may have been due to an enterprising Webmistress.[9] Moreover, occasional personal enquiries, both in the Americas and Western Europe, suggest that critically minded international labour specialists were not much interested in participating in this experiment, although they may have lurked (participated passively) there.

However, none of this means that the experiment should be dismissed. On the contrary, this criticism should be considered a provocation to systematic research on COL21, including its sponsorship and management, its subjects, discourses, participation and impact and the similarities and differences between the English and Spanish sites. The point is that we (I risk speaking also for the reader here) quite urgently need such a discussion site, and it does not yet really exist.[10]

The Unofficial Conferences:
Which Dialogue of the Millennium?

To the seven conferences I have noted elsewhere (Waterman 1999), I have to add a significant forerunner from 1988 and two latecomers from the end of 2000.[11] These events have been taking place on the institutional, political, educational and academic margins, or bases, of the international trade union structures. Most have taken place within the traditional capitalist core. However, several have not (those in Korea, South Africa, Mexico and Brazil). And, in most cases of which I am aware, those that have been US-sited have involved Southern participants, although only exceptionally those from the ex-communist world.

I have commented elsewhere on another such conference/network (Waterman 1999), so I will confine myself here to the Open World Conference in Defence of Trade Union Independence and Democratic Rights (OWC), held in San Francisco, CA on 11–14 February 2000 (Open World Conference 2000b). This was probably the largest of the informal millennial events, attended by 560 people from 56 countries, 200 of them from outside North America. It was a Trotskyist initiative and was addressed by the leaders of the party concerned, but it restricted the blowing of this particular trumpet and succeeded in involving people from beyond the traditional left. Moreover, it was entirely funded by unions and community and labour movement organisations, which raised $11,000–14,000 to cover the costs of the event. Nine workshops were held, covering such subjects as women workers, immigrant workers, privatisation and deregulation, civil society and NGOs, peace and self-determination, racism and democratic rights, union incorporation into corporate and/or state structures (at every level) and labour and the environment. The conference also paid considerable attention to the role of the UN and to the ILO, both of which were seen as abandoning their traditional roles and being incorporated, in subordinate position, into the neoliberal globalisation project (Sandri 1999). This was an impressive, even heroic, initiative, revealing the capacity of a traditional vanguardist socialist party to come out energetically, broadly and internationally against neoliberal globalisation, and suggesting the willingness of organisations representing hundreds of thousands of members to respond to such an appeal. The OWC eventually established its own Web site, produced a video and printed reports (see References and Other Resources). Much of this has been reproduced in other languages.

However, I have to question certain features of this event, some shared with the other "alternative" conferences mentioned and some with the ICFTU itself. The first is its defensive character, from its title forward. The language is that of militant resistance. I quote randomly from the OWC's on-line and printed conference materials: "denounce", "preserve", "steer clear of ... attempts to co-opt", "beat back", "fight against", "defend", "halt", "renationalise", "refuse". Here there is no sign of the movement, in Latin American feminist parlance, "from opposition to proposition".

For me, the second notable feature is the assumption that the working class is the primary victim of neoliberalism. "Working class" is here stretched to embrace all poor people (women, peasants, indigenous peoples, urban residents), who are thus denied any other significant interest or identity than that of unionised male urban workers in large-scale enterprise. There follows from this, thirdly, the assumption that the (inter)national union movement is or should be the leading force for the "reversal" of neoliberalism, and the assumption that all nontraditional institutions, practices and discourses —NGOs, civil society, so-called globalisation, even national or international union mergers—are, as such, instruments of the class enemy, that they debilitate or disorient the class struggle. (This is particularly paradoxical given that the International Liaison Committee behind the OWC is itself, of course, an NGO.)

Fourth, I note significant lacunae in areas covered at the OWC. Although there was a session on/of women, the sole demand of the conference concerned an ILO instrument on pregnancy leave; there was no mention of sexual harassment and rights, and therefore nothing about patriarchy *within* either the inter/national union movement or the ILC/IWC itself. And despite one woman's proposal for an international committee of working-class women, led by women, there was no reference to feminism—surely the major theoretical/ ideological force both informing and stimulating international working women's struggles over the last 20 years. Fifth, there was no critique of traditional international trade unionism as such.[12] And finally, consistent with this, there was no workshop, no statement and certainly no discussion of the *meaning* of internationalism: whether yesterday or today; whether that of the unions, labour or socialists, or more generally. In sum, the conference was marked not only by a posture of radical oppositionism but also by the ideology of labourism/classism. Its internationalism, by default, remains largely that of the NIC period.

Let me risk a generalisation—or offer a proposition—about informal labour events: they customarily have their feet on the new terrain of neoliberal globalisation, but their heads are often in an old world of ideologies and institutions. This is, of course, a criticism, but it also has to be a recognition. The organisers and participants in most of these often innovative events still seem more at home with the discourses of imperialism/national-developmentalism, continuing to be wedded to the union (and/or labour/socialist party) as the primary or sole institutions for struggle against globalisation, thinking of inter-nationalism in terms of relations between national, local, industrial or company-based unions and understanding international dialogue as "exchange of experiences" and, often, of "the national" as the privil-eged or sole terrain of resistance and reassertion (contrast ICTUR 2000). Their procedures, too—sometimes despite intentions to the contrary—tend to reproduce traditional union or party practices. Some of these projects still consider theirs as the privileged voice of the new labour internationalism (the vanguard conference? the vanguard network?). Even if they do not have such pretensions, they do not seem to be aware or take account of the others, even where they overlap in focus and intent, and even where some participants are present at one or more of the other conferences! All of this could and possibly should be taken as a sign of (1) the novelty of the networks and networking and (2) a continuing globalisation shock, as (3) militant inter/nationalist activists grasp for old tools to dislocate a radically transformed capitalism, a process which, as suggested above, really requires radically transformed tools.

I think that there is every reason to avoid posing the informal events in opposition to COL21, or even to the ICFTU's Millennium Congress. In some ways, in certain areas, on certain issues, the ICFTU may be in advance of the OWC (eg on women, on relations with NGOs). Rather, I think we need to see all these conferences as a single new international *agora* (both public space and market place) for which a new map is necessary, of which a fuller picture still has to be painted.

Communications, Culture and Computers:
From Space to Cyberspace?

The necessity for labour and its internationalism to have com-
municational/cultural and electronic form was revealed dramatically
by the "Battle of Seattle" against the World Trade Organisation in late
1999. The initiative for the demonstration came from a network of
NGOs, or a network of networks of NGOs. US and international
unions participated significantly but neither led nor determined the
nature of this event. Rather, it was the other way round: international
union participants and observers tended to distance themselves from
those parts of the event they did not themselves either participate in
or control. International mobilisation took place largely through the
Internet. Protest activity was largely in the hands of the Direct Action
Network, which trained people in flexible but combined forms of
action. Naomi Klein (2000:23–24) notes the novelty and richness of
this multifaceted event:

> Despite … common ground, these campaigns have not coalesced
> into a single movement. Rather they are intricately and tightly
> linked to one another, much as "hotlinks" connect their Web sites
> on the Internet. This analogy is more than coincidental: the
> communication technology that facilitates these campaigns is
> shaping the movement in its own image. Thanks to the net,
> mobilisations unfold with sparse bureaucracy and minimal hier-
> archy; forced consensus and laboured manifestos are fading
> into the background, replaced by a culture of constant, loosely
> structured and sometimes compulsive information-swapping [...]
> The decentralised nature of these campaigns is not a source of
> incoherence and fragmentation but *a reasonable, even ingenious,
> adaptation to changes in the broader culture.* (emphasis added)

The US unions, providing some 50% of total participation, got
involved late, organised separate activities (in a stadium and a hall)
and tried to marshal their march away from where the police were
brutalising nonviolent resisters (Thomas 2000:190–191). The international trade unions were invisible in the dominant media, although
more so in the alternative videos made (see Other Resources—
Videos). Some national or international union leaders strayed from or
even rejected the cautious AFL-CIO policy and strategy. A number of
major US unions, and numerous unionists, simply broke ranks and
joined the rest of the demonstrators. However, whilst the ecologists
turned out dressed as turtles, the trade unionists turned out dressed

as ... trade unionists. Where the nonviolent resisters put their bodies on the line, the US union leaders went down momentarily on their knees in prayerful attitude.[13] Result: the 50% of unionists got 5% of the visual coverage in the major international (meaning US) news magazines! One could only put this down to "media bias" if the forms of union expression had been as original, dramatic or ludic as those of the other demonstrators.

With a few notable exceptions, the international union movement has yet to understand the significance of all this. Jean-Paul Marthoz (2000:30), a journalist long associated with the ICFTU, recognises the increasing centrality of the media within the globalisation process and the potential of both the media and media workers in the struggle against globalisation. However, confronted by media coverage of the radicals and radicalism at Seattle, he considers the public projection of Seattle a matter for "caution rather than euphoria". *Why not both?* And why—to return to international unions and the international media—is international labour not prominently identified with and involved in the new international movement for the democratisation of communication (Voices 21 1999)? Again, it seems, international labour is responding to the new globalised public sphere and new forms of collective self-expression in defensive/aggressive rather than in learning/creative mode.

Such a literally conservative response has long been identifiable in international union attitudes toward the new information and communication technology (ICT). This became evident almost 20 years ago, with the ICFTU's failure to take up a Scandinavian social-democratic computer specialist's free offer of an open-access database, called—ironically—Unite.[14] It continues today with what one must call the ICFTU's misguided attempt to establish and control a "union" domain name (like .com, .uk and .org) on the Internet.[15] Increasing numbers of international union Web sites do provide a welcome increase in access to information on their own activities. However, this represents a belated response to ICT as *instrument* (faster, cheaper and further-reaching), not as *cyberspace* (another kind of space, with unlimited possibilities for international dialogue, creativity and the invention/discovery/development of new values, new attitudes and new dialogues). Even the brave new multiunion Website *Global Unions* only represents a bigger, faster, further-reaching union magazine and news and—possibly—mobilisation service.[16] These are, then, primarily organs of *propaganda*,[17] which can only incidentally serve the creation of those dialogical practices and dialectical understandings necessary to our new complex, globalised, capitalist reality.

For more globalisation-appropriate practices, we have to turn to international labour's more marginal media, whether magazines such as *International Trade Union Rights* (which has run a quite extensive discussion on the problematic issue of international trade/rights linkage) or Web sites run by NGOs and/or individuals, such as Eric Lee's news (plus) service, *LabourStart* We can also turn to to left communication specialist Richard Barbrook's provocative proposals for new principles of labour organisation (1999). Barbrook understands that ICT is not simply something workers or unions can use; it is something that they produce and that also produces workers and workers needing unions of another kind: "As well as reforming the structures of existing labour organisations, digital workers should start co-operating with each other using their own methods. As they're already on-line, people could organise to advance their common interests through the Net. Formed within the digital economy, a virtual trade union should emphasise new principles of labour organisation: artisanal, networked and global" (Barbrook 1999). And, for a yet more general understanding of the role of ICT in relationship to internationalism, we again need to go beyond the particular world and worldview of labour to a reflection on "Women@Internet":

> Networks—such as women's, environmental, ethnic and other social movements networks—are the location of new political actors and the source of promising cultural practices and possibilities. It is thus possible to speak of a cultural politics of cyberspace and the production of cybercultures that resist, transform or present alternatives to the dominant virtual and real worlds. This cybercultural politics can be most effective if it fulfils two conditions: awareness of the dominant worlds that are being created by the same technologies on which the progressive networks rely (including awareness of how power works in the world of transnational networks and flows); and an ongoing tacking back and forth between cyberpolitics (political activism of the Internet) and what I call place politics, or political activism in the physical locations at which the networker sits and lives. (Escobar 1999:32)

Conclusion: Networking, Communication, Dialogue

I suggested earlier that the fundamental problem of trade union internationalism under a GNC is one of forms and practices, with those of the trade union being heavily marked by the NIC capitalism in and against which they took shape. This means that criticism of union bureaucracy, hierarchy and ideology—the Portnoy's Complaints of the traditional left—are somewhat out of place, or out of date. We really need an additional, even an alternative, principle of worker self-articulation (both joining and expression) appropriate to our era. In other words, we need one that would continually and effectively undermine the reproduction of bureaucracy, hierarchy and dogma that occurs also within "radical" and "revolutionary" unions.

As the last two quotes above suggest, this principle is the *network*, and the practice is *networking*. There is no need to fetishise the network or to demonise the organisation. "Networking" is also a way of understanding human interrelations, and we can therefore see an organisation in network terms, just as we can look at a network in organisational ones. Nonetheless, it remains true that the movement from an NIC to a GNI capitalism is also one from an organised to a networked capitalism (Castells 1996, 1997, 1998). It is from the international labour networks and networking that the new initiatives, speed, creativity and flexibility tend to come. For unions or socialists to condemn, or even criticise, NGOs as lacking in "democracy" or "representativity" is to misunderstand the new principles, forms and practices of radical-democratic social movements. The latter are centrally concerned with empowerment through information, ideas, images, values, *son et lumière*. Insofar as we are talking of radical-democratic networks, networking or, indeed, NGOs, they represent a major source of, or resource for, renovation and movement within civil society, in relation to capital and state and within or between such organisations as trade unions. An international unionism concerned with being radical-democratic and internationalist will learn this, or it will stagnate. International union networking itself will stagnate if it does not recognise itself as a part of a radical-democratic internationalist project that goes far beyond the unions, far beyond labour problems.

"Networking" relates to communication rather than institutions. If international labour networking is not to reproduce the dominant values of a GNI capitalism, it must be informed by and produce a radical-democratic style of communication and sense of culture. I call this a "global solidarity culture". This finds dramatic expression in Voices 21, produced by an international network of democratic communications academics, activists and practitioners (1999). This movement concerns itself with increasing access to the media, the right to communicate, diversity of expression, security and privacy. As earlier indicated, the international trade union organisations are notably absent from this new international social movement. This is in part because of their institutional self-definition and in part because communications workers and unions tend to be as fearful of "public interference" in their territory as they are of media magnates or state censorship. Yet labour has a long and rich cultural history and has in the past innovated and even led popular, democratic and even avant-garde cultural movements. Once again, international trade unionism has to either surpass its reductionist self-definition or remain invisible in the international media arena, which is increasingly challenging and even replacing the institutional terrain as the central site of democratic contestation and deliberation.

Debate is a continuation of war by other means. The intention is to defeat or destroy the other, whether this is an idea, movement or person. *Discussion* implies listening to the other, with no necessary implication of surpassing or transforming the exchange. *Dialogue* implies a dialectic, a process in which initial positions are transformed or a new synthesis reached. In talking above about international labour's millennial dialogue, I spoke both descriptively and prescriptively. There *are* such debates and discussions taking place; they *ought* to take dialogical form, within, between and without (outside) the international labour movement (Waterman 2001b).[18]

International and internationalist dialogue on labour internationally is not simply *facilitated* by the Web. The *logic* of the computer is one of feedback. A unidirectional, one-to-many, centralising use of the computer for purposes of control is a denial of this logic and its possibilities. The military/industrial/commercial/statist Internet and hypercapitalist Web are themselves *subversive* of capitalist institutions and institutionalisation. As Marx (Marx and Engels [1848] 1935:209) said of capitalism itself—somewhat prematurely—150 years ago, "All fixed, fast frozen relations, with their train of ancient and venerable prejudices and opinions are swept away, all new-formed ones become antiquated before they can ossify. All that is solid melts into air". There is no other way for us to operate within both our globalised world and the "real virtuality" surrounding it and literally informing it than to overcome our fear of flying (Castells 1996:327–375). This requires of labour internationalists—whether within the institutions, on their peripheries or somewhere-else-but-concerned-with-such—that we become, as Enzensburger (1976:21–22) said of the electronic media, "as free as dancers, as aware as football players, as surprising as guerrillas". And it requires of all of us that we learn to engage in dialogue with each other as we continue our struggles—that we make a road beyond capitalism whilst both walking and talking.

If this suggests a certain utopianism, then this, too, is a requirement of a reinvented labour internationalism. In criticising contemporary understandings of our present dilemma, Ruth Levitas (2000) reminds us of the necessity of combining a dialogical utopianism (process) with visions of a postcapitalist society (place and space?). However, she also reminds us that an undifferentiated notion of dialogical transformation—one that ignores the increasingly conflictual interests within contemporary capitalist society—will obscure these conflicts and leave us where we are. Relevantly, for our subject matter, she illustrates her argument with a European Commission document that urges "solidarity" between those who "earn income from work and those who earn [sic] their income from investments" (Levitas 2000:208–209; sic in original). A meaningful basis for a transformatory dialogue, she suggests, requires "a critical analysis of capitalism— aimed not (just) at saying isn't it awful, but at identifying potential points of intervention which might lead to transformation, and potential agents of that transformation" (Levitas 2000:209). Enough said?

Acknowledgements

This chapter draws from a long working paper (Waterman 1999), as well as a book (Waterman 1998, 2001a). Thanks are due to Kim Scipes, Bruce Nissen and particularly Dan Gallin and Jane Wills for comments on earlier drafts. For an interesting supplement and challenging (social democratic) contrast to this chapter, see O'Brien (2000).

Endnotes

[1] The following analysis should be compared with that of Dan Gallin (1999), who, as past General Secretary of the International Union of Food and Allied Workers (IUF), has been a participant in as well as a critical commentator on union and labour internationalism. See also Gallin (2001).

[2] Van der Linden (2000) is the major source for the history of the ICFTU. Sarah Ashwin (2000) provides an informative and perceptive critique of its latest period, particularly in relationship to the ex-Communist world. She (2000:113) also raises the question of whether the ICFTU is not now moving toward "social movement unionism", a notion to which I will return.

[3] "Tripartite" suggests a pie with three equal parts. In terms of relative power, however, the ILO should surely be rather represented as a pizza, with capital and state as the rich upper layer (75%) and labour as the supporting base (25%).

[4] Some years ago the ICFTU appeared to recognize the ambiguities or limitations of the word "free" by changing the title of its magazine from *Free Labour World* to *Trade Union World*.

⁵ Kjeld Aagard Jakobsen (this collection), International Secretary of the major Brazilian left union confederation, the CUT, even argues that both the ICFTU and the WFTU are based on a Bolshevik model! I believe that this Bolshevik model was an adaptation of the classical German Social-Democratic one. The notion of comparing/contrasting, rather than opposing, the models and behaviour of the ICFTU and the WFTU has the makings of an original MA or PhD research project.

⁶ There is little evidence that such an understanding is forthcoming. The ICFTU is currently identified with the UN's "Global Compact", an attempt by the United Nations to ingratiate itself with and give an ethical aura to multinational capital. With respect to labour, the UN's Kofi Annan has "asked" world business to uphold a number of principles that exclude any explicit right to strike (ICFTU 2000a, b). The ICFTU also seems to be ingratiating itself with tomorrow's world power, China, despite that country's hostility to worker rights and union independence (China Labour Bulletin 2000). The ICFTU and some ITSs are also married to the idea of establishing a "social clause" or 'labour standards' through the World Trade Organisation, despite the increasing disrepute accruing to that and other international financial institutions (Gumbrell-McCormick 2000:508–15; Waterman 2001a, b).

⁷ I have abandoned my original concept of "social movement unionism" to those who, as we will see below, have given this wider currency, albeit in a more traditionally "classist" form.

⁸ I am thinking here primarily of Lambert and Webster (1988) on apartheid South Africa, Munck (1988:117) on the Third World generally, Seidman (1994:2–3) on South Africa and Brazil and Scipes (1996:viii–ix) on the Philippines. Munck (2000:93–94) has qualified and extended his formulation. Regrettably, none of these authors has attempted the more extensive (re)formulation that my initial typology surely requires. Most influential recently has been Moody's impressive overview of global labour (1997). Indeed, his last chapter is entitled "Toward an International Social Movement Unionism"! However, his (1997:290) account of this phenomenon amounts to a description/ prescription of a more activist and democratic unionism that still assumes the leading role of the working class in the struggle against neoliberalism. Whilst promoting a more flexible, open and internationalist unionism, he remains therefore limited by traditional workerist assumptions. Seattle—a discussion of which follows—shows how, under a GNI capitalism, a network of social movements can have a broader vision and more sophisticated and militant strategy than workers and unions do. Assertion of the working class's vanguard role in the struggle against neoliberalism would seem to be empirically in error and prescriptively counterproductive (compare Cowie 1999).

⁹ Despite my own several attempts to get messages of different types and lengths onto COL21, and despite several promises that this would happen, it took almost a year before one was published—on the Spanish site, and in English!

¹⁰ An exception might be Labor-List (see Resources), which has hosted one or two intensive discussions on certain international labour issues. However, it is my impression that participants on this list are either uninterested in discussing or feel unqualified to discuss matters relating to the international organisations and institutions.

¹¹ These include the following, sources for which, where extant, are listed in the Resources:
- A "premillennial" event, sponsored in 1998 on an anniversary by the Danish General Workers Union: *A New Global Agenda: Visions and Strategies for the 21st century*;
- A union-sponsored *World Meeting Against Globalisation and Neoliberalism*, held in Brazil in September 1999;

- A Trotskyist-initiated *Open World Conference in Defence of Trade Union Independence and Democratic Rights*, held February 2000 in San Francisco, which I discuss below;
- A national union/academic/education event, *Unions and the Global Economy: Labour Education at the Crossroads*, held in Milwaukee, Wisconsin, 13–15 April 2000;
- An international conference/festival on labour and the electronic media under globalisation, *Labour Media 99*—the second such event—held in Seoul in November 1999;
- A conference on *Trade Unionism in the 21st Century*, in Johannesburg in October 1999, organised by the Southern Initiative on Globalisation and Trade Union Rights (SIGTUR);
- An international conference on *Building a Labour Movement for Radical Change*, organised in Cologne, Germany in March 2000 by the Amsterdam-based Transnationals Information Exchange, in which one major topic was "A New Internationalism?";
- A seminar on *The Present Panorama of International Trade Union Structures: New Challenges and Union Strategies in the Face of Globalisation*, organized with foreign/international contributions in Mexico City in November 1999. Although addressed to a local audience, this shared concerns and orientations with the earlier events;
- A workshop on *Promoting International Labour Rights and Solidarity* at Wellesley College, outside Boston, MA, USA in November 2000, which allowed for an intensive exchange amongst academic, union and NGO specialists, including those from Asia, Latin America and elsewhere;
- LaborTECH 2000: *Building New Global Unionism through Labour Media*, at the University of Wisconsin, Milwaukee, WI, USA, 1–3 December 2000. The latest in a series of such events, with significant international address and participation.

[12] Rather, such criticism as there was of international trade unionism was directed towards the new forms thereof, particularly the earlier-mentioned Union Network International. Although the US AFL-CIO was criticised, particularly in relationship to Seattle, the ILC/OWC may have been nervous about criticising organisations to which conference participants owed allegiance.

[13] US observers tell me that such religious rituals are common in the US union movement, but no more than I could they guess to whom or for what these leaders might have been praying. To a foreign observer (and an international audience?) the sight was pathetic, especially when contrasted with the rituals of other demonstrators —possibly inspired more by an internationally familiar Gandhian tradition.

[14] This proposal was even publicly promoted *within* the ICFTU by the then-editor of the then *Free Labour World*, Ian Graham (1982a, b). Graham later moved to the distinctly more communication- and computer-friendly International Chemical, Energy and Mineworkers Federation (ICEM).

[15] This is my initial interpretation of evidence from Eric Lee (2000). ICFTU thinking here was, it seems to me, bureaucratic, technocratic and territorial. It was *bureaucratic* in so far as (1) it would have been a relationship between offices/officers (the other party being the corporate-dominated committee that assigns Internet domain names), and (2) the fact that it has thus far apparently involved neither publicity, consultation with nonunion specialists, mobilisation of the ICFTU membership, nor even consultation with the concerned public. It was *technocratic* in its belief that there is a technical fix for problems of labour or democratic rights. Finally, it was *territorial* in that it was

to be the ICFTU and its allied or member unions that would decide which unions were "real", with the right to use the domain name. The notion of creating a territorial *place* in cyber*space* suggests a lack of understanding of the nature of the latter. Lee suggests there are a number of cyberspace-relevant ways of establishing a union presence and of finding labour-relevant material on the Internet, none of which require a domain name (2000). Moreover, these ways appear to be open to labour activists armed with basic Web skills, imagination and an interest in international solidarity.

[16] And even the best of the new international printed union magazines, the International Metalworker Federation's excellent *Metal World*, has no letter page, much less some kind of open space for more extensive discussion. Contrast this with the recent two pages (out of 16—ie over 10%) provided by the left *Labour Notes* in the US.

[17] As defined in the *Shorter Oxford English Dictionary*: "disseminate, diffuse (statement, belief, practice)".

[18] A personal note: Coming from the tradition of Marxist polemic (including that of Lenin, whose major works are all profoundly marked by their polemical form and intent), I have had to fight my way out of this box and toward something more like a discussion or a dialogue. Another box, of course, could be that of "overblown academic drivel" (an international union officer's response to me on an electronic discussion list, in 1990, toward the end of the international union Ice Age). To have established at least a public discussion with Bill Jordan (Waterman 2000) is a minor sign that the times may be a-changin'. There are other indications that the international union institutions are beginning to surpass the defensive/aggressive mode in responding to public criticism. Over the last years I have been finding myself in increasing—and increasingly meaningful—dialogue with union and other internationalists. More recent, and tentative, have been public or private exchanges with inter/national union organisations and officers. Whilst private discussions could be interpreted (by my street-fighting political/academic friends) as a sign of my naïveté on the one hand and of institutional incorporation on the other, I see them rather as a discussion—an experience or experiment—from which both parties could later move to an open dialogue. In any case, I place no value on any such private discussion, any more than paid consultations or evaluations, unless they permit one to improve on published pieces like the present one that serve to better forward an open dialogue. I hope that such a dialogical intention is present in this piece of writing, despite forceful criticism of the traditional institutions—and the alternative networks! Readers will inform me to the contrary; indeed, one already has.

References
Extended Bibliography
Ashwin S (2000) International labour solidarity after the cold war. In R Cohen and S Rai (eds) *Global Social Movements* (pp 101–116). London: Athlone
Barbrook R (1999) "Frequently Asked Questions: Digital Work—Digital Workers and Artisans: Get Organised!" HTML file: <URL: http://www.labournet.org/1999/March/digiwork.html>, last accessed March 2001
Bezuidenhout A (1999) *Towards Global Social Movement Unionism? Trade Union Responses to Globalisation in South Africa*. Geneva: International Labour Organisation/International Institute for Labour Studies. HTML file: <URL: http://www.ilo.org/public/english/bureau/inst/papers/2000/dp115/?>, last accessed March 2001

Brecher J, Costello T and Smith B (2000) *Globalisation from Below: The Power of Solidarity.* Boston: South End Press

Carew T (2000) A false dawn: The World Federation of Trade Unions. In M van der Linden (ed) *The International Confederation of Free Trade Unions* (pp 165–186). Bern: Peter Lang

Castells M (1996) *The Information Age: Economy, Society and Culture.* Vol 1, *The Rise of the Network Society.* Oxford: Blackwell

Castells M (1997) *The Information Age: Economy, Society and Culture.* Vol 2, *The Power of Identity.* Oxford: Blackwell

Castells M (1998) *The Information Age: Economy, Society and Culture.* Vol 3, *End of Millennium.* Oxford: Blackwell

CEDAL (1999) *Impacto de la globalización en los derechos del trabajo* [Impact of Globalisation on Labour Rights]. La Paz: Centro de Estudios para el Desarrollo Laboral y Agrario

China Labour Bulletin (2000) "Feature: Political Tourism Revisited". CLB #35. HTML file: <URL: http://www.china-labour.org.hk/2005e/feature_icftu.htm>, last accessed March 2001

Couper A D (1999) *Voyages of Abuse: Seafarers, Human Rights and International Shipping.* London: Pluto

Cowie J (1999) Kim Moody, workers in a lean world: Unions in the international economy. *International Labour and Working-Class* 56:134–136

Enzensberger H M (1976) *Raids and Reconstructions: Essays in Politics, Crime and Culture.* London: Pluto

Escobar A (1999) Gender, place and networks: A political ecology of cyberculture. In W Harcourt (ed) *Women@Internet: Creating New Cultures in Cyberspace* (pp 31–55). London: Zed Books

Fimmen E (1924) *Labour's Alternative: The United States of Europe or Europe Limited.* London: Labour Publishing Co

Gallin D (1999a) "Organised Labour as a Global Social Force". Paper to a Workshop on International Relations plus Industrial Relations, Conference of the International Studies Association, Washington, 20 February. Global Labour Institute, Geneva

Gallin D (2001) Trade unions and NGOs in social development: A necessary partnership for "social development", *Transnational Associations*, No 1, pp 17–36

Graham I (1982a) Computers of the world UNITE? *Free Labour World* 1:2–3

Graham I (1982b) Programmed solidarity? First studies on a union computer network. *Free Labour World* 6:32–33

Gumbrell-McCormick R (2000) Facing new challenges: The International Confederation of Free Trade Unions (1972–1990s). In M van der Linden (ed) *The International Confederation of Free Trade Unions* (pp 341–518). Bern: Peter Lang

Hyman R (1999) "An Emerging Agenda for Trade Unions?" HTML file <URL: http://www.ilo.org/public/english/bureau/inst/papers/1999/dp98/index.htm>, last accessed March 2001

International Centre for Trade Union Rights (ICTUR) (2000) *"Going Global"—Globalisation or Glo-baloney?* London: International Centre for Trade Union Rights

International Confederation of Free Trade Unions (ICFTU) (2000a) "ICFTU On-line ... Global Compact an Opportunity for Global Dialogue". 31 July. HTML file: <URL: http://www.icftu.org/displaydocument.asp?Index=991210514&Language=EN>, last accessed March 2001

International Confederation of Free Trade Unions (ICFTU) (2000b) The global compact: For a socially responsible business world. *Trade Union World* 9:22

International Transportworkers Federation (1996) *Solidarity—ITF Centenary Book*. London: Pluto

Jordan B (2000) Remarks of Bill Jordan, ICFTU General Secretary, at the Reception of the International Conference "The Past and Future of International Trade Unionism". *Gent* 18 May. E-mail received 24 August

Klein N (2000) Does protest need a vision? *New Statesman* (UK), July 3, pp 23–25

Lambert R and Webster E (1988) The re-emergence of political unionism in contemporary South Africa? In W Cobbett and R Cohen (eds) *Popular Struggles in South Africa* (pp 20–41). London: James Currey

Lee E (2000) "The Internet Belongs To Everyone". HTML file: <URL: http://www.labourstart.org/icann/ericleebook.shtml>, last accessed March 2001

Levitas R (2000) Discourses of risk and utopia. In B Adam, U Beck and J van Loon (eds) *The Risk Society and Beyond: Critical Issues for Social Theory* (pp 199–210). London: Sage

MacShane D (1992) *International Labour and the Origins of the Cold War*. Oxford: Clarendon

Marthoz J-P (2000) The media and globalisation. *Trade Union World* No 7–8:30

Marx K and Engels F (1935[1848]) The manifesto of the communist party. In *Karl Marx: Selected Works*, vol 1 (pp 204–241). Moscow: Cooperative Publishing Society of Foreign Workers in the USSR

Moody K (1997) *Workers in a Lean World: Unions in the International Economy*. London: Verso

Munck R (1988) *The New International Labour Studies: An Introduction*. London: Zed

Munck R (2000) Labour in the global: Challenges and prospects. In R Cohen and S Rai (eds) *Global Social Movements* (pp 83–100). London: Athlone

National Minority Movement (nd) *Strike Strategy and Tactics: The Lessons of the Industrial Struggles. Thesis Adopted by the Strassburg Conference Held under the Auspices of the Red International of Labour Unions*. Foreword by P. Gladding

O'Brien R (2000) Workers and world order: The tentative transformation of the international union movement. *Review of International Studies* 26:533–555

Open World Conference (2000a) HTML file: <URL: http://www.info.org/>, last accessed March 2001

Open World Conference (2000b) Open World Conference in Defence of Trade Union Independence and Democratic Rights. *OWC Report Back Bulletin, No 1*. San Francisco: Open World Conference

Quinteros C (2000) Acciones y actores no sindicales, para causas sindicales. El caso del monitoreo independiente en Centroamérica [Nonunion action and actors for union causes. The case of independent monitoring in Central America]. *Nueva Sociedad* (Caracas), 169:162–176

Reinalda B (ed) (1997) *The International Transportworkers Federation 1914–1945: The Edo Fimmen Era*. Amsterdam: International Institute of Social History

Sandri R (1999) "Confronting Neototalitarianism: Globalisation and the Struggle for Trade Union Independence". Contribution for the Open World Conference of Workers in Defence of Trade Union Independence and Democratic Rights, February 2000, San Francisco. HTML file: <URL: http://www.owcinfo.org/campaign/discuss01.htm>, last accessed March 2001

Scipes K (1996) *KMU: Building Genuine Trade Unionism in the Philippines, 1980–1994*. Quezon City: New Day

Seidman G (1994) *Manufacturing Militance: Workers' Movements in Brazil and South Africa, 1970–1985*. Berkeley: California University Press

Silverman V (2000) *Imagining Internationalism in American and British Labour, 1939–49*. Urbana: University of Illinois Press

South African Labour Bulletin (2000) Com Com: A series of irreverent postcards. Our inside reporter sends a series of postcards from Durban at the time of the ICFTU congress. *South African Labour Bulletin* 24(3):112–116

Thomas J (2000) *The Battle in Seattle: The Story Behind and Beyond the WTO Demonstrations*. Golden, CO: Fulcrum

Trade Union World (1999) Special 50th anniversary edition: How the ICFTU has influenced global developments year after year. *Trade Union World* 7:5–70

Van der Linden M (ed) (2000) *The International Confederation of Free Trade Unions*. Bern: Peter Lang

Voices 21 (1999) "A Global Movement for People's Voices in Media and Communications in the 21st Century". HTML file: <URL: http://www.comunica.org/v21/statement.htm>, last accessed March 2001

Waterman P (1998) *Globalisation, Social Movements and the New Internationalisms*. London: Mansell

Waterman P (1999) *International Labour's Y2K Problem: A Debate, a Discussion and a Dialogue (A Contribution to the ILO/ICFTU Conference on Organised Labour in the 21st Century)*. Working Paper Series No 306. The Hague: Institute of Social Studies

Waterman P (2000) "From an International Union Congress to an International Labour Dialogue: An Exchange between Peter Waterman, Global Solidarity Dialogue/Dialogo Solidaridad Global, and Bill Jordan, General Secretary of the International Confederation of Free Trade Unions". HTML file: <URL: http://www.antenna.nl/~waterman/jordan2.html>, last accessed March 2001

Waterman P (2001c) Capitalist trade privileges and social labour rights. *Working USA*, 4(5):1–17

Waterman P (2001a) *Globalisation, Social Movements and the New Internationalisms*. Paperback, with new preface. London: Continuum

Waterman P (ed) (2001b) A social clause for labour's cause? Guest-edited special issue of *Working USA*. Forthcoming

Other Resources
Serials
International Union Rights. International Centre for Trade Union Rights. UCATT House, 177 Abbeville Rd, London SW4 9RL, UK. E-mail: ictur@gn.apc.org.

Labour Notes. Labour Education and Research Project. 7435 Michigan Ave, Detroit MI 48210, USA. E-mail: labornotes@labornotes.org. Web site: HTML file: <URL: http://www.labornotes.org>

Metal World. International Metalworkers Federation. POB 1516, 54 bis, route des Acasias, CH-1227 Geneva, Switzerland. E-mail: Sjutterstrom@imfmetal.org.

Videos
Labour Battles the WTO in Seattle '99—Workers of the World Unite. 38 min. VHS, NTSC. Labour Video Project, POB 425584, San Francisco, CA 94142, USA. E-mail: lvpsf@labornet.org.

Open World Conference in Defence of Trade Union Independence and Democratic Rights, San Francisco, 11–14 February 2000: Selected Speech Excerpts. VHS, NTSC. 60 min. OWC, c/o San Francisco Labour Council, 1188 Franklin St, Rm. 203, San Francisco, CA 94109. E-mail: owc@igc.org.

Showdown in Seattle: Five Days That Shook the WTO. VHS, NTSC. 150 min. Independent Media Project/Deep Dish Television, 339 Lafayette Street, New York, NY 10012. Web site: HTML file: <URL: http://www.papertiger.org>

Web sites/E-dresses:

Global Compact: Human Rights, Labour, Environment. HTML file: <URL: http:// www.unglobalcompact.org/>

Global Labour Directory of Directories, put together by LabourStart. HTML file: <URL: http://www.labourstart.org/gldod.shtml>

Global Solidarity Dialogue/Dialogo Solidaridad Global. HTML file: <URL: http://www.antenna.nl/~waterman/>

Global Unions. HTML file: <URL: http://www.global-unions.org/>

Interactive Conference on Organised Labour in the 21st Century. HTML file: <URL: http://www.ilo.org/public/english/bureau/inst/project/network/index.htm>

International Confederation of Free Trade Unions. HTML file: <URL: http://www.icftu.org>

Labor-List, LAB-L@YORK-U.CA

LabourStart. HTML file: <URL: http://www.labourstart.org/

Nueva Sociedad. HTML file: <URL: http://www.nuevasoc.org.ve>

Open Directory Project. HTML file: <URL: http://dmoz.org/Society/Work/ Labor_Movement/Unions/>

Open World Conference. HTML file: <URL: http://www.owcinfo.org/>

SiD's Global Labour Summit. HTML file: <URL: http://www.antenna.nl/~ waterman/sid.html>

Union Network International. HTML file: <URL: http://www.union-network.org>

Voices 21. HTML file: <URL: http://www.comunica.org/v21/>

World Federation of Trade Unions. HTML file: <URL: http://www.wftu.cz>

Workshop on Promoting International Labour Standards and Solidarity, ccandlan@ wellesley.edu.

Peter Waterman (London, 1936) describes himself as a pensioned but unretired researcher/writer, resident in The Hague, Netherlands. He is the author of *Globalisation, Social Movements and the New Internationalisms* (1998, Cassell; paperback 2000, Continuum), and coeditor of *Labour Worldwide in the Era of Globalisation: Alternative Union Models in the New World Order* (1999, Macmillan; Korean edition 2000). His current interests include globalisation, communication, culture and solidarity; the life histories of internationalists and his long-suffering Global Solidarity Dialogue Web site, <http://www. antenna.nl/~waterman/>.

3

Southern Unionism and the New Labour Internationalism

Rob Lambert and Eddie Webster

The chapter traces the genesis of SIGTUR, a new network/organization of southern unions that has been built over the past decade, which brings together democratic unions from Latin America, Southern Africa, Asia and Australasia. The impact of neoliberal globalisation has spurred this action, and Australian unions—with their rich tradition of labour internationalism—have been at the forefront. The chapter shows how the initial hostility of the established trade union internationals has been transformed into strategic alliances as the internationals have come to value SIGTUR's campaign orientation. The chapter argues that SIGTUR has continued to expand because of its strong emphasis on internal democracy. The new southern alliance is one instance of a search for a new form of unionism—global social movement unionism—that may offer greater scope for a more effective resistance to the logic of globalisation. In the new millennium, this search is critical if unions are to rekindle the vision and the confidence that drove the early movement.

Millennium Movements, Ideological Crisis and the End of History

For the past 200 years, private corporations have spearheaded global capitalist expansionism. These profit-driven companies transcended national boundaries in an endless drive for new markets. Various forms of government support, including a willingness to intervene militarily in certain instances and advances in communications and transportation systems, facilitated the global reach of capitalist corporations. The success of this drive to organise globally was matched by the relative failure of emerging union movements to internationalise as effectively as companies. Certainly, there were glimmers of labour internationalism, brief moments when unions did indeed turn outwards as a form of defence. These flourishes were without exception short-lived. There appeared to be a certain inevitable cycle, as fleeting moments inexorably gave way to the national. National organisation was viewed as a lever to force compromise.

Perhaps the greatest opportunity for forging an effective labour internationalism was present between the 1860s and the 1940s—an age of class ideology, an historical moment when the labour movement appeared inspired, self-confident, independent and internationalist. The initiative that flowed from this self-confidence was reflected in the first tentative steps to internationalise. In the mid-19th century there was a burgeoning of activity when building employers sought to break strikes in England by importing strike-breakers from Europe. The young English labour movement responded by reaching out to continental workers. A leader of the London Trades Council proposed "regular and systematic communication between the industrious classes of all countries" as the solution to this practice (Fernbach 1974:12). The First International, the International Working Men's Association (IWMA), formed in this context in 1864 and became a vehicle for promoting such contact and communication. When English building workers took strike action against their employers' attempt to reduce wages and increase working hours, they recognised that international support from continental workers in France, Germany, and Belgium was "a matter of life or death" (Olle and Schoeller 1984:142).

These first tentative steps preceded an expansionary phase in the European movement, with its leading sections determined to win political power and assert working class interests.[1] Marxism was the dominant ideology. The works of Kautsky and Bebel, which popularised Marxism, attracted the leaders of the working class movement and the activists who followed them. Theory was condensed into three simple propositions (Sassoon 1996:6). First, the capitalist system is unfair. Juridical equality between parties disguises a real inequality: the capitalists "cheat" workers by appropriating far more than they pay in wages and other necessary production costs. This appropriation is the source of the disproportionate wealth, power and influence of this class. Second, history proceeds through stages; the present stage is transient. Finally, workers are a fundamentally homogeneous class, despite the obvious differences that exist. All workers are united by the struggle to improve their conditions and achieve real rather than mere formal equality. To realise this, workers need to organise into political parties and unions that seek to attain these goals.

These propositions proved to be a dynamic and effective mobilizing ideology. They embodied a statement about the present ("the existing social order is unfair"), a statement about the future ("the existing social order can be changed") and, finally, a strategic statement about the transition from the present to the realisation of a future vision. Belief in these propositions created a *social movement,* committed to changing the status quo. What gave the socialist movement its winning edge over rivals within the working class movement was the powerful ideas it developed regarding the third proposition—"what is to be done?" The socialist movement came to the fore through its intuitive recognition that the working class represented a social subject "with tremendous political potentialities" (Sassoon, 1996:7). Sassoon (1996:7) argues, "By thinking of the working class as a political class, ascribing to it a specific politics and rejecting the vaguer categories ('the poor') of earlier reformers, the pioneers of socialism thus virtually invented the working class". He (1996:7) then makes the vital point that "[t]hose who define, create.... 'Democratic' politics—that is, modern mass politics—is a battlefield in which the most important move is that which decides what the battle is about, what the issue is. To be able to define the contending parties, name them and thus establish where the barricades should go up or where the trenches should be dug gives one a powerful and at times decisive advantage. This is what all major movements for social change have had to do."

Building such a movement was challenging, because the proletariat at this time was certainly no homogeneous mass, divided as it was by occupations, skills, territories, nationalism and religion. What was significant was the way in which the socialist movement gave ideological cohesion and an organisational unity to these fragments. "Class consciousness was constructed by political activists, just as nationalism was constructed by nationalists, feminism by feminists, racism by racists" (Sassoon 1996:8).

The contrast between this movement at the turn of the last century and labour movements venturing into the new millennium is striking. First, with few exceptions, most contemporary labour movements are not in an expansionary phase. Instead, they have experienced substantial membership declines, which accelerated during the 1980s and 1990s as economic liberalisation and the accompanying work restructuring took effect. Secondly, these movements appear to be in worldwide ideological disarray and confusion. The dissipation of Marxism as a mobilising ideology is matched by the dominance of neoliberalism in the sphere of economic management, where even social democratic parties in power accept these parameters of economic governance. The three propositions that were the source of the early movement's dynamism have been substantially modified. Critiques of the present system are ad hoc and piecemeal, lacking in focus. Injustice is no longer related to capitalism as an economic system. Whilst certain union movements have begun to attack the effects of globalisation, the underlying logic of this expansionary dynamic is not analysed. In short, statements about the present lack power and rigor. They have failed to have any significant impact or attract citizens into their ranks to do serious battle against economic and social change.

This ideological crisis of labour is most apparent when the second and third statements are considered. The notion that the existing social order can be changed has given way to a pervasive pessimism that the social order *cannot* be changed in any fundamental sense. Whilst unions remain committed to defending worker rights and conditions, the linkage between these immediate struggles and a longer-term vision is absent. The third proposition concerning what is to be done has given way to the bleak notion that "*nothing* can be done". Globalisation, materialised through tariff reduction, financial deregulation and workplace restructuring, is generally viewed as inevitable; these are facets of the economic landscape that cannot be altered. Whilst national federations have begun to organise and support acts of resistance against these changes in varying degrees, and whilst international union organisation has begun to debate new approaches, a coherent alternative strategy grounded in ideology has yet to be devised. The helplessness of citizens before these forces of change is matched by the absence of an independent labour movement response.

The tables have been turned. A hundred years ago, the labour movement had a vision and a future plan and had gained the initiative, and it was industrial and finance capital that were in disarray. The great crash of the late 1920s undermined the credibility of market ideology at a time when the working class was increasingly assertive. However, this golden age of class ideology was also an age of lost opportunity through deep ideological division. This is a complex, often tragic story. Here it suffices to say that the three internationals that emerged were all, for different reasons and under changing circumstances, unable to resolve political differences through effective democratic processes. This is not to underplay the depth or the complexity of the differences over nationalism and World War I, responses to the rise of Fascism in Europe, or Stalinism, Soviet nationalism and the plight of the working class internationally. What is of immense significance for this chapter's argument is that these divisions fatally weakened labour movements and emasculated labour internationalism as promising initiatives swiftly disintegrated.

This failure opened the way for the ascendancy of corporate interests, which came to control the agenda, define the issues and decide what the battle was about. At this moment in time, nowhere is this more evident than in the evolution of the World Trade Organisation (WTO). For example, the Transatlantic Business Dialogue (TABD), a working group of the West's one hundred most influential chief executives, provides the agenda for the WTO (Palast 2000). The TABD has developed an "implementation table" that currently contains 33 items. These include environmental, consumer and worker protection laws that the TABD wishes to see defeated or watered down. Armed with their "scorecard" and agenda items for the WTO, TABD leaders have direct access to the American president and the president of the European Commission.

Business leadership's strategic focus contrasts starkly with labour's confused response. In the main, the movement has simply responded to set terms—market efficiency, international competitiveness and enterprising individualism. This predicament exists because labour leadership has been outmanoeuvred on the big-picture strategy of inter-national trade, investment and global economic governance. Labour's political construction of class consciousness has withered before this powerful, coherent, alternative worldview. Fukuyama would have us believe that this "unabashed victory" of economic liberalism signals "the end of history" (Fukuyama 1989: 16). Competitive individualism, the unifying spirit of the age has displaced political struggle that "called forth daring, courage, imagination, and idealism" (Fukuyama 1989: 16).

Recognition of the nature of this decline is vital to renewal, and awareness of the contrasts thus sketched is a starting point for debate on new labour internationalism's prospects. Such a debate is a pre-condition for halting the decline and reigniting a vision for a just and equitable social order. In considering these prospects, history's irony is ever-present: labour internationalism's historic failure is incon-trovertible, yet this very failure contributes to the creation of a set of objective conditions favourable to the construction of labour internationalism. Past ideological division is being transcended as movements recognize that a unifying, coalition-building strategy is essential to challenging globalisation's ruthless logic, and the cyber-space communications technologies offer immense possibilities for an internationalist project.

This chapter analyses the emergence of the Southern Initiative on Globalisation and Trade Union Rights (SIGTUR) as one instance amongst many others of a new labour internationalism emerging as a consequence of these changes. This new southern organisation of independent democratic trade unions in Asia, Australia, New Zealand, Africa and Latin America was formed in March 1999 at a meeting in

Australia. The organisation's formation was an outcome of close on a decade of intense activity.[2] The "Southern" in the organisation's title is defined *politically*, not *geographically*: that is, SIGTUR is one initiative to bring together some of the most exploited working classes all over the world, where union rights are negated or constrained, and political situations restricted.[3]

Unions participating in SIGTUR include the Congress of South African Trade Unions (COSATU), the Center of Indian Trade Unions (CITU), the All India Trade Union Congress (AITUC), the Korean Council of Trade Unions (KCTU) and the Kilusang Mayo Uno (KMU) in the Philippines. SIGTUR has also embraced newly emerging unions in Indonesia, Malaysia, Thailand, Sri Lanka, Pakistan and China. CUT in Brazil has recently joined. Trade union democracy and independence are the essential foundation of SIGTUR.[4]

The genesis of SIGTUR reflects the struggle to enkindle a *new* labour internationalism, one that seeks to learn from history, transcend the fatally divided past and seize cyberspatial opportunities.

The Genesis of SIGTUR

SIGTUR's genesis reflects the melding of two rich working class traditions: the unique internationalism of Australian left unions and the organising style and ideological orientation of the new South African unions that emerged after 1970. Labour internationalism has always been a central feature of left unions in Australia. When ships arrived in Australia carrying Dutch troops to reclaim their Indonesian colony, the Maritime Union of Australia (MUA) imposed bans relating to the docking and departure of the ships. Australian unions were also active in the international campaign against the South African apartheid regime, and South African shipping was often subjected to bans. This international solidarity culture stood the unions in good stead when the newly elected Labor Government initiated a grand experiment of deregulating the highly protected Australian economy at a faster rate than any other economy in the world. The leadership sensed that such a dramatic change could devastate unions, given the country's proximity to the Asian region, where trade union rights are circumscribed. Instead of turning inwards in search of a purely national solution, their internationalist culture led to an outward orientation. In their view, the most effective defence against deregulation's destructive consequences was international solidarity with southern unions where union rights were negated.

Initially, the strategy was poorly formulated. In 1988, the Assistant General Secretary of the Western Australian Trades and Labour Council (WATLC) set up a meeting with the three Western Australian universities to involve them in developing strategy. They planned a large-scale conference of union leaders in the Indian Ocean Region and applied for International Labour Organisation (ILO) funding. An academic conference agenda was formulated to the point where keynote speakers were approached. However, ILO funding was not forthcoming, and the idea remained dormant.

In late 1988 the WATLC was persuaded to adopt a different strategy, which displaced an academic orientation with a more modest organising one. The WATLC accepted that the priority should be relationships with genuine, democratic Asian unions that were fighting for recognition. As a result, they visited countries in the region during 1989 and 1990 and made contact with democratic unions. These organisations were in similar circumstances to those that had pertained during the South African union's long and difficult struggle for recognition during the 1970s and 1980s, and suffering under similar forms of repression. The WATLC committed to organising a small workshop of these unions to explore whether or not there existed the possibility of working together on a common strategy against globalisation.

The General Secretary of COSATU was committed, having argued that the internationally nonaligned COSATU should develop a Southern alliance of democratic unions so as to more effectively challenge globalisation's logic. This meant that COSATU became a strong ally in the venture from the outset, contributing their rich vein of experience to unionists who were facing precisely the same issues that the aspirant South African unions had faced 20 years earlier. Organising and mobilizing workers in a situation where rights were negated and where both state and employers are hostile was the cardinal strategic issue.

The first small workshop was held in Perth in May 1991. There were 24 delegates, evenly divided between Australian participants and those from the region.[5] Even at this early stage in the process, South African leaders played a key role in sharing experiences of how to build democratic unionism in a hostile environment. The meeting focused on building strong unionism committed to social emancipation, under repressive conditions.

This first tentative step was immediately challenged. Despite the crumbling of the Berlin wall in 1989, Cold War politics lingered. A right-wing national organisation in Australia with strong links to the Catholic Church and active in the right wing of the Australian Labor Party (ALP) and the Australian trade union movement, the National

Civic Council (NCC), launched a scathing attack on the initiative in their national magazine, *Social Action*. Immediately following the first workshop, the NCC reiterated its view that the WFTU was the force driving the initiative. They went on to criticize the meeting as "unrepresentative ... The delegates did not necessarily represent recognized trade unions in their respective countries" (*Social Action* May 1991:11). Their logic here was that the WATLC's initiative should have aligned with the established unions in the region. However, these unions were products of American post-World War II intervention, unrepresentative of the working class and reflecting instead the interests of authoritarian statism, local economic elites and multinational corporations. The initiative had little option but to search out the unions in the forefront of the struggle to establish democratic unions, which often stood in opposition to the established client unions. The reason for commitment to democratic unionism was obvious: how else could globalisation logic be challenged? This required new forms of international solidarity action, which clearly would never be forthcoming from state-sponsored or employer-dominated unionism created as a Cold War stratagem.

The successful launch of the Indian Ocean Trade Union Initiative led to a much larger conference attended by 140 delegates in Perth in November 1992. The base of the network expanded to include other Asian countries.[6] Debate at this conference focused on the denial of trade union rights in the Asian region and strategies to highlight and struggle for these. A third meeting, also attended by 140 delegates, was held in Perth in November 1994.

A turning point for the network came in 1995, when the recently elected government in Western Australia intensified its antiunion stance by undermining freedom of association through legal amendments. This radicalised the Western Australian union movement, and it launched a militant campaign involving a protest march of over 20,000 workers. Drawing on the network, the WATLC invited COSATU to speak at this rally. Significantly, the COSATU leader, drawing on the solidarity shown by the Fremantle dockers during the antiapartheid struggle, threatened to reciprocate with boycott action if the laws went ahead. COSATU's boycott threats were backed by a similar commitment from CITU in India. Unions participating in the network organised protest action outside Australian embassies throughout the region. Here was solidarity of historical import, for it was possibly the first time ever that severely exploited workers from developing nations had led mass protest action in solidarity with workers' struggles in a developed industrialised nation. These pressures reinforced the militant local campaign and led to the withdrawal of the legislation. This provided a model of an internationalism where the local and the global fuse in a new, more powerful dynamic of resistance that has yet to be fully developed. Tony Cooke, leader of the union negotiating team, concluded that this linked international action was the key factor in defeating the proposed laws.

These events were of enormous import for the future of this new, fragile network of democratic unions. Key elements of the established international trade union movement, which had been extremely wary of and even hostile to the initiative, shifted their position dramatically. They realised that the initiative was not about "replaying cold war politics" and that the network, fragile as it was, heralded new forms of resistance against the logic of globalisation (*Social Action* 1991:11). They acknowledged that the orientation was to the building of global solidarity, regardless of politics, the only criteria being commitment to democratic unionism.

One outcome of these events was a new relationship with the established labour internationals. Dan Gallin, then General Secretary of the International Union of Food Workers (IUF), who had previously been openly hostile to the network, flew to Perth to discuss "coalition-building" between the network and the ITS. This was a real breakthrough. Subsequently, Gallin played a constructive role in developing links between the network and many of the established ITSs.[7]

The ensuing strategic debates placed a new emphasis on understanding the restructuring dynamics of industry sectors in order to more effectively ground strategy. This new dimension gained momentum within the network's Fourth Regional Congress, held in Calcutta in 1997 and hosted by CITU, with some 260 delegates. The success of this Indian meeting consolidated the vision of a *Southern* rather than a *geographically bound* network of democratic unions, where a Southern identity denoted a *political experience* of exploitation and marginalisation that arose out of a particular position of subordination in the new global economy. At an RCC meeting in Perth in March 1999 that included a range of ITSs, the initiative's identity was transformed: the Indian Ocean Initiative became identified as SIGTUR.

The India meeting had another significant impact on the evolution of SIGTUR's strategy. The 1997 workshop-based meeting in Calcutta brought to the fore the devastating effect of downsizing, outsourcing, casualisation and the sale of state assets on the condition of the working class across all sectors and all countries. Whilst the workshop outcomes provided a damning indictment of the social and economic impacts of neoliberal globalisation, there appeared to be no clear vision on how this restructuring could be effectively resisted. This weakness was addressed at the fifth regional meeting, hosted by COSATU in Johannesburg in October 1999. The meeting took a new direction: a limited set of objectives was established prior to the meeting, and its focus was on formulating modest, realisable organising goals and campaign tasks.

SIGTUR's ten-year genesis was marked by advances and challenges. In moments of deep crisis, it appeared as if this fragile experiment would not survive. However, SIGTUR has endured because of the organising principles that informed the initiative from the outset.

SIGTUR's Organising Principles

The core principles underlying SIGTUR's organising strategy bring a certain fresh perspective to the notion of a *new* labour internationalism. These principles are based on positions deemed vital to a renewal of struggle against neoliberal globalisation.[8] SIGTUR's essential policy position includes commitment to:

- the broadest possible political embrace through constituting SIGTUR as an organisation of *democratic and independent* trade unions;
- an alliance of *Southern* unionism as a critical constituency in a renewed globalisation struggle;
- *global* social movement unionism as a distinctive new form of unionism, appropriate to the present conditions;
- a program of *global action* as the pathway to global social movement unionism; and
- the fullest possible exploitation of cyberspace communications systems in propagating and coordinating global action.

These principled policy commitments will now be elaborated to demonstrate that these are not merely a body of fresh *ideas* on the new labour internationalism.[9] Indeed, they are being materialised, albeit unevenly, in the decisions and mass actions of large Southern organisations.

Democratic and Independent Unionism

At an Indian Ocean Initiative RCC meeting in Johannesburg in 1996, a document on *Principles for Participation* was formally endorsed on 2 August. These principles were the outcome of two years of intense debate.[10] Essentially, the document stated that the initiative would only work with those organisations that conformed to ILO Conventions 87 (freedom of association), 98 (collective bargaining) and 151 (public employees). The document went on to state that this should be reflected in "organisational structures and practices".[11] This was carefully defined in the second principle, which stated that "[u]nions which are established by the state or are part of the state which seek to control workers in the interests of capital and the state cannot be part of the initiative. Furthermore, unions which are established with the assistance of employers and are dominated by employers should be excluded". Principle Three asserted that "[t]his initiative will include independent unions, which are active at the grass roots level in organising and representing the interests of the working class". Time and resources were not going to be expended on those organisations that were inactive and ineffectual. The adoption of Principle Four was crucial to ensuring the broadest possible resistance base. It stated that "[t]his initiative will not exclude or include unions/federations solely on the basis of their political and ideological orientation, or their tactical and strategic goals within their countries, which aim to further the interests of the working class". The document concluded:

> To the extent that we achieve a principled and broad-based, inclusive orientation, we will become a forum for intense, creative debate on working-class interests. In an era when the powerful forces of global capital and finance capital, represented by international institutions such as the IMF and the World Bank, are ranged against the working class movement, such an approach is of paramount importance. We must be a catalyst for dialogue and debate, as well as strategic initiatives aimed at the protection and renewal of the working class movement.

At certain moments since the passage of the *Principles,* there have been intense pressures to include union federations that would not meet these criteria. These moves have been successfully resisted. SIGTUR's biannual meetings have been forums for debate on various issues connected with the *Principles*. Structured to promote the fullest possible delegate participation, they have had as their backbone small workshops and report-backs, rather than the endless speeches and engineered resolutions common to many international union forums. The International Secretary of the KCTU has stated that:

> SIGTUR is complementary to many of the official meetings of the international trade union movement. It creates space and meets needs.

SIGTUR provides the opportunity to highlight what workers are going through; what key struggles are being fought; what are the landmarks?

SIGTUR provides the basis for strengthening campaigning and the rapid interchange of information. The emphasis will always be on bringing together genuinely democratic and independent union movements. (Youngmo 1999)

Internal democracy has facilitated debate on vexed questions of union strategy in developing nations. Could militarised state unions in Indonesia be reformed? Two years after the launch of the initiative, the KMU split politically. This led to debate with the advancement of the view that both factions should be included unless it could be proven that the breakaway unions contravened the *Principles*. Efforts to transform and democratise the Malaysian Trade Union Congress were also discussed. Certainly the China question has been the most difficult of issues.

Clearly there are unresolved questions. That this venture has held together for a decade despite these differences is testimony to the power of internal democracy. More positively, participating unions are the most active at grass roots level when compared to the older unions established during the Cold War period by states and employers. In varying degrees, all are critical of neoliberal globalisation. They therefore offer the best prospects of building a genuine resistance to globalisation. Their Southern identity makes such resistance an imperative—hence the importance of the second strategic commitment.

Alliance of Southern Unionism

"Southern" represents a political reality for SIGTUR. Rather than being solely a geographic signifier, this term captures the experience of exploitative relations central to the identity of movements. These relations are reflected in the denial of political and labour organising rights by authoritarian states. The participant unions reveal a distinct locus in the global economy: all are similarly located within the new international division of labour. Australia, a prime mover of the initiative, would appear to be the odd one out, given its developed nation status, and its only claim to Southern identity would seem to be its geography. However, Australia is now being stripped back to Southern status in a political sense, as union rights there are increasingly constrained, the manufacturing sector dismantled, and tourism hailed as an economic saviour.

Neoliberal globalisation's impact on the developed nations of the North has also created a horizon of opportunity for a historically unprecedented unity of international labour organisation. For most of the 1990s, the Indian Ocean Initiative had to fight for its right to exist. The ICFTU was implacably opposed to it, since an organisation linking continents East/West did not fit with the ICFTU model tying geographic regions to the European center. Founding the initiative on national unions often at war with ICFTU affiliates in the Asian region only served to exacerbate the tensions.[12] In 1994, the initiative launched a public attack on ICFTU structures in the Asian region and counselled COSATU against ICFTU affiliation. This attack included a scathing critique of the work of certain ITSs in Asia, most notably the IMF, who were accused of colluding with corrupt union leaders in Malaysia and thereby failing to take up the cause of the Malaysian electronics workers. These tensions destabilized the initiative in Australia, given the fact that the ACTU was a significant ICFTU affiliate. Despite being under attack, the initiative survived between 1990 and 1996 due to iron-clad support from all the major left unions in Australia.

These divisive years reflect the old internationalism, driven by Cold War logic. The ICFTU and many of the ITSs fanned these flames. This was indeed a cold climate in which to give birth to a genuinely new internationalism. As shown in the previous section, the pressures of globalisation transformed this hostility. Southern organisation was not in opposition to the North, but existed as an essential complementary component in a unified struggle against globalisation. Thus neoliberal globalisation has, ironically, created an unparalleled opportunity for forging a vibrant, powerful internationalism the likes of which has not been witnessed before. There are significant signs that this is no romantic dream. At every level now, past political and ideological differences are swept aside by these overriding goals: the assertion of worker rights, the rebuilding of a strong movement and the challenging of a socially destructive logic of pure market relations now cutting a swathe through all nations. Whereas new initiatives were previously perceived as a threat to existing structures, they are now viewed as complementary to them, enhancing the movement more generally. Every level of the movement is finding new forms of uniting around a common cause. Both the ICFTU and the ITSs are working closely with SIGTUR to build a strong Southern unionism focused on global action campaigns. The ACTU passed a resolution at their 1996 Congress endorsing SIGTUR for the first time.

Global Social Movement Unionism

SIGTUR's commitment to global social movement unionism (GSMU) is one of many distinctive contributions to the new internationalisms that are evolving.[13] At this stage, this does not mean that union leaders in SIGTUR identify the strategic shifts in union organising and campaigning that are occurring as GSMU. However, as will be shown in this section, the changes, which are uneven at this point in time, are best captured in the concept of GSMU.[14]

GSMU may be said to exist when unions move beyond their traditional workplace boundaries to form alliances with other civil society movements within the nation state, whilst at the same time creating a new global union form. The latter transcends the nation-state by linking internationally with similar unions with the express goal of global campaigning as a new form of resistance to globalisation. Social movements come into being through *social action*—through mobilizing citizens. SIGTUR is tentatively exploring the possibilities of such action assuming a global reach, through effective cyberspace communications and grounded in new global union structures. This should not be read as a formalistic definition of GSMU, but rather as an attempt to capture real shifts in strategy. GSMU is unlikely to appear in an instant, but will evolve through experimentation and struggle, through striving to find new ways to challenge the legitimacy of neoliberal globalisation. This transition to a new style of unionism, only in its infancy and certainly not present in all SIGTUR constituents, will be elaborated below.

One feature of neoliberal globalisation's ascendancy is the forging of an alliance of powerful interests. New cyberspace systems liberated by wide-ranging deregulation have further empowered investment funds and large corporations. Liberal economics dominates across the political spectrum, maintaining pride of place for competition policy. To date, trade unions have had no answer to the ways in which market rationalism has undermined their membership base. Strengthened corporate and financial interests have been matched by a weakened union movement.

Reversing this imbalance assumes David-and-Goliath-like proportions. Despite the daunting character of the challenge, however, there is no option but to take the first hesitant steps. Traditional strategies, under which unions only organise full-time workers *at the workplace,* bargaining over wages and conditions, need to be rethought. Unions will have to discover how to best track and organise workers spun out of full-time work through the processes of downsizing, outsourcing and casualisation that neoliberal globalisation has legitimated. This could take many forms. Unions may set up their own new structures (general unions) to recapture the new part time, casualised workforce. They may well be able to forge new relationships with civil society organisations concerned about the plight of this growing underclass of working poor.

However, the drive for social movement unionism is produced by more than labour market change. The impact of market rationalism on all spheres of society means that a new political voice has to be found. In a developed economy such as Australia's, the ALP seems unable to break from their commitment to the essential logic of globalisation, hoping instead to secure a human face to an *inevitable* process of competitive change by maintaining the social welfare commitments underpinning social democracy. When compared to the conservative alternative, Labor carries a corresponding economic banner of reform combined with a vital distinction: acceptance of the trade union role.[15] In Asia, both authoritarian and democratic regimes are committed to global engagement based on cheap, controlled labour. At this historical juncture, there appears to be no alternative programme and no political party willing to assert—or capable of asserting —political and social control over the process of global restructuring.

Yet the lives of citizens are being transformed. Even a conservative Australian newspaper asked in a lead article what it called "The Billion Dollar Question: If the economy is booming, then why are so many of us suffering?" (*The Australian* 6–7 May 2000:29–35, weekend magazine). Workplace restructuring has created a "tense, mistrustful, anxiety-haunted society" (*The Guardian Weekly* 30 June 1996). In Asia's postcrisis booming economies, the condition of labour mirrors the worst excesses of 19th-century Britain.[16] In the absence of an alternative program, workers and citizens worldwide are condemned to declining conditions, long working hours, increased insecurity, and psychologically damaging managerialism as unimaginable wealth is accumulated by the share-holding, business-owning class.

SIGTUR plans to take a modest first step in researching present restructuring and imagining an alternative. The Sixth SIGTUR Congress will take place in Seoul, Korea, in November 2001. Over the next 18 months, work will proceed within three commissions: manufacturing, the state/public sector and international regulatory institutions. These commissions are mandated to present an analysis of restructuring and an alternative. This alternative will be embodied in a "Seoul Declaration" that will propose both an alternative vision *and* an organising strategy to begin to reshape national political agendas. The declaration will serve as a signpost, signalling a direction. It will be a focus within a process, and will therefore subject to regular deepening and revision, as more substantial research data becomes available and as new union initiatives are reviewed and refined. The declaration is likely to stimulate debate on union strategy that could bring the greatest possible pressure to bear on globalisation politics—that is, on a position where existing parties claim *there is no alternative* to liberal economic restructuring. This may well lead to a renewal of interest in social movement unionism. The existing programme, representing the interests and consolidated power of international finance, corporations and traditional parties, can only be challenged by a new popular alliance between organised labour and the wider community—that is, through the strengthening of civil society against the current form of global change.

Many of SIGTUR's constituents have had some experience of transcending the workplace. COSATU's opposition to the apartheid regime was characterised by a strong alliance with community organisations and innovative, community-based shop steward organisations that developed effective campaigns. COSATU's present campaign against casualisation is premised on a strong alliance with community-based organisations. CUT, KMU and the KCTU have had similar experiences. The 1998 maritime dispute in Australia forced the issue onto the union agenda, as it was generally recognised that community support on the pickets was crucial to the resistance.

However, an alternative power base will only emerge when alliances built out of spontaneous upsurges of support at moments of crisis demonstrate an *enduring effect* on the actual form of trade unionism. Spontaneous, fleeting alliances such as those arising out of the attack on the MUA cannot be said to be building social movement unionism (SMU) when traditional union structures and traditional collective bargaining within national industrial relations systems are unchanged after the event. Hence, there are problems that require further national debate over reinventing national organisation. Leaders of SIGTUR constituents speak positively of the importance of SMU. "We must involve the community and become involved in the community" has become a watch-cry. Yet the construction of this alternative union form is yet to be realised in any enduring sense.

SIGTUR has taken the debate about alternative unionism a step further by advancing the notion of *global* SMU. Kim Moody (1997:3) posited this as an alternative to the emergence of global business unionism, which has been a dominant response to global change. In our view, GSMU is realised when nationally based sectoral unions create *enduring* organisational linkages across national boundaries that aim to impact on national workplace and political strategies. Again, what is crucial is to move beyond the episodic encounters that have characterised trade union internationalism to date. International visits of union leaders have been a core activity. Politically serious visits can have a value. However, as with SMU, GSMU cannot be built on fleeting encounters. Unions have to choose to link organically across territory, oceans and continents. This has resource implications.

SIGTUR has chosen to experiment in this direction. At the Fifth SIGTUR Congress in Johannesburg in October 1999, the MUA and the South African Transport and Allied Workers Union (SATAWU) signed a declaration of intent to create a global union. Such a union would link the ports of Fremantle in Western Australia with South Africa's east coast port of Durban. Such a linkage is highly symbolic. History resonates: During the apartheid years, Fremantle warfies often delayed South African shipping in protest against the regime. Ship owners were forced to refurbish the cabins of black seamen before the ships were allowed to be offloaded. More recently, the South African transport unions came out in solidarity with Australian workers fighting against the imposition of antiunion laws. In 1995, the unions threatened a boycott of Australian shipping on route from Fremantle to Durban unless the Western Australian laws restricting trade union rights were withdrawn. On the understanding that the boycotts would be cancelled, the Western Australian government retreated.[17] When a new version of the laws was reintroduced in 1997, dock workers in all South Africa's major ports withdrew their labour for a day and marched to the city centres in protest against the renewed attack on Australian unions. Large numbers participated in the Durban marches, holding aloft banners proclaiming their commitment to Australian workers who had stood by them in their fight against apartheid. During the 1998 maritime dispute, shipping was actually boycotted: in early May of that year, Australian ships were stranded with unloaded cargo.

Significant lessons were drawn from this experience, notably the idea that global integration and the trade dependence of nations render governments vulnerable to militant, global union action. In 1995, the Western Australian government was determined to press ahead with its labour market flexibilisation agenda, yet they eventually crumbled before the pressures outlined above. A sensible strategy, therefore, requires that the global unionism experiment should first be applied to this strategic sector. From this arose the statement of intent signed by the Assistant General Secretary of the MUA and the

SATAWU President at the Fifth SIGTUR Congress. This statement argued that

> [t]he challenge for the two unions is to consolidate and build the foundation for international unionism on an ongoing basis. Workers cannot be called into action if they know little about the history, culture and current challenges of workers in other nations. These understandings and consciousness have to be built. Organisation has to develop to foster this new internationalism. With this in mind, the leaderships of the MUA and SATAWA (TGWU) wish to state their commitment to advancing this process.
>
> The leaderships here present commit to advancing the process of linking the ports of Fremantle in Western Australia and Durban in South Africa organisationally. We commit to advancing this idea through their respective democratic structures.
>
> Let us commit ourselves to build an international unionism, step by step, just as we organise individual workplaces step by step. Let us mark the beginning of the new Century with a vision, a commitment, optimism that we can build a new unionism for a new Century. This statement of intent is a small step in this long march. (SIGTUR Action Plan 1999:13)

Since the fifth congress, steady progress has been made on implementing this agreement. It was endorsed at the November 1999 National Conference of the MUA, which is the union's policy-making body. An MUA delegate attended a SATAWU meeting in May 2000. At that meeting, the two unions reached the following agreement as the first tentative step towards establishing a global union: "It was agreed that we would exchange two delegates and that the country would host the two delegates for one month. We established that in order for the visiting delegates to appreciate fully the cultural differences of its sister port as well as the political and industrial environment, the delegates should stay with families of workers in that port" (Summers 2000:1).[18] The commitment has been consolidated, opening the way to the tough decisions on the form of the linkage and the way in which this will be resourced. If SIGTUR can succeed in this modest first step, it may provide something of a general route map to where unions should aim in the 21st century.

Global Action as a Pathway to GSMU
GSMU will be built through action, through striving to develop the capacity to initiate and then coordinate borderless solidarity. To this

end, the SIGTUR congress in Johannesburg set modest goals to begin the slow and difficult process of organisational change. Unions committed to a campaign against mining giant Rio Tinto. Following the South African meeting, materials were distributed to SIGTUR constituents. The issue of Rio will be integrated into routine union training in order to raise consciousness, not just on this MNC, but on the more general role of MNCs in the new global economy. The strategic thinking is that if this campaign is successful it may serve as a template for future actions. Over the past year SIGTUR has promoted protest action against Rio Tinto, in Pakistan and Western Australia to date.

In Johannesburg, SIGTUR also committed to trying to organise a common May Day campaign building to May 2001. In this first round, a common theme of work restructuring and casualisation under globalisation was adopted, which focused concretely on job loss and job insecurity as a consequence of downsizing, outsourcing and casualisation. Delegates committed to working towards a common May Day throughout the South, to be trailed in the year 2000 with a view to a more extensive event in 2001. May Day was viewed as an opportunity to highlight the devastation neoliberal globalisation had imposed on job security and conditions. Participant countries that mobilized on this common issue were South Africa, India, Indonesia, the Philippines, Korea and Western Australia.

As part of their efforts, South Africa, India and Korea organised a general strike. Four million workers responded to the general strike call in South Africa, two million in India, and 100,000 in Korea. This action and others highlight significant facets of the new labour internationalism. Networks such as SIGTUR do not organise action at the local national level. Instead, these decisions are taken by national unions. In this strike situation, COSATU, CITU and KCTU were all solely responsible for the decision to strike in order to highlight the crisis. SIGTUR's role was to utilize cyberspatial communication to ensure that all participant unions learnt of the actions and communicated them to their memberships. The mass actions were *for* job security and humane conditions and *against* the effects of economic globalisation, indicating a new ideological position being forged in the process of struggle. Again, SIGTUR's role is to capture this shift and communicate it effectively, so that individual national movements are not left isolated to face their own power elites, challenging their loyalty to the nation's well-being. The elites assert that actions such as the strike damage a nation's competitive interests, placing investment-driven job creation at risk. Future jobs are at stake as a consequence of these "reckless" strikes. Grounded cyberspatial communications allows a dialogue of common emancipatory interests that dissolves this national perspective. This is an essential counterbalance to the intense elite-defined nationalism.[19]

In sum, what is distinctive in these mass actions is this. First, organised labour is hesitantly evolving an independent ideological stance. Second, far from being a spent force "in the new transformative social dynamics", organised labour is in fact proving to be a *leading* force (Castells 1997:360). And third, the labour movement is prepared to take *radical action* to pressure for an end to the liberal economic policies being pursued by political parties in power.

The challenge of coordinating global action has served to highlight serious organisational weaknesses. Whilst unions are increasingly aware of the necessary local/global linkage in virtually every dispute, as yet there have been no moves to restructure and allocate resources. At present, union federations have only one international secretary running inadequately staffed and resourced International Departments. COSATU is a step ahead in that certain of its affiliates have created full-time international officer positions. As a result of underresourcing, communications break down frequently and follow-up is often poor. As trade union internationalism moves towards coordinated action, this is a fatal flaw. Campaigns only happen if human and financial resources are properly allocated. This is perhaps the greatest of all challenges in building a new internationalism.

Over the next two years, SIGTUR's leadership expects only partial success in the implementation of the action plan. However, this weakness can be turned to advantage if it leads to a debate about the need to allocate resources to international work. SIGTUR is already promoting the establishment of subregional coordinating committees to promote and coordinate the action plan. Such committees are in the process of being established in Southern Africa, South Asia, Australia, East Asia, and Brazil. As yet, COSATU has no international committee, so their commitment to establishing a SIGTUR committee is a breakthrough. SIGTUR is currently establishing a Web site, which will enhance communications and the effectiveness of the campaigns. Relationships with the major ITSs are strong and evolving.

Challenges SIGTUR Faces

SIGTUR faces four significant hurdles: the conflict of interests underpinning the new international division of labour; difficulties in searching for a appropriate model of labour internationalism; organisational weakness; and the separation of the economic and political spheres.

At an elementary level, Haworth and Ramsay (1986) are correct: when corporations restructure, jobs lost in Australia are jobs gained in China. However, the situation is more complex than this. SIGTUR's Asian leadership has argued that unions should not accept the notion of a conflict of interest without also recognising the way in which neoliberal globalisation, in accelerating the relocation of production, has highlighted potential common interests. So, for example, young Malay electronics workers, who have been struggling against US micro-chip company Harris for more than a decade, view their conditions as slave-like. They are hostile to the collusion between the company and the Malaysian state in the denial of union rights. SIGTUR leaders from such developing countries have argued that jobs under slave conditions are unacceptable. They have therefore joined SIGTUR in the belief that the struggle for the retention and strengthening of labour rights and standards and jobs in the developed world and the fight for precisely the same conditions in the South are inextricably linked. The development of democratic trade unions in the South is SIGTUR's first priority. Who can predict the impact on trade, investment flows and the distribution of jobs if these battles were to be won? Surely moving wages up from below subsistence levels in the developing nations of the South will create a stronger domestic market, more stable than overdependence on foreign companies and export industrialisation.

The second hurdle is lack of clarity on an appropriate model of labour internationalism. Levinson's (1972) intervention stimulated a wide range of critiques, notable in which is their failure to specify an alternative to multinational collective bargaining (MNCB). SIGTUR strategy is at an early stage in this respect. The new organisation is promoting GSMU, initially in the most strategic of sectors, as a way of strengthening unions' capacity to successfully resist the current attacks. This is a very different orientation from MNCB and the liberal democratic industrial relations model that underpins it. SIGTUR is characterised by its Southern identity and experience. The SIGTUR model of internationalism is a resistance model—hence the attractive-ness of a social movement orientation. The challenge resides in working through the building of global unionism in mainstream manufacturing, where effective collective bargaining is critical. We are searching for an alternative that integrates MNCB and GSMU. The new unionism is about increasing bargaining power within the framework of trans-formed union organisation.

Hurdle three is organisational weakness. National unions are threatened by declining memberships, driven by strategic failure, lean production restructuring, casualisation and an aggressive managerial ideology individualising work relations. A vibrant internationalism can only be founded on strong, nationally based unions in alliance with other social forces. Unless resources are allocated to building this global movement, present weakness—both national and international—will be exacerbated.

The fourth obstacle to building a solid internationalism is the domination of unions by the political parties to which they are allied. SIGTUR has no magic wand, no formula to *instantly* move towards a new political response to globalisation that might challenge conventional politics and traditional union/party relations. Union/party relationships such as those between COSATU, the South African Communist Party (SACP) and the African National Congress (ANC), the Australian Council of Trade Unions (ACTU) and the ALP, and the CITU and the CPI (Marxist) are all products of complex national histories. No international organisation can impose perspectives on these historic relationships. Hence, at one level SIGTUR's strategy can be viewed as economistic with a strong "pragmatic" focus. The singular focus is: how can movements be empowered to challenge the destructive logic of globalisation?

However, the pragmatic route of practical action may, in the longer term, lead to and consolidate a new kind of labour movement (GSMU) that would redefine the political/economic divide. The Seoul declaration may advance new political ideas on the future shape and institutional architecture of global relations. This search for new organisational forms and for new ideas could well have an impact on national politics. Indeed, this is already occurring, as COSATU forces the issue of the relationship between massive job loss and economic liberalism onto the political agenda through its four-million-strong May Day strike in 2000. The *new* internationalism involves a struggle to reintegrate politics into labour internationalism. Globalisation offers the prospects of this integration on the basis of a visionary, democratic politics of freedom, equality and dignity. The plight of the majority, the extremes of inequality, the psychological damage of workplace relations and the severe exploitation of workers in developing nations are giving impetus to a return to values currently subsumed by a singular, all-encompassing value: market freedom.

This possible renaissance lies somewhat ahead of present opportunity. The immediate task is to continue to build SIGTUR as an enduring force capable of promoting a new internationalism. SIGTUR is still a fragile structure; it has been sustained for a decade by sheer political will and determination. The successes achieved in this decade would not have been possible had this will not been nurtured in the fertile soil of resistance generated by neoliberal globalisation.

Endnotes

[1] In this introduction, I draw on the work of Sassoon (1996). See also Hobsbawm (1982), Salvadori (1979), Schorske (1955), and Touraine, Wieviorka and Dubet (1984).

[2] SIGTUR grew out of the Indian Ocean Initiative, which had its founding conference in May 1991. Participating unions met regularly, and conferences were held in 1992, 1994, 1997 and 1999.

[3] Whilst it is important to stress that this is only one initiative and that there are many other significant moves being made by Southern unionism, SIGTUR's leadership—which represents some of the most significant unions in the south—will be struggling to establish SIGTUR as the dominant Southern force in the international trade union movement. This in no way detracts from other valuable initiatives; it is a simple statement of the importance of thinking politically about the restructuring of trade union internationalism.

[4] This is defined in terms of ILO Convention 87 on freedom of association, and 98 on collective bargaining rights.

[5] The latter included leaders from the KMU in the Philippines, the newly established Solidarity trade unions in Indonesia, independent union activists from Malaysia (including Arokia Dass, recently released from prison), and activists from Sri Lanka, Pakistan and Papua New Guinea. COSATU sent a strong delegation of four senior leaders.

[6] The network was expanded to include Thailand, Vietnam, Korea and India. The Center of Indian Trade Unions (CITU) had a large delegation that contributed significantly to the debates. Cosatu was again strongly represented.

[7] These included the International Metal Federation (IMF), the International Chemical, Energy and Mining Federation (ICEM), the Public Sector International (PSI), the International Union of Food Workers (IUF), and the International Transport Federation (ITF). Significantly, these organisations have since participated in SIGTUR's Regional Coordinating Committee (RCC).

[8] Obviously, one cannot simply assume that trade unions are opposed to neoliberal globalisation. Through the past two decades, Australian unions, led by the ACTU, advanced the notion of *strategic or best practice* unionism, which posited constructive engagement with the workplace efficiency drive associated with deregulation. This is beginning to be reassessed within certain ACTU affiliates. For a critique of Australian best practice unionism, see the article that I wrote for *Politics and Society*.

SIGTUR's international engagement has meant that its leadership was confronted with the negative dynamic of global openness in a political world where labour rights and standards varied enormously. From the outset, therefore, SIGTUR adopted a critical stance on the present form of global restructuring and has worked to assist unions in rethinking the whole question of constructive engagement.

[9] The first four of these commitments are discussed. Cyberspace communications is considered briefly at the end of section four and is mentioned throughout the analysis.

[10] A statement of *Principles for Participation* was first floated at an RCC meeting in August 1994. CITU was concerned that the adoption of such a set of principles might exclude unions with which they were working closely. They were also concerned that the term "independent" might signify independence of political parties, creating difficulties for them given their very close relations with the Communist Party of India (CPI) (Marxist). The KMU was also ambiguous on this issue. Finally, it was agreed to

refer the issue to the 3rd Regional Conference in November 1994 in Perth. At that meeting, the document was again deferred, this time to the next RCC meeting. It was at this meeting in South Africa in August 1996 that the *Principles* were finally adopted after further lengthy debate.

[11] All quotes in this paragraph are taken from Indian Ocean Initiative (1996:1).

[12] In the postwar period, an element of the anticommunist strategy of the US was the construction of either state- or company-dominated unionism that was distant from the real interests and needs of workers. SIGTUR established relations with the independent unions in the region, which had to fight against company and state unionism in an intense struggle to secure their base. The ICFTU's Asia Pacific Regional Organisation (APRO) relates the older, established, US-promoted Asian unions.

[13] There are other significant new labour internationalisms evolving in the Americas. The core of this might be an "anti-NAFTA internationalism", developing in Mexican unions. I am grateful to Peter Waterman for drawing my attention to these developments.

[14] The notion of a global social movement unionism was introduced by Kim Moody in his 1997 book, *Workers in a Lean World*. In my view, Moody has introduced a creative new dimension to the social movement unionism concept, even though the concept of GSMU is inadequately developed in his book. So there is much theoretical work to be done, following close on the tail of real changes in union strategy as unions attempt to empower citizens and workers and begin the long journey of transformation.

[15] A key question in Australian politics is whether or not the ALP can be pressured to re-evaluate their commitment to neoliberalism's competitive project. The leadership of the Australian Manufacturing Workers Union (AMWU) is increasing the pressure in this regard as it witnesses the continued rationalisation of Australian manufacturing.

[16] See Lambert (1999a), in which I present ethnographic data on the experience of young Indonesian workers in the new industrialisation's factories.

[17] For an account of this remarkable experience, see Lambert (1996).

[18] Extract of the report by Dean Summers, Assistant General Secretary of the Seaman's division of the MUA, Western Australia.

[19] There is an obvious irony here. Corporate leadership and the political parties that support their agenda strive to weaken the social resolve and civil commitment of the nation-state, while at the same time calling on the working class and their organisations not to undermine the nation-state through a failure to commit to global competitive restructuring, which itself erodes the economic capacity of the nation state.

References

The Australian (2000) Beneath the bottom line. 6–7 May:29–35

Boaventura de Sousa S (1995) *Toward a New Common Sense: Law, Science and Politics in the Paradigmatic Transition*. London: Routledge

Burawoy M (2000) *Global Ethnography: Forces, Connections, and Imaginations in a Postmodern World*. Berkeley: University of California Press

Castells M (1996) *The Information Age: Economy, Society and Culture*. Vol 1, *The Rise of the Network Society*. Oxford: Blackwell

Castells M (1997) *The Information Age: Economy, Society and Culture*. Vol 2, *The Power of Identity*. Oxford: Blackwell

Castells M (1998) *The Information Age: Economy, Society and Culture*. Vol 3, *End of Millennium*. Oxford: Blackwell

Cohen R (1991) *Contested Domains: Debates in International Labour Studies.* London: Zed Press

Fernbach D (1974) *The First International and After.* London: Penguin (p 12)

Fukuyama F (1989) The end of history? *The National Interest,* Summer.

Haworth N and Ramsay H (1986) Workers of the world untied: A critical analysis of the labour response to the internationalization of capital. *International Journal of Sociology and Social Policy* 6(2):55–82

Hirst P and Thompson G (1992) *Globalisation in Question.* Cambridge, UK: Polity Press

Hobsbawm E (1982) *The History of Marxism.* London: Harvester Press

Indian Ocean Initiative (1996) *Principles for Participation.* Document formally endorsed at RCC meeting, 2 August, Johannesburg

Lambert R (1996) Regional Solidarity and Trade Union Rights *International Trade Union Rights* 3(2):6–7

Lambert R (1999a) An emerging force? Independent labour in Indonesia. *Labour, Capital and Society* 32(1):70–107

Lambert R (1999b) Global dance: Factory regimes, Asian labour standards and corporate restructuring. In J Waddington (ed) *Globalisation: Patterns of Labour Resistance.* London: Mansell (pp 72–105)

Levinson C (1971) *Capitalism, Inflation and the Multinationals.* London: Allen and Unwin

Levinson C (1972) *International Trade Unionism.* London: Allen and Unwin

Levinson C (ed) (1974) *Industry's Democratic Revolution.* London: Allen and Unwin

Marx K (1970) *Capital,* vol 1. London: Penguin

Moody K (1997) *Workers in a Lean World: Unions in the International Economy.* London: Verso

Olle W and Schoeller W (1984) World market competition and restrictions on international trade union policies. Reprinted in P Waterman (ed) *For a New Labour Internationalism.* The Hague: Institute of Social Studies Publication (pp 39–60)

Palast G (2000) How US business sets the globalisation agenda for the WTO. *Guardian Weekly* 26–31 May:14

Press M (1984) The lost vision: Trade unions and internationalism. In P Waterman (ed) *For a New Labour Internationalism.* The Hague: Institute of Social Studies Publication (pp 88–108)

Press M (1989) A critique of trade union internationalism. In M Press and D Thomson (eds) *Solidarity for Survival: The Don Thomson Reader.* Nottingham: Spokesman.

Ramsay H (1999) In search of international union theory. In J Waddington (ed) *Globalisation: Patterns of Labour Resistance* (pp 192–219). London: Mansell.

Salvadori M (1979) *Karl Kautsky and the Socialist Revolution, 1880–1938.* London: New Left Books

Sassoon D (1996) *One Hundred Years of Socialism: The West European Left in the Twentieth Century.* London: IB Taurus Publishers

Schorske C (1955) *German Social Democracy, 1905–1917.* Cambridge MA: Harvard University Press

SIGTUR (1999) *Action Plan.* Unpublished; available from SIGTUR

Social Action (1991) May:11

South African Labour Bulletin (1999) Special edition on 5th SIGTUR Congress, Building Internationalism

Summers D 2000 Report by Assistant General Secretary of the Seaman's division of the Maritime Union of Australia, Western Australia, on May 2000 SAWATU meeting. Unpublished; available from SIGTUR

Thomson D and Larson R (1978) *Where Were You Brother? An Account of Trade Union Imperialism.* London: War on Want
Touraine A, Wieviorka M and Dubet F (1984) *The Workers' Movement.* Cambridge, UK: Cambridge University Press
Waterman P (1984) *For a New Labour Internationalism.* The Hague: Institute of Social Studies Publication
Waterman P (1999) The brave new world of Manuel Castells: What on earth (or in the ether) is going on? *Development and Change* 30:357–380
Waterman P (2000) Labour Internationalism in the Transition from a National/Industrial/Colonial Capitalism to an Informatised/Globalised One ... and Beyond. Unpublished paper
Waterman P (2001) *Globalisation, Social Movements and the New Internationalisms.* London: Continuum
Youngmo Y (1999) International Secretary of the KCTU. Intervention at SIGTUR's Regional Coordinating Committee meeting, 29–30 March, Fremantle, Western Australia. Unpublished

Rob Lambert is the Coordinator of the Southern Initiative on Globalisation and Trade Union Rights (SIGTUR), a network organization of independent and progressive trade unions spanning Latin America, Africa, Asia and Australasia that has been built over the past decade. He was a trade union organizer in South Africa during the 1970s when the new unions were emerging. He is an Associate Professor at the University of Western Australia and heads the Department of Organisational and Labour Studies. He has published widely on the issue of international labour standards and manufacturing change and has edited a book on the new unions in Indonesia, *State and Labour in New Order Indonesia* (1997, UWA Press). He is presently coordinating an international research project on the globalisation of whitegoods manufacturing.

Eddie Webster is a Professor of Sociology at the University of the Witwatersrand in South Africa. He is the Director of the Sociology of Work Project (SWOP), which is engaged in a wide range of labour research. Professor Webster has had a 30-year association with the new independent labour movements in South Africa and has published widely on labour movement issues.

4

Rethinking the International Confederation of Free Trade Unions and its Inter-American Regional Organization[1]

Kjeld A Jakobsen

In responding to the impact of corporate globalization on the working class, the trade union movement needs not only to rethink its strategies, but also to review its international organization. This chapter highlights changes in the labour market such as the increase in unemployment, deregulation, informality, the stronger presence of women, and the issue of child labour. In this context, the chapter goes on to consider the growing social movements that might form alliances with trade unions for social change.

The present international confederations of trade unions—the International Confederation of Free Trade Unions (ICFTU), the World Confederation of Labor (WCL), and the World Federation of Trade Unions (WFTU)—were profoundly engaged in the cold war. Their structure today, particularly that of the ICFTU, is the same as 50 years ago. The ICFTU's structure mirrors the Leninist model of centralized direction practiced by its traditional opponent, the WFTU. Many national confederations resisted this East-West pressure during the Cold War, and chose to stay outside all of the international confederations. Post-Cold War, most have elected to become members of the ICFTU, believing it to be a democratic space for an open political debate, and in the hope of reform. However, expected change has been slow to materialize. This chapter explores the way in which changes already made in the Organización Regional Interamericana de Trabajadores (ORIT) might shape ongoing discussions in the ICFTU.

Faced with the far-reaching economic, political, and social changes that have occurred in the world, and their effects on the working class, the trade union movement has the considerable challenge of redefining its political priorities and structures. This was one of the concerns of the Brazilian trade union congress (CUT) and of similar organizations in other countries before the 17th World Congress of the International Confederation of Free Trade Unions (ICFTU) held in Durban, South Africa, in April 2000. However, we found ourselves frustrated, because, although the ICFTU may have politically outgrown the logic of the Cold War, it has yet to find its place within the new world order. It does not appear to have realized that this new global economic order cannot be confronted by using the old strategy, and that neoliberalism is not an inexorable process, the consequences of which must be accepted or even welcomed since we can have a minimum effect on them.

All of the proposals for structural reform of the ICFTU were referred to a "Millennium Debate" (also called the "Millennium Review"). This is legitimate because, although the majority of affiliated organizations want changes, there are different views of the direction that these should take. However, the "debate" in itself does not guarantee any practical outcome. The aim of the present chapter is to draw attention to some prior efforts to reform the ICFTU and its American regional organization, ORIT (Organización Regional Interamericana de Trabajadores), to present an assessment of the results of these efforts and to make some suggestions as to the way forward.

The Significance of the International Trade Union Movement in the Modern World

This is the first issue to be analyzed in attempting to arrive at a correct evaluation of the current balance of power and the characteristics of the class struggle. When Karl Marx issued the call "Workers of the world, unite!" in *The Communist Manifesto* in 1848, he was referring basically to the workers in the newly emerging industries of the countries of Western Europe. When the ICFTU was founded a hundred years later, the founding unions were labour organizations of this same Western Europe and North America, with a few trade union organizations from other continents. All of the prior attempts to create international organizations, from the First International onwards, including the ICFTU, had their merits and made important contributions to the history of the working class. However, it has to be recognized that these attempts also had their limitations, and that the cultures from which they emerged and which they produced are in many ways outdated. The working class today is not the same as it was in the time of Marx, and not even the same as it was when the ICFTU was founded.

We should also mention here the two other international labour organizations. The World Confederation of Labor (WCL) was founded in 1921, based on Christian principles, and operates in Latin America through the CLAT (Confederación Latino Americana de Trabajadores). The World Federation of Trade Unions (WFTU) was founded in 1945, although its origins go back to before World War II, to organizations influenced by Communism. Its Latin American organization is the CPUSTAL (Congresso Permanente de la Unidad Sindical de los Trabajadores de America Latina). At its foundation, the WFTU represented trade union organizations of the Allied countries that had opposed the Axis during World War II. When the US government proposed the Marshall Plan for funding the reconstruction of war-ravaged Europe, the countries of Eastern Europe, influenced by the Soviet Union, voiced their opposition to the political influence that this would obviously give the United States. This marked the beginning of the Cold War, and discussion of the subject within the WFTU led to the emergence of two distinct points of view. The organizations of the western countries were in the main favorable to the plan because it would aid European industrial reconstruction and result in the generation of employment. The organizations affiliated to Communist parties, on the other hand, were absolutely opposed, arguing that the Marshall Plan represented an external interference in European politics. This polarization was the justification for the withdrawal from the WFTU of the majority of the organizations in the western countries, to create the ICFTU in 1949.

The repercussions of the Cold War are still with us. In Latin America, we are still suffering the aftermath of military dictatorships, civil war in Central America, the revolution in Cuba, armed struggles in various countries, the money distributed so liberally by the AIFLD (American Institute for Free Labor Development), and the conflicting activities of the three international labour organizations. The ORIT is one of the fruits of this period of history, being founded in 1951 largely on the initiative of the American Federation of Labor-Congress of Industrial Organizations (AFL-CIO) and under its control. This was the Latin American representative of "free trade unionism," with strong anticommunist undertones but with an organic link to the ICFTU, founded only two years before. Its status was reinforced in 1963 when an agreement was signed with the US government and the AFL-CIO became responsible for 90% of the ORIT's budget. When the AFL-CIO withdrew from the ICFTU in 1969, because of condemnation of the war in Vietnam (among other reasons), it remained affiliated to the ORIT and increased its influence over that organization. The ORIT only resumed normal relations with the European trade union organizations and the ICFTU itself in the 1980s, after the AFL-CIO reaffiliated to the ICFTU in 1982.

This normalization of relations paved the way for a greater influence of European trade union organizations in South America.

Until that time, there had been only a few isolated bilateral programs between European organizations and Latin American trade unions. However, the involvement of the ORIT and its affiliates in these projects led to new confrontation between different concepts already present within the ICFTU.

Today, we are forced to live with a new capitalist model in the form of financial domination, rather than the material domination of the "30 golden years of capitalism" from the 1940s to the 1970s. Most countries have revived old theories of economic liberalism, the collapse of which at the beginning of the last century provoked two world wars, serious economic crises, the rise of Fascism and Nazism, and other specters. The economic importance of industrial and agricultural workers has declined, and the number of workers in the private service sector has increased, while employment in the public sector has decreased as the result of neoliberalism and the establishment of the "minimal state." Although the number of women and of children under 14 in the labour market has increased, the restructuring of production, privatization, and the fall of trade barriers have resulted in an overall fall in employment. Within our continent of South America in particular, we have seen the failure of the "import substitution model," foreign debt crises, and mediocre economic growth over the last 20 years. This has had serious consequences for workers, forcing the trade union movement to reorganize in order to face up to these new challenges.

In countries such as those of Latin America that entered late on the industrial scene, there was a mass migration of rural workers during the period between 1950 and 1980, seeking work in industry. Many found work, but many also had to be content with casual labour without security or formal contracts. In recent years, the restructuring of production has also forced the descendants of these rural workers into the informal labour market, in significant numbers. Many countries in the southern hemisphere have yet to experience industrial activity on any scale, and in these countries the only workers who have formal contracts are public employees. The remainder are poor and engage in unregulated activities that require little technical knowledge and offer little security.

The economically active population worldwide is currently estimated at approximately 2.4 billion. According to the International Labor Organization (ILO), in 1998 approximately 1 billion people— or approximately 17% of the world population—were unemployed or only casually employed. These figures include some 200 million working children under 14, often working under the most intolerable conditions, in prostitution, drug-related, or war-related activities. The cuts in expenditure on social services, which are occurring nearly everywhere in the world, have also contributed to forcing retired workers back into employment, generally on a casual basis, or have brought pensions below subsistence level. They also prevent young people from obtaining better educational and professional qualifications by forcing them into employment prematurely.

Unemployment, precarious working conditions, and casual employment primarily affect the more vulnerable sectors of society, such as women, the young, the old, and ethnic groups already subject to social discrimination. The trade union movement has the task of defending the rights and interests of all workers, including those who lack qualifications, those who are poorly paid, those who are at the bottom of the social hierarchy, and those who are unemployed, casually employed, or subject to forced labour. This role demands changes in focus and strategy. Strategies and forms of organization that were successful during the other periods of capitalism cannot deliver the desired results in the face of this different model.

The final phase of the period of "developmentalism" in Latin America occurred at a time when the majority of the countries were ruled by military dictators. The end of this period was a time of struggle for democracy and for the release of political prisoners and the amnesty of exiles, a struggle in which the trade unions played an important part, leading in some countries to a new trade unionism rooted in the utility and high-tech sectors, as well as in vigorous peasant movements. This is true of the national trade union confederations in Brazil, Chile, and Paraguay, for example, which have adopted new democratic trade union concepts and practices and have influenced the labour movement within the continent as a whole, including the ORIT, to which they later became affiliated. This period also saw the victory of the Sandinista revolution in Nicaragua and civil war in the majority of the countries of Central America, leading to direct US political and military intervention in the region, polarizing opinion within Latin American trade unions, where the majority were against this intervention and in favor of peace.

The repercussions of this period have been complex, especially given the historical background of trade unionism in the Americas, with its numerous streams such as anarchism, populism, Christianity, and nationalism, not to mention the influence of the three international organizations, which in some cases led to the founding of totally artificial movements. In contrast to the ICFTU, the ORIT has not been invulnerable to these changes. There has been a decline in the political influence of the organizations that supported military dictatorships, and at the same time there has been a general struggle for democracy throughout Latin America. This has permitted the intro-duction of significant changes that I will comment on below. The ORIT reflects a variety of trade union experiences and incorporates organ-izations of different sizes and capacities for mobilization, operating in very different social and economic conditions within the different countries of Latin America, but recent changes speak to the wider concerns facing the international trade union movement.

The Organization of World Trade Unionism

Like the national trade unions, the international labour movement has a geographically based structure in the form of the ICFTU, the WFTU, and the WCL and their regional organizations, and an indus-trially based structure in the form of the International Trade Secretariats. The ITSs follow the same principles as the ICFTU, although they are independent bodies. The total number of workers organized into trade unions represented by these international organizations and those represented by "independent" national organizations (not affili-ated to any international organization) is something over 300 million, or approximately 15% of the economically active population of the world. This includes the 150 million members claimed by the All China Federation of Trade Unions (ACFTU). Although the percentage of unionized workers is relatively small, these workers would represent a formidable political power if they were effectively organized and co-ordinated. However, this is not the case. We also need to give serious consideration to the problem that 85% of all the workers of the world are outside the trade union movement.

While the numbers of bodies affiliated to the WFTU and the WCL have remained the same or have decreased, the ICFTU is growing. There is little doubt that it is the most representative trade union body, both in the industrialized countries and in the underdeveloped or developing countries, although it still has a long way to go to become an ideal organization. Table 1 shows the distribution of trade unions affiliated to the ICFTU, distinguishing between the developed countries (G7 and other OECD countries) and the rest of the world. The table demonstrates that the representation of less developed countries (48%) is almost the same as for the developed countries (52%), and greater than that of the G7 countries (36%). However, the majority of the 90 organizations that affiliated between 1990 and 1999

Table 1: Organizations Affiliated with the ICFTU

Group	No. of Countries	Organizations	Members	%
G-7	7	12	44,357,416	35.6
Other OECD	17	19	21,019,959	16.9
Non-OECD	121	184	59,221,909	47.5
TOTAL	145	215	124,599,284	100.0

Source: ICFTU, November 1999. Hungary, Poland, the Czech Republic, Mexico, and South Korea, although members of the OECD, do not meet the same standards of development as the others and have therefore been included in the "Non-OECD" category. The five OECD countries included within "Non-OECD" have eight national centres, with 5,649,959 members, representing 4.6% of the total.

were from less developed countries, which is where the potential new members are. There are few organizations in the industrialized countries that are not already members of the ICFTU; the only way to grow in these countries is to increase the proportion of workers that are unionized.

The leadership of the ICFTU and most of the ITSs does not reflect potential trade union growth. These organizations are largely led by representatives from a minority of labour organizations in the industrialized countries, especially the G7 countries. Moreover, the leadership structure paradoxically copies the very Bolshevik model of the regimes which "free trade unionism" so vehemently opposes. This clandestine industry-based structure, devised by the Russian Social-Democratic Workers' Party at the beginning of last century (1903) and consisting of Congress delegates, a Central Committee and a General Secretary, is largely reflected in the hierarchy of both the ICFTU and the WFTU. This leadership model was fully justified in the context of the struggle against the authoritarian regime of Czarist Russia, in which revolutionaries were arrested, tortured and often executed, so that they needed a safe and efficient organization. However, 83 years after the fall of the Czar, in a climate of democracy and pluralism, this is an outdated structure for an international trade union organization. It needs to be changed to reflect the composition of the membership and the world in which we live. Hardly any of the national organizations retain such a centralized leadership structure, and even many of the ITSs and at least one regional organization, ORIT, have already modified their structures so as to broaden the leadership and spread the power and responsibilities, at least minimally.

The North-South Divide Within the Trade Union Movement

We have already seen that, understood as a division between the developed and less developed world, the representation of workers from the North and the South in the ICFTU and the ITSs is about equal, and that members from the South could possibly become a majority within a few years. In future, this needs to be reflected in the leadership and politics of these organizations. The major challenge for the international trade union movement is to integrate the struggles and concerns of workers both North and South. If it is to succeed, international trade unionism needs to find common ground between these workers. Without such initiative, the trade unions are at risk of falling victim to competition between the two hemispheres, with the eventual loss or erosion of workers' rights, to the detriment of all.

The unions need to address the fact that the effects of neoliberalism are different for the industrialized countries, which are conducting the process and are able to protect their economies should the need arise, and the surrounding countries, which are forced to adopt the model without any power to influence and adapt the way things are done. When it comes to discussions about the effects of globalization in the form of "free trade," the restructuring of production, or the liberalization of investment, it is not sufficient to demand that the basic rights of workers be safeguarded. What is the good of guaranteeing the right to freely organize and to bargain collectively, for example, after the jobs have been destroyed? For the workers of the South, it is fundamentally important that the international trade union agenda also includes unambiguous opposition to the neoliberal experiment and the discussion of alternatives that allow sustainable development with the generation of employment and income and the preservation of basic human and trade union rights.

The ICFTU's insufficient concern with such preoccupations led, for example, to the embarrassing situation in which the affiliated organizations in the industrialized countries unanimously support the World Trade Organization's (WTO) "Social Clause" (to protect workers in less developed countries against ultraexploitation as a result of the fall of trade barriers), while many of the affiliated organizations of Asia, Africa, and Latin America are still not sufficiently engaged in this campaign because of the lack of debate and remaining concerns about possible protectionist uses that could aggravate their already difficult economic situation. In other words, drawing up proposals in a bureaucratic fashion, without considering the real situation of all—or at least the majority—of the membership and without in-depth discussion of the issues involved, could divide and weaken workers in the face of globalization.

This situation was illustrated even more seriously in relation to the Multilateral Agreement on Investment (MAI). Various social organizations, trade union bodies, nongovernmental organizations (NGOs), and even governments were opposed to the content of these negotiations because of the radical neoliberalism of the proposals, which advocated subordinating national sovereignty to the interests of transnational corporations. Nonetheless, instead of joining forces against the MAI, the Trade Union Advisory Committee (TUAC) to the Organization for Economic Cooperation and Development (OECD) restricted itself to demanding, as a condition for the liberalization of investments, that reference to basic workers' rights and the environment be added to the preamble of the agreement and that other safeguards be included in the body of the proposal.

Discussions about these and other matters such as foreign debt, reform of multilateral institutions, international cooperation and free trade, and the liberalization of foreign direct investment (FDI) need to take the Southern perspective into account. It is not enough to call upon the International Monetary Fund and the World Bank to rethink their positions on human rights, workers' rights and the environment. These institutions continue to impose economic policies and structural adjustment on countries that request loans, and they actually cause poverty and the violation of human rights as they do so. The G7 countries have discussed canceling the foreign debts of poor countries —a very just proposal—but it has been suggested that debt cancelation should be linked to respect for the basic standards of the ILO. Between 1982 and 1998, the Third World countries paid four times what they borrowed; the right of nonpayment should therefore be conceded to all of them with no strings attached. We demand that trade agreements respect the basic standards of the ILO so as to avoid "social dumping," but not as a condition for conceding a right. Delay in the pardoning or nonpayment of foreign debt has been a crucial factor in obstructing the development of the majority of the world's peoples.

Finally, many regret the failure of the beginning of the Millennium Round, arguing that the less developed countries have lost the opportunity to increase their participation in world trade. However, this is a complete fallacy: to date, the results of free trade have only benefited the developed countries, which have led the process of globalization, to the detriment of the less-developed countries. The increase in the volume of trade has seen the less-developed countries absorbing more imports while the quality of their traded goods has declined. The beginning of a new round was not going to alter this situation. Seventy-one and a half percent of FDI has taken place in the developed world, and about 80% of what has reached the developing countries has been directed to privatization, acquisitions, mergers, and the restructuring of existing companies—processes that do not create new opportunities, but only increase unemployment.

In Europe, negotiation with governments and between workers and employees has deep cultural roots as the result of long years of struggle during the first half of the last century. In these countries, there is less need to resort to strike action. In the US, many companies have adopted antiunion policies. Together with legislation hindering organization, this means that the percentage of unionized workers is low, and millions of US workers are not covered by collective labour contracts. In Japan, company trade unions, seniority, and lifetime employment lead to a different situation, with more collaboration between unions and company management. In the South, however, it is still not uncommon for activists to be dismissed, imprisoned, or even murdered, simply for trying to organize workers into unions. This leads to serious workplace conflicts and means that it is nearly always only possible to make meaningful progress through negotiation if this is accompanied by a show of force. Until all those concerned properly appreciate these differing realities, it will remain difficult to define strategies for trade union campaigns at the global level. This demonstrates that the workers of the South need to have a greater say in the policy and practice of international trade union organization.

An Unsuccessful Attempt to Bring Change to the ICFTU

The first effective attempt to bring about substantive changes in the ICFTU occurred with the sudden resignation in 1994 of Enzo Friso as General Secretary of the organization. One of the candidates proposed as a replacement was Luis Anderson, a Panamanian trade union leader who, as General Secretary of ORIT since 1983, had given that body a more social-democratic emphasis. A group of leaders of European and American organizations gathered around him and, in proposing his candidature, suggested a series of changes in the ICFTU to meet the demands of the new situation of neoliberal ascendancy, globalization, and the end of the Cold War.

We all know the outcome. The other candidate, Englishman Bill Jordan, former General Secretary of the European Metalworkers

Federation, was elected, with the support of the largest affiliated organizations, the TUC (United Kingdom), DGB (Germany), JTUC-Rengo (Japan), the AFL-CIO (USA) and a majority of the African and Asian members. In Latin America he was also supported by the CTM of Mexico and the CTV of Venezuela.

Nevertheless, these discussions led to mature proposals being put before the 16th World Congress of the ICFTU in Brussels in 1996, supported by those organizations that had previously supported Luis Anderson. These proposals advocated the following four priorities for action and structural change:

1) Strengthening the united action of the international trade union movement by seeking to affiliate new, emergent, progressive organizations, establishing better relationships with independent organizations and those affiliated to other international organizations, and forming alliances with other social organizations;

2) A global campaign for employment, with the construction of a platform fighting for greater and better employment, an issue common to all, giving the ICFTU—for the first time—the role of coordinating trade union action on a global scale;

3) Intervention in regional, continental, and global trade agreements, in defense of workers' rights and the social dimension —another theme of common interest to the members; and

4) Establishment of the role of the ICFTU as the effective representative of workers in relation to such multilateral bodies as the IMF, the World Bank, the WTO, and others, questioning the policy of structural adjustment and proposing alternatives to it.

In addition to these policy changes, changes in the leadership structure were also proposed, including the creation of a Confederal Secretariat to direct the day-to-day administration of the organization. The Secretariat would have consisted of the President, General Secretary, and Assistant General Secretary of the ICFTU, the co-ordinator of the International Trade Secretariats, and the three general secretaries of the ICFTU regional organizations in the Americas, Africa, and Asia—respectively, the ORIT, the African Regional Organization (AFRO), and the Asia-Pacific Regional Organization (APRO). Luis Anderson's supporters believed that a global organization needs to reflect its globalness in its leadership. This stands in contrast to what has occurred ever since the foundation of the ICFTU, in which Europeans have always occupied the principal posts. The forces opposed to change at this level, however, united to prevent our proposals from being approved.

At the Durban Congress in April 2000, the CUT and others tried to present a more modest proposal through a motion to amend the statutes of the ICFTU. This would allow for the direct election at the congress of more than one Assistant General Secretary. At least one would come from an organization from a less developed country, as a way of ensuring a Southern presence and at least minimally sharing the power and day-to-day administrative responsibilities. The reaction of the "powers that be" was, after much discussion, to refer this amendment for consideration at the Millennium Debate. It was also to recommend that another Assistant General Secretary should be selected at the subsequent meeting of the Executive Committee, as provided for in the existing statutes, with the current Secretary General being disposed to support the candidature of a woman from the developing world.

A further amendment to the statutes was proposed to oblige member organizations, especially those entitled to more than two delegates, to make at least 50% of their nominated delegates to future congresses female. After considerable pressure the principle was approved, but on the condition that, if they could not meet this requirement, organizations would provide justification to the relevant committee. Both this reluctance and the position of the current Secretary General in reserving the second Assistant Secretary post for a woman—despite the argument made by the ICFTU women's committee that they wanted to discuss their participation in the Secretariat as including the possibility of occupying *any* of the seats, not just a "second assistant" one—illustrate how difficult it is to get gender considerations accepted within the union movement. And this occurs despite all the rhetoric favorable to the participation of women at all levels of the leadership.

The political and structural stagnation of the ICFTU is worrying. Many affiliated organizations are calling for change, but there is controversy as to the form that reform should take, and there is the risk that future change will lead to the regionalization and fragmentation of international policy. Thus, the European organizations could defend interests within the European Union through the European Trade Union Confederation (ETUC), while ORIT defended interests within the Mercosur, System of Central American Integration (SICA), and Caribbean Community (CARICOM), and the Asia-Pacific Regional Organization defended interests within the Asian Pacific Economic Cooperation and the Association of South-East Asian Nations (ASEAN), leaving the ICFTU with the role of coordinating trade union solidarity at global level. This would be a major error, given the process of globalization. Although global change affects regional policies in different ways, the scope of change means that we need a global organization more than ever before.

A Successful Reform of the ORIT

When these proposals for reform were discussed at the continental level, conditions for restructuring the ORIT proved to be more favorable. The experience within ORIT could serve as an example for the international trade union movement as a whole. The majority of affiliated organizations supported the proposals, including the new leadership of the AFL-CIO. The structural changes sought for the ORIT were basically the following:

- Decentralization and power sharing in the day-to-day running of the organization;
- Greater representation of the subregions in the leadership structure; and
- Division of executive responsibilities to meet growing demands.

Discussion within the ORIT began with the vacancy for the post of Assistant General Secretary in 1995. This opened a process of replacement and brought the opportunity to approve a new composition of the Executive Council. This was not accepted, so the process of consulting member organizations began, under the coordination of a Restructuring Commission, to draw up proposals to be presented to the congress. The run-up to the 1996 Congress began with a series of symposia designed to consult the affiliated organizations in the subregions. This concerned the priorities to be discussed at the congress and a definition of the tasks of the next leadership of ORIT.

At the same time, a detailed study of trade agreements within the continent was begun, with the setting up of a specific working group entitled "The Integration and Globalization Working Party." This was given the task of analyzing the implication of the trade agreements for workers and of organizing appropriate action by ORIT and its member organizations. The working party organized missions of union leaders, who met with government representatives, businessmen, and union organizations in different countries. They sought support for the adoption of the Social Clause at the WTO, for the creation of a Trade Union Forum in the Free Trade Area for the Americas (FTAA) on the same lines as the Business Forum, and for the establishment of a working party to evaluate the impact of the FTAA on jobs and workers' rights. The experience of attending the Ministerial Meetings at the FTAA in Denver and Cartagena also demonstrated that simply holding parallel interunion meetings and forwarding well-framed documents with analyses and demands to governments was completely ineffective, given the scope of the processes and interests involved and the inequality of the opposing forces.[2]

The Parallel Workers' Forum held in Belo Horizonte, Brazil, in May 1997 was a response to the preoccupations raised by the assessment for a new approach. It provided an opportunity to deliberate in more detail on the real significance of the FTAA for workers. The following quotation from the Manifesto of Working Men and Women of America is representative of the consensus: "As it is being implemented, the FTAA is an unjust and antidemocratic process which we oppose" (*Workers of the Americas Manifesto* 1997:n/a). We were also able to work together with other social organizations (NGOs and groups representing Indians, blacks, women, environmentalists, small businesses, and others) in various countries, including Canada, USA, Mexico, Chile, and Brazil. This effort produced a joint resolution. We also held a protest march and public demonstration which attracted approximately 10,000 people. During the march, demonstrators who were not part of the forum clashed with police, leading the authorities to block the avenue down which we were marching. It was really moving to see the major union leaders of the Americas, arm in arm, forcing their way through the riot police.

Belo Horizonte pointed the way toward a new direction for trade union intervention in trade agreements within the continent, based on reinforcing unity and integration with popular movements. The next stage of this struggle was to prepare a continental campaign for a social dimension to trade, and another parallel forum during the Second Conference of American Heads of State in Santiago, Chile, 1998. The ORIT contributed greatly to the success of this event. Hundreds of trade union bodies, social organizations, and NGOs gathered in Santiago and approved a document entitled "An Alternative for the Americas," proposing a policy for sustainable economic development with safeguards for the rights and interests of the more vulnerable sectors of society as a social alternative to neoliberal economic policies and free trade agreements within the continent. The meeting also saw the launch of the Continental Social Alliance (CSA), an informal network of social organizations, including the ORIT, which has continued to grow through the adhesion of other Brazilian networks. Some of these, like Rede Brasileira pela Integração dos Povos, Brazilian

Network for the Integration of Peoples (REBRIP), have been formed as a result of the stimulus provided by the CSA itself.

Finally a new leadership structure for the ORIT was approved at its 14th Congress, held on 22–25 April 1997 in Santo Domingo, the Dominican Republic, with more than 200 delegates and observers of whom 30% were women. A proposal on structural reform presented by the Restructuring Committee was approved, creating a Secretariat of five members with at least one being a woman.[3] This decision was particularly important, because it was the first time that a decision had been taken at an international union level to change the traditional power structure, centralized in the figure of the Secretary General. At this congress, delegates also focused on questions of employment, human and trade union rights, defense of collective bargaining, social security, education, organization, and unionization. Two other political discussions are worthy of note.

1) For the first time, an ORIT congress showed its unambiguous opposition to privatization, despite the fact that some organizations had supported privatization programs in their own countries.

2) When a resolution was presented condemning the US blockade of Cuba and the Helms-Burton Act (in the midst of consideration of the violation of human rights in that country), an objection was raised that this formulation would weaken the supportive nature of the resolution and provide the US government with more ammunition for the application of the act. After various arguments, both in favor and against this objection, it was agreed to refer this subject to the Executive Council for a decision.

Suggestions for the Future

Although there have been advances, the ORIT still has a way to go before it can truly be called an "inter-American trade union organization." This is also the case for the ICFTU in its sphere of representation. Despite the claims of some of the older staff members that there have been significant changes during the last decade, the whole structure of the ICFTU needs reform. We would like to note here some suggestions for the future direction of the two organizations:

1) The Millennium Debate launched at the 17th ICFTU World Congress in Durban led to the formation of a working

committee (Progress Group) consisting of the Secretary General, the President of the Administrative Committee, representatives of the Women's and Youth Committees, and representatives of the regional organizations. In addition, the committee will include representatives of the affiliated organizations in Western and Eastern Europe and of the TUAC and the ITSs, and two major figures of the trade union world, Bob White (former president of the CLC of Canada) and Leroy Trotman (of Barbados, former President of the ICFTU). Although the methodology, scope and time of the discussion will be defined by the committee itself, there are still many issues to be faced. These include meaningful discussion with the other international trade union movements and the willingness of the ITSs to participate effectively in the formation of a forum which will take the final decisions, especially those which will bring about changes in the articles of the ICFTU Constitution.

2) In the case of the ORIT, the Secretariat, with representatives of all the subregions except for the Caribbean, permits greater integration, respect, and exchange between the different trade union cultures. However, this is still not enough; the organization still suffers from the legacy of the historical North-South divide. One of the challenges before us is the absolute necessity of building a closer-knit and more unified organization. The organization of united fronts in relation to multinational companies, free trade, and the multilateral financial institutions could contribute to this. We also need to initiate discussion on the introduction of workers' committees in multinational companies.

3) Given the current situation, we need to strengthen trade union solidarity in the Americas, both internally among the affiliated organizations and externally by strengthening relations with the independent national organizations and other international organizations. Historically, the worst feature of the labour movement has been sectarianism. This has divided the movement both organically and politically to such a point that organizations have frequently been at odds with one another and even fought one another, much to the delight of the moguls of industry and government.

In order to avoid this within ORIT, it has been necessary to devise strategies for each subregion and each country, as well as to create a willingness to live with other concepts of trade unionism. Errors have been committed in the past. For example, in Peru the CGTP, affiliated with the WFTU, has undoubtedly been the most representative national trade union organization for many years. When the Confederación de Trabajadores del Peru, traditionally affiliated with the ICFTU/ORIT, was suspended for embezzling money from international sources, instead of working with the real trade union movement it created the Central Unica de Trabajadores (CUT) Peru. This claims 2 million members, mostly in casual employment, whose existence is, to say the least, suspect.

A somewhat similar error was made when the CUT, with a clearly leftist political tendency, became the largest national trade union organization in Colombia. The ICFTU/ORIT later ended up affiliating one of its offshoots, the Frente Unitária de Trabajadores Democráticos (FUTD), in violation of all the criteria that guide the acceptance of new members and at the risk of dividing the organization. This particular situation has been overcome because the FUTD has disappeared.

4) The region of Central America warrants special attention. Nearly all of the countries in this area have been involved in long civil wars with thousands being left dead, wounded, and homeless. This has had serious repercussions for the union movement, because in these conflicts the trade unions have been forced to take the side either of the rebels or the government. There has been no middle ground, and thus regular trade union activity has not been possible during this period.

Now that peace has been achieved, the reconstruction of the unions faces numerous difficulties. When those who joined the rebels attempt to organize trade unions, they tend to start from their political and military experience, resulting in vertically structured organizations that are not suited to their function. The others are faced with a dilemma concerning their relationship with governments that have implemented neoliberal policies, with their well-known attacks on worker rights. Central America nowadays is the paradise of export processing zones and *maquiladoras* (assembly plants).

The effects of the Cold War and of misguided international aid have also caused considerable fragmentation within the trade union movement in the region, to the extent that in El Salvador, the smallest of the countries, there are six organizations that claim to represent the workers nationally.

Mexico has not suffered the consequences of war to quite the same degree, but the trade union movement within the country finds itself in a special situation. This is a heavily populated and industrialized country with the potential for a strong trade union movement. However, the close past relationship of the CTM (Confederación de Trabajadores Mexicanos) with the PRI (Partido Revolucionario Institucional), and consequently with the government, has prevented this potential from being realized. The neoliberal policies of the government and the existing trade union structure have made it difficult for alternatives to emerge. Recently, however, a new representative body, the UNT (Unión Nacional de Trabajadores) emerged out of agreement between democratic trade unions and dissidents from the CTM. This movement promises to be independent of government and political parties and to break with the corporatism traditional to Mexico. Although there are internal divisions due to its mixed origins, it could become a viable alternative for trade unionists.

5) The recent affiliation to ICFTU and ORIT of the Canadian CSN and the Nicaraguan CST still leaves other national organizations that may also join in the future, such as the CUTs of Colombia and Honduras, the PIT-CNT in Uruguay, the CTA in Argentina, the COB in Bolivia and Unsitrágua in Guatemala. The affiliation of these organizations should be a target in strengthening ORIT, because they can contribute to its plans for action (especially in Central America, with considerable emphasis on agriculture, which is the principal activity in the area).

6) It is also necessary to make an effort to be self-supporting. The annual contributions of organizations affiliated to ORIT add up, at the very most, to around US$200,000, which is completely inadequate to sustain international work of this scope. The remainder of the budget is covered by donations from the ICFTU and international aid.

7) On the subject of funding, international aid is another important issue which needs to be assessed by ORIT, in relation not so much to the funding of its own projects as to funds channeled through it to its affiliated organizations. Without a clear union strategy and without targets, deadlines and policies directed to making the projects self-sustaining, collaboration can do more harm than good, as has already been proven in some cases. (The Peruvian CTP was recently

expelled from the ICFTU/ORIT for misappropriation of international funds; and FENASTRAS of El Salvador was also expelled for supporting the government policy of installing *maquiladoras* and for slandering another affiliated organization in El Salvador, the CTD.)

8) Finally, it is crucial to develop unity among workers in the face of neoliberal globalization. During the Cold War, it was easier to call for unity because this was in support of a struggle against dictatorship and in favor of democracy. Today, however, the situation is more complex: the political and economic model against which this unity is directed has democracy as one of its formal pillars. The ORIT is not the only organization to be faced with this dilemma. It affects any international trade union organization actively involved in the problems of movements in different countries, when such involvement manifests itself supranationally in the criticism of neoliberal policies (as in the case of recent popular demonstrations in Bolivia, Peru, Ecuador, and Colombia).

Closing Remarks

Over the past few years, the trade union movement throughout the world has had the opportunity to reassess its future. Twenty years of neoliberalism have convinced the public that alternatives are needed. The movements against unemployment and the erosion of social rights that have occurred in different European countries in recent years demonstrate a reaction against the more perverse effects of the neoliberal experiment. They force new themes onto the trade union agenda, in addition to establishing a new unity and solidarity; we are seeing the employed fighting for the rights of the unemployed and workers with a right to social security defending those who are denied this right.

The general strike in South Korea in 1997 attacked government reforms intended to flexibilize workers' rights and smashed one of the pillars of neoliberalism, the flexibility of labour rights, with supranational repercussions. The strike received massive international support, coordinated by the ICFTU. In the same way, the successful strike of the US United Postal Service workers against part-time working gave the lie to the neoliberal claim that the flexibilization of workers' rights in the country was leading to the creation of employment and improvement in the conditions of North American workers. The demonstration organized in the four Mercosur countries in December

1996 by the Coordination of Trade Union Organizations of the Southern Cone in support of the right of workers in the region was also a first, like the joint demonstration with other social bodies in Belo Horizonte during the FTAA Conference.

Recent decisions by the ORIT with regard to both its structure and its policies have brought it closely into tune with the current situation and given it an agenda which allows it to take specific offensive actions, such as the continental campaigns for increased employment (by decreasing the length of the working day), and action in support of agrarian reform, and the extension of ILO Convention 58 on the termination of employment. With the efforts of the new leadership and the collaboration of the member organizations, this campaign could become a factor in bringing about change and could provide a model for united action on a continental and world scale. Unity occurs among equals with the same objectives, but alliances can be made with independent bodies that have at least partially overlapping objectives. For all its 300 million unionized workers, the world trade union movement cannot bring the neoliberal experiment to an end on its own.

A recent high point of these new initiatives was the demonstration in Seattle against the WTO, or at least against the adverse effects of globalization. This was called for by the North American trade unions together with social organizations and NGOs, and it attracted almost 50,000 people. Together with the failure of the beginning of the Millennium Round, this demonstration has had a considerable impact on public opinion by showing that "something is rotten in the state of globalization." We can be sure that there will be more such demonstrations.

The ORIT has the potential and the confidence to play a new role in coordinating supranational action in support of trade union development where it is weakest, and in pointing the international trade union movement in new, more authentic, and more progressive directions. In the meantime, we continue to await a positive response from the ICFTU about its reforms.

Endnotes

[1] Editorial note: This chapter was translated from the Portuguese original by B W Howells. It has been checked by Peter Waterman and Jane Wills. Given the large number of organizational acronyms, we have decided to provide only those considered central to the argument. This has been done in English, Portuguese, or Spanish as seemed appropriate. Responsibility for the result must rest with us. For an earlier Spanish version of this chapter, see Jakobsen (1998).

[2] The international trade union movement is not unaccustomed to holding meetings to discuss big issues that it has little power to influence, either because of lack of union involvement or because of the extent of the problem. A well-known example is the meeting held in São Paulo in 1995 during the war between Peru and Ecuador. This was intended to discuss the position of the ORIT. Representatives of the affiliated organizations of the two warring countries and of the countries of the so-called Rio Group responsible for negotiating a peace agreement were present. The meeting took nine hours to draw up a document of five paragraphs, with the representatives of Peru and Ecuador both trying to persuade the meeting to support the positions of their respective countries. It could well be asked what contribution this meeting made to resolving the conflict.

[3] The Secretariat consisted of the following posts: President, General Secretary, Administrative and Finance Secretary, Trade Union Policy Secretary, and Economic and Social Policy Secretary. The people elected to these posts were, respectively, Dick Martin of the CLC, Canada; Luis Anderson of the CTRP, Panama; Angel Zerpa Mirabal of the CTV, Venezuela; Amanda Viatorro of the CTD, El Salvador; and Vitor Baez Mosqueira of the CUT, Paraguay.

References

Jakobsen K A (1998) Nuevos rumbos en la ORIT? (New challenges in the ORIT?). In Maria Silvia Portella de Castro and Achim Wachendorfer (eds) *Sindicalismo y Globalización: La Dolorosa Inserción en un Mundo Incierto* (pp 307–318). Caracas: Nueva Sociedad

Workers of the Americas Manifesto (1997) Parallel Workers' Forum, 11–15 May, Belo Horizonte, Brazil

Kjeld Aagaard Jakobsen is a Brazilian and a trade unionist from the electrical sector. He has been a member of the CUT's Executive Board since 1991 and its International Secretary since 1994, and served as its Acting President from May to August 2000. He has been Vice President of the ORIT since 1995 and a Director of the ICFTU since 1996. He is the author of articles on globalization and international trade unionism as well as free trade and labour rights.

5

Transnational Capital, Urban Globalisation and Cross-Border Solidarity: the Case of the South African Municipal Workers

Franco Barchiesi

The chapter discusses the redefinition of strategies of international solidarity and action in South African organised labour, with particular regard to the South African Municipal Workers' Union (SAMWU). SAMWU has recently been challenged by the pervasive penetration of global capital and multinational corporations in schemes of "Public–Private partnership" in the delivery of municipal infrastructures. These developments carry potential dangers for trade union organisation and for public services in a context of extreme inequality. SAMWU has identified international action against global capitalism as a decisive terrain of struggle for workers' and citizens' rights. However, the union's difficulties in articulating an effective confrontation at this level reflects broader problems in internationalist approaches adopted by South African labour. These refer primarily to a problematic conceptualisation of new subjects of opposition and of alliances with emerging global social movements.

Neoliberal Transitions and the Crisis of Union Internationalism

Recent changes in policy priorities—spurred by the globalisation of financial flows and macroeconomic liberalisation—have emphasised on a global scale the role of transnational corporate actors, in ways that substantially affect national labour organisations, their forms of representation vis-à-vis states and employers and forms of international solidarity. For many observers, these processes have caused a decline of patterns of union internationalism based on Western-style national organisations of a predominantly male industrial proletariat. At the same time, new questions are arising about the possibility of rebuilding forms of labour internationalism that—far from automatically reproducing the centrality of the trade union organisational form

—define relationships with new and diversified oppositional subjects and resistance practices. These are emerging, and connecting on a global scale, to respond to the new configuration of capitalist corporate power in the age of neoliberalism.

The following pages will assess these dynamics with a focus on the South African Municipal Workers Union (SAMWU), one of the country's largest worker organisations, with a reputation for entrenched grassroots radicalism. SAMWU's strategies of international solidarity and cross-border linkages will be assessed with regard to the restructuring of municipal services, particularly the deepening private sector participation in water provision.

The South African case acquires a peculiar significance for three main reasons. First, South Africa is a recently democratised developing country in which globalised capital has played a decisive role in the transition from authoritarianism to democracy. This has contradicted previous emphases on the state's developmental functions. Second, these developments have challenged the decisive role that working-class organisation and mobilisation had gained in opposition to apartheid. Third, South Africa provides a laboratory for Public–Private partnership schemes in basic services and infrastructures. The nature of these goods as social needs emphasises the role of neoliberal restructuring in defining new terrains of worker and citizens' opposition to what is often perceived as privatisation driven by the profit motive to the detriment of equal rights. At the same time, the predominant role that foreign companies have assumed in such shifts immediately internationalises the issue for SAMWU and its allies, which are faced with the task of reconstructing new forms of global solidarity and cross-border alliances.

The concept of globalisation implies the ability of transnational capital to valorise specific localities in ways that are decreasingly dependent on the regulatory capacity of the state to bind investment to social conditions, fiscal obligations and developmental goals (Mittelman 1996; Teeple 1995). At the same time, new forms of international regulation have emerged, exemplified by the structural adjustment policies (SAPs) sponsored by the International Monetary Fund (IMF) and the World Bank (WB) and trade liberalisation advanced by the World Trade Organisation (WTO). These facilitate a general macroeconomic consensus around free trade and the attraction of international investment as desired policy goals (Ghai 1996). Conversely, the opportunities provided by the liberalisation of financial investment make the immediate aim of development efforts integration in the capitalist world economy, rather than the satisfaction of domestic demand and local needs. This emphasises the role of multinational corporations (MNCs) as engines of integration (Hirst and Thompson 1994; Hoogveldt 1997). At the same time, the benefits of this process have been unequally distributed. New divisions of labour in developing countries are based on the externalisation by core countries of labour-intensive segments of production, performed by largely informalised, vulnerable and unorganised sectors of the labour force (Munck 1998; Thomas 1995). Finally, a loss of juridical sovereignty by nation-states has often been lamented and the role of subnational actors such as municipalities concomitantly been emphasised in the provision of fiscal incentives, infrastructures, funding and partnership arrangements for transnational capital (Feagin and Smith 1987; Sassen 1992, 1996). This often reproduces forms of dualism in urban labour markets, with a high-tech finance-based economy contrasting with new peripheries of low-skill, low-wage, unprotected workers (Benner 2000).

From labour's point of view, rising capital mobility and the variety and unevenness of the arrangements by which specific localities are valorised by transnational investment flows imply important challenges. It has been noticed that capital mobility has undermined nationally based class compacts (Coates 1999), weakened national union organisations (Moody 1997) and stimulated the emergence of a new transnational working-class solidarity (Davis 2000; Sassen 1998). A number of diverse cases show how the marginalisation of labour organisations from their traditional sites of power and influence, coupled with worsening living conditions and precariousness, has increased the sensitivity of worker activists to issues of workplace-community linkages, deindustrialisation, poverty, unemployment, and prices, standards and availability of social services (Jonas 1998; Needleman 1998; Witheford 1997). These linkages popularise, at a local level, the systemic connections between transnational capital, new forms of supranational economic and financial regulation, and the promotion of liberalisation, privatisation and fiscal discipline policies, leading to the decline of employment, working standards, environmental protection and social welfare (Gills 2000; Klein 2000). As a result, an increasingly globalised imagery has emerged to provide arguments and analyses to localised workers' and community struggles.

This new spirit has been demonstrated by episodes such as the 1999 demonstrations against the Seattle summit of the WTO and the anti-IMF/WB demonstrations in Washington in April 2000 and Prague in September 2000. However, these developments present labour organisations with the problem of relating to new social movements in ways that require the rethinking of longstanding and established notions of labour internationalism (O'Brien et al 2000). Michael Hardt and Antonio Negri (2000) have recently provided a convincing analysis of the relations between the rise of new forms of transnational capitalism and the crisis of established patterns of internationalism. Their concept of "empire" defines the social form of globalised capitalism and its political structures. This is characterised by the absence of national boundaries in a form of corporate capitalist domination, where social welfare provisions, rights and services have undergone a pervasive privatisation and commodification. The process ends up in an articulation of local spaces and functions by deterritorialised transnational companies that are networked by immaterial flows of information and finance. In moving onto this level, the globalisation of capitalist domination represents a response to previous patterns of international solidarity, linking separate national working classes into a single class around common struggles and socialist objectives. While the power of this class was recognised by state-based Keynesian and welfarist deals, capital could ultimately prevail over working-class power only by accepting and turning to its advantage the new global terrain of confrontation that working-class internationalism had envisaged. The resultant globalisation of investment flows, technological practices, forms of work and production organisation substantially weakened the national workers' organisations that had nurtured the "old" internationalism.

Another factor that has queried a proletarian internationalism based on the national organisations of the industrial working class is the role played by social movements and their cultures in developing societies (Alvarez, Dagnino and Escobar 1998). In these cases, the advance of neoliberal policies, the erosion of public services and the deepening of inequality and marginality multiply the terrains of radical organising and mobilisation, bringing to the fore a plurality of social subjects. These include women's struggles against the unequal gendered burden of structural adjustment policies, intellectuals and students contesting the commodification of education, church-based activism against foreign debt repayment, environmental resistance to the corporate plunder of nonrenewable resources, opposition to military spending and movements for the enforcement of indigenous rights and against the enclosure of communal land. These organisations can be invaluable allies to worker organisations as unions forge new networks of opposition to capitalism (Waterman 2000).

As a result of these contemporary challenges, the model of labour internationalism inherited from the now endangered industrial working class faces two broad alternatives. As Eric Lee (1996) observes, although the "old" labour internationalism has virtually collapsed under the blows of the current configuration of global corporate power, attempts have been made to adapt the outlook and strategies of worker solidarity to face a globalised capitalism. Tentative steps in this direction include forms of international action against productive delocalisation (as in the case of the cross-border mobilisation by Spanish, French and Belgian unions against the closure of the Renault plant in Vilvoorde (Belgium), announced in 1997) and the embryonic forms of unitary wage strategies around the European works councils (see Wills this issue). However, these have generally failed to make significant inroads into managerial prerogatives on productive, locational and employment strategies. This is largely due to the steady decline in union density in all the countries concerned, the growing diversification of labour markets and the fact that unions are usually part of national productivity deals and corporate identities that weaken their grassroots radicalism and transnational mobilising potential (Schmitthenner 1999; Wills 2000). In these cases, unions could try to internationalise their wage and productivity bargaining strategies inside major corporations. However, factors such as the lack of social security for migrant, atypical, unwaged workers and the use of environmentally destructive means of production seem to require that the union movement be part of programmes and coalitions of different social actors, if the movement is to be able to change social policy priorities and the utilisation of resources. The conflict between environmentalism and organised labour on the conversion of heavy industry in many European countries seems to be a case in point.

Issues of social integration, expansion of social entitlements and the protection of fair labour standards feature prominently in recent positions assumed by the main international union centre, the International Confederation of Free Trade Unions (ICFTU 2000). However, this orientation falls short of demands expressed globally by rising anticorporate and antineoliberal social movements. The organisation's response to the Seattle demonstrations, while recognising that trade policy can no longer remain the WTO's exclusive precinct, does not go beyond the demand to include specific mechanisms for the treatment of developing countries and labour standards in the WTO. Therefore, it is given the power to solve imbalances created by its own liberalising agenda. This misses the fundamental criticism of the WTO expressed in Seattle. As Peter Waterman (2000) concludes, advocating such a lobbying role for trade union internationals in relation to national and supranational institutions and in the context of an unchanged tripartite bargaining framework is a hindrance, even if it is occasionally included in demands for new global coalitions. In practice, the networking strategies adopted by new social movements to identify common orientations out of different experiences and values are hardly in accordance with the traditional centrality of the factory working class and the hierarchical structure of mainstream unions (Borgers 2000; Danaher and Burbach 2000).

In conclusion, the decline of the "old" internationalism has left union movements with new challenges in their search for new ways to articulate international solidarity. On the one hand, unions have tried to update the old internationalism, adapting it to the new terrains of confrontation marked by global corporate penetration. However, this strategy carries with it the risk of confirming union centrality in solidarity processes that do not represent the growing areas of exclusion generated by the current phase of global capitalist restructuring (Lambert 1998). On the other hand, unions are also presented with opportunities to enrich their objectives and priorities, multiply their points of contact and alliance with social movements and reach out towards diversified constituencies. In the final analysis, this bifurcation of alternatives for labour internationalism highlights the ability of trade unions to reinvent themselves as actors in broader patterns of global solidarity (Waterman 2001). As the following case study from South Africa will show, individual unions, organising in sectors more exposed to capitalist globalisation and transnational corporate dominance, are confronted in their local or industry-specific struggles with the implications arising from these global challenges.

A Rude Awakening: Unions and Neoliberalism in the New South Africa

The transition to a democratic political system in postapartheid South Africa has been influenced by the global hegemony of market-orientated approaches. These have profoundly modified, before and after the 1994 electoral victory of the African National Congress (ANC), the perceptions and perspectives of all the main social and political actors involved (Marais 1998). Conversely, options of state-led and demand-driven developmentalism have gradually been marginalised (Bond 2000a). The redress of deep class, gender and spatial inequalities inherited from the past has come increasingly to depend on a notion of economic growth premised on fiscal discipline, containment of public spending and strengthening business confidence. This has also implied attempts to involve local and foreign private capital in the provision of basic services and infrastructures in different schemes of "partnership" with the state. This shift was expressed in the Growth, Employment and Redistribution (GEAR) strategy in 1996. The strategy subordinated, in particular, the expansion of public spending and state intervention, to results in terms of deficit-to-gross-domestic-product ratios and overall growth targets that have hardly proven achievable.

The scarcity of resources for social service delivery and the decision to reduce public spending have been generally disguised as painful but necessary fiscal constraints, imposed by the priority of growth in macroeconomic indicators, in an essentially "trickle-down" approach (Marais 1998). However, imposed scarcity has been unable to link growth and social development. South Africa remains heavily dependent on the disproportionate role of financial capital (Standard Bank Economic Division 1999), which has shifted patterns of accumulation and investment away from job-creating activities and labour-intensive production sensitive towards domestic needs. Vast areas of unsatisfied social needs, especially among the black population, reflect the gaps between urban and rural areas, between shrinking formal employment and the expanding (largely female) informal and casualised workforce and between black townships and predominantly white suburbs. This latter divide is inherited from the separate institutions and discriminatory residential patterns for the reproduction of the labour force put in place by the past racist regime. As a result, with an unemployment rate of about 30%, half of the population survives with little more than 10% of the national income (May 2000), a fifth of urban households have no electricity and a quarter have no running water. The cost of providing extremely basic household services like an outdoor tap, a flush toilet and electricity is twice the amount currently allocated by the government (Cashdan 2000).

Organised labour's position in South African society is threatened by the modification of the social status of waged labour. The stability of the wage relation—now the linchpin of life strategies and income prospects for a declining number of households—is in crisis, undermining its past function as a mechanism of socialisation for a working class capable of demanding social rights and equality (Barchiesi 2000). According to recent research, waged employment is no longer able to provide an effective barrier against poverty. In fact, formal wages provide the most important source of income to the poorest 40% of South African households, while 47% of the "poor households" and 35% of the "very poor households" have at least one economically active member employed (NALEDI 1999:40). In the case of the "poor", this figure is higher than the one for households with all active members unemployed. Full-time employment is a reality for just 42.6% of the economically active population and for only about a third of Africans. For the rest, waged employment largely means casual or temporary jobs (NEDLAC 2000). These data reflect new areas of working-class poverty and exclusion that are no longer confined to the experience of unemployment.

Finally, the pattern of transition adopted by the South African democratic state has severely reduced the space for the union movement within political initiative and programmes. As a special case in postcolonial Africa, trade unions were decisive in the demise of apartheid. Their organisational strength, mass base and capacity for mobilisation provided the most important source of internal opposition during the decades of repression that drove the ANC to largely underground and foreign-based operations (Baskin 1991; Friedman 1987). Working-class struggles were revived in the first half of the 1970s, and black trade unions retained a predominantly factory workplace orientation. This allowed them significant gains and survival in the face of repression, until popular opposition in the townships was resumed in the first half of the 1980s and a new generation of ANC-aligned worker organisations emerged. A hotly contested debate then led the union movement in a direction defined as "social movement unionism" (Webster 1988). Workers' participation in popular protests and stayaways for political democratisation, the end of state brutality, the upgrading of social services and improvements in the quality of life forged new alliances between unions and community organisations. In 1985 the Congress of South African Trade Unions (COSATU) was founded, the culmination of a union unity process whose outcome was the definition of a formal alliance between COSATU and the ANC.[1] After the 1994 elections, COSATU became a partner of the ANC-led ruling alliance, together with the South African Communist Party (SACP). This federation acquired a decisive role in policy-making forums and institutions, with several national and local union leaders elected via the ANC lists. However, this also meant that the union federation was confined to defending workers' rights in the framework of modernisation defined by the free-market policies of the ruling party. COSATU has therefore been hampered in advancing an alternative to the rise of a neoliberal orientation inside the ANC leadership. Other factors have also contributed to this outcome, such as the exodus of experienced union leaders and organisers towards the party's ranks, the permanently high levels of unemployment, the links of personal patronage that tied many COSATU cadres to the ANC and an increasingly fashionable image of waged workers as relatively privileged compared to the vast masses of the poor and marginalised (Buhlungu 1997).

For some writers, a combination of political democratisation, macro-economic conservatism and institutionalisation of social inequality is an outcome of ten years of South African transition (Bond 2000a; Desai 1999; Marais 1998; McKinley 1997). At the same time, new actors have come to the fore in the policy process, including trans-national financial institutions and companies, layers of technocrats and consultants, a new black corporate elite, rising forms of local microentrepreneurship and marginalised masses to be gratified with at least a symbolic semblance of "delivery". The ANC's need to strike deals with this plurality of actors has eroded the authority that old and established allies gained during "the struggle", imposing renewed sacrifices on a working-class constituency whose loyalty to the ruling party was guaranteed by the union's position in the "alliance".

COSATU and its affiliates retain a crucial position in self-styled "corporatist" bodies of tripartite economic and social policy-making —which also include state and business representatives—and in a host of forums of industrial restructuring and workplace participation and cooperation. However, they have found the agenda of these structures increasingly determined by the need to raise business confidence and reduce social conflict. This has led unions to fight from a defensive position against proposals involving the privatisation of state assets, labour market flexibility and limitation of the public role to "safety nets" for the extremely poor. Important signs of disaffection and scepticism have recently emerged at union grassroots level towards the COSATU-ANC-SACP alliance and the role played in it by the union federation (Buhlungu 1997). It is not uncommon today to see COSATU affiliates and local sections of many unions being involved in "antiprivatisation" and "antineoliberal" coalitions and alliances with other social movements.[2] This scenario carries important challenges for the solidarity politics of the federation and its affiliates, particu-larly in terms of defining new relations with global social movements.

Local Government Restructuring, Global Capital and the Commodification of Basic Needs: The Case of Water Services

South African municipal workers' struggles underline the relevance of issues of privatisation both in linking union activism to the broader demands of grassroots communities and in providing new potential connections between the discourses of local specificity and globalised resistance. The ways in which such connections are elaborated, however, contain unresolved questions for rebuilding forms of labour internationalism. SAMWU's opposition to the privatisation of urban social services and its defence of their decommodification have highlighted the contradictions arising from the involvement of transnational corporations in public service delivery (Bond 2000b; Van Niekerk et al 1999). This new political landscape has been reflected in a language of opposition that expresses workers' struggles that stretch beyond the workplace to relate to demands for social citizenship rights.

A new form of local state is emerging in South Africa, one that replaces the "redistributive" state advocated in previous stages of the transition (Bond, Dor and Reuters 2000). In fact, the process tends to separate authority from service provision at the local level, where the latter is increasingly contracted to the private sector. Services tend therefore to be reorganised as independent business units and cost-centres, respondent to the profit motive, organised along managerial criteria and subject to business assessment of viability and sustainability, with decreasing subsidization from other levels of government (Ruiters and Bond 1998). The local state redefines its role as an agency whose main priority becomes that of channelling global capital flows through a balance between socially accessible levels of delivery and private corporate economic advantages. These are codified in the type of contract adopted, its length, its regulation, its subdivision of risks and the scope it allows the private managers of the contracted utility.

This restructuring of municipal services takes place in the context of a racially based subdivision of local government structures and finances from the apartheid era, which was responsible for unequal and discriminatory access to land, housing, water, electricity and other social services (Bond 2000b). In the past four years, budget constraints imposed on local government have facilitated an increasing number of concession contracts, where transnational corporations with widespread global interests have been called upon to organise, build, manage and maintain the delivery of basic social necessities.

The contracting out of services to private companies has been accompanied by a radical downsizing of local level subsidization from other tiers of government. South African municipalities are expected to raise from local sources (mainly fees and rents) a particularly high level of their budget—approximately 90%. At the same time, inter-governmental transfers, used to finance operating costs and provide basic services and therefore highly redistributive in nature, have been slashed (by 85% between 1991 and 1998; Friedrich Ebert Stiftung 1998). The programmatic and ideological underpinnings of such developments are contained in the 1998 "White Paper on Local Government" (Department of Constitutional Development 1998) and "Framework for the Restructuring of Municipal Service Provision" (South African Local Government Association 1998), the latter signed by COSATU and the South African Local Government Association. The Framework defines the public sector as the "preferred method" for service delivery aimed at universal coverage, and it commits the parties involved to mutual consensus over the restructuring and implementation of Public–Private partnerships (PPPs). The "White Paper", on the other hand, lists a series of possible contracting options for municipal services. Research conducted into existing PPPs reveals that the government favours contracts of concession, rather than simple maintenance of services (Bond 2000b; Van Niekerk et al 1999). Under a concessionary regime, private companies assume extremely broad responsibilities for service management, extension of infra-structures, new "greenfield" developments and collection of tariffs from end-users. The high level of commercial risk implied in this kind of contract often requires extensions of up to 30 years of its duration. Researchers therefore define this delegation as a form of privatisation: even without the sale of state assets, the production and delivery of services are transferred to companies operating on the basis of profit-making and cost-recovery principles.

This process tends to facilitate job reductions, deterioration of wages and working conditions, limitations on union power and geographically uneven quality of service. In particular, impoverished communities receive lower quality and relatively high cost services, coupled to intensified rates of disconnections for "rate-defaulters". In March 1999 the South African government admitted that between 50% and 90% of water projects being implemented had suffered interruptions or complete failure, largely due to poor maintenance and people's inability to pay (African Eye News Service 9 May 1999).

Water services have provided the most advanced area of experi-mentation, and the most relevant testing ground for SAMWU's strat-egies of international solidarity. The 1997 Water Services Act explicitly separates the functions of the water services regulatory authority and the water services provider. It commits the Department of Water Affairs to consider recovery of operating and maintenance expenses from consumers, regardless of income structures. At the same time, the government's Municipal Infrastructures Investment Framework

(MIIF) explicitly limits the extent of service subsidisation by the state only to extreme areas of socioeconomic disadvantage. For these, in any case, the funding of communal facilities (such as collective pit latrines and taps) rather than household ones has been suggested (Bond, Dor and Ruiters 2000).

Transnational companies engaged in water services management in developing countries have grown at an impressive speed during the past twenty years, largely as a result of privatisation policies conducted by Western European governments. The sector now shows a high degree of oligopolistic concentration based on a few global players, with diversified interests (including banking, media, chemical and construction) and market presence in several countries (Hall 1999). All the major players operating in the South African market, in particular, greatly benefited from water privatisation in the 1980s neoliberal season in France (companies include SAUR-Bouygues, Vivendi and Suez-Lyonnaise) and the United Kingdom (Biwater). Some of these were already involved in water services for the black "homelands" established by apartheid.

The first municipal privatisation projects in "white" South Africa took place in the first half of the 1990s in Fort Beaufort, Queenstown and Stutterheim, all in the Eastern Cape (Bond, Dor and Ruiters 2000:27). Following these, the government recently embarked on a very ambitious water PPP by the Nelspruit (Mpumalanga) municipality with a consortium led by Biwater. This 30-year "BOTT" (Build, Operate, Train and Transfer) concession, the first major water PPP in South Africa, was launched in October 1999. The choice of this type of contract was justified on the grounds that only the private provider could generate funds capable of integrating previously excluded townships in the town's water system. SAMWU publicly complained that the contract was enforced under provisions for tariff payment that were not disclosed to the union, after Biwater unilaterally reviewed the employees' conditions of service (*Star Business Report* 20 October 1999). SAMWU is faced with urgent new organisational challenges if it is to resist such developments.

COSATU's Dilemmas and SAMWU's Struggle against Water Privatisation: Between Community Politics and the Elusive New Internationalism

The history of international labour solidarity with the struggles of the South African unions is inextricably linked to that of the global antiapartheid mobilisation and to the ideological divisions in international trade union bodies during the Cold War. When organisations of black workers started to emerge out of the 1973 Durban strikes, the ANC-aligned South African Congress of Trade Unions (SACTU)—which had ties with the Soviet-oriented World Federation of Trade Unions (WFTU)—was still the most influential voice of the black South African working class overseas, even if repression had forced it underground. The development in the 1970s of an independent trade union movement largely outside the ANC tradition, which resulted in the formation of the Federation of South African Trade Unions (FOSATU) in 1979, defined international solidarity as a terrain of contestation. On one hand, SACTU claimed the exclusive right to represent South African black workers before the international antiapartheid movement and trade unions, explicitly denying legitimacy to "direct links" between emerging South African unions and overseas organisations that could sidestep SACTU. At the same time, international union solidarity was from the very beginning far from foreign to the new worker organisations (Bezuidenhout 2000). Apartheid South Africa's position in the world economy was that of a semiperipheral producer of raw materials and a manufacturer of semidurable and durable consumer goods mainly addressed to the white minority. This facilitated the penetration of multinational corporations in many sectors (including automotive, electrical and chemical), often in partnership with domestic capital, in the broader context of state interventionist and protectionist industrial policies.

The pro-Western ICFTU, in particular, adopted policies of material support for the embryonic black worker organisations. These were met with increasing suspicion by the South African unions, especially as a consequence of the greater AFL-CIO influence over the ICFTU during the 1980s. However, although accusations of trade union imperialism continued to be made about relations between South African unions and international bodies, this did not prevent the creation and consolidation of enduring links on specific projects with national affiliates of both the ICFTU and the smaller World Confederation of Labour (Forrest 1994).

Southall (1995:269) defines the unions' approach, attentive to the practical usefulness of situational links and suspicious of structured ideological international affiliations, as being to "use rather than being used by the international labour network". It led to a policy of flexible, pragmatic, cross-national union alliances. This was translated into a policy of international nonalignment, when unions in COSATU (which absorbed FOSATU in 1985) initially decided not to belong to any international body; many of them chose to become members of International Trade Secretariats (ITSs) only in the 1990s. At the same time, ICFTU's funding and support were particularly oriented to legal and humanitarian aid to put pressure on governments and employers with interests in South Africa (Southall 1995:327–339).

The centrality assumed by the ICFTU and the ITSs in COSATU's international networking eventually led to COSATU's affiliation to the ICFTU in 1998. However, this centrality also caused a substantial neglect of two areas of engagement for the democratic union movement, which were particularly felt after the demise of apartheid. First, COSATU's contribution to building an African and Southern African union movement was inadequate, even after COSATU's decision to follow the Organisation of African Trade Union Unity (OATUU) and the Southern African Trade Union Co-ordinating Council (SATUCC) in 1991 (Southall 1995:351). Second, the role of the ICFTU in channeling funds and assistance tended to deter unions from exploring new solidarity links with social movements, community struggles and gender-based mobilisation. Capacity problems played a part in this situation: the federation's first international officer was appointed only in 1991 (Bezuidenhout 2000:18), and sector- and region-specific initiatives have become a priority only in the past five to six years. These have been aimed at building links primarily with unions in countries with sizeable manufacturing sectors facing the challenge of democratisation and liberalisation, as in the case of the "Indian Ocean Rim initiatives", the 1999 Southern Initiative on Globalisation and Trade Union Rights (SIGTUR; see Lambert this issue) and links with Brazilian and Korean unions. New relations have also started to unfold with unions in potential "competitor" countries in Southern Africa. These initiatives privilege co-operation on tariff reduction, social clauses, the enforcement of labour standards and the impact of export processing zones, particularly in those industries such as textile and clothing where liberalisation is a particularly pressing concern for South African unions.

At the same time, relations with global social movements and anti-corporate resistance outside workplace-based and industrial relations structures have been marginalised in these forums and initiatives. While the events in Seattle have contributed to a sense of urgency for social movement alliances inside the country, COSATU's approach has been characterised by a failure to reflect on the significance and implications of such events. COSATU's response to Seattle emphasised the progressive aspect of protests against international economic institutions, but it also underlined how protesters constituted a "motley crew" with no common agenda or centralised coordination, which exposes them to the danger of being co-opted or of becoming a mere "sideshow" (COSATU 2000). The presence of COSATU's General Secretary in the government's delegation at the Seattle talks, or at the yearly World Economic Forum in Davos, is explained by the federation's priority of "democratising" the WTO and similar institutions. The fact that global linkages with social movements do not figure high in COSATU's international agenda reflects the federation's institutionalisation at home, as well as its growing inability to provide alternatives to the free-market macroeconomic approaches of the government.

Confronted by this situation, many COSATU affiliates have defined their own global strategies in a context of high uncertainty. SAMWU's case illustrates these dilemmas in a particularly clear way. Currently the largest municipal union in the country, with nearly 150,000 members, SAMWU was founded in 1987 as a merger of organisations coming from different political traditions (*Workers' News* November 1997). Some organisations were the municipal unions that had revived black workers' militancy in the sector in Johannesburg and the Eastern Cape during the 1980s. These bodies gravitated around the ANC-aligned United Democratic Front (UDF), rejected FOSATU's political abstensionism and its predominantly workplace orientation and opted for a style of "community unionism" that included forms of activism like rent boycotts and stayaways. However, the core organisation in launching SAMWU was the Cape Town Municipal Workers' Association (CTMWA), once a conservative staff association. This organisation started moving in a progressive direction during the 1960s under a new leadership, although it did not align itself with nationalist politics or with the UDF. Together with the particular location of SAMWU members in the South African economy, this peculiar mix of radical community unionism and radicalised established unionism probably explains the union's sensitivity to worker-community alliances, which has been prominent in its antiprivatisation and anticommodification discourse and strategy.

At the same time, the international solidarity policies adopted at SAMWU's founding congress reflected FOSATU's tradition of rejecting international affiliations (including to ITSs) and privileging direct links with progressive worker organisations, especially in developing countries.[3] At its 1991 congress, SAMWU decided to affiliate to the ITS for the sector, the Public Services International (PSI), but as late as 1997 the union was recognising that its participation in PSI activities was "a bit inconsistent" (*Workers' News* November 1997:3).

The general secretary and the national officers followed international relations on a largely ad hoc basis.

Only since 1997 has this relative neglect of international solidarity activity dramatically changed. In July 1997 the union decided to appoint a full-time International Relations Officer (IRO); they were one of the last COSATU unions to do so. This officer was required to report directly to the general secretary and the first deputy president. At the same time, SAMWU arranged for special officials to be appointed to follow international issues in each of its nine provincial structures. These were charged not only with the task of informing members about SAMWU's international policy and organising international visits, but also with that of monitoring operations of foreign companies at local level and the public–private partnerships involving these companies. The International Subcommittee (ISC) was restructured to include the IRO, together with two permanent delegates from each province, two delegates from the National Women's Committee and SAMWU's General Secretary and First Deputy President (Mhlongo 2000). Finally, SAMWU's participation in the PSI's structures was reinforced by the decision of the PSI 1997 World Congress to establish subregional advisory committees, four of which were constituted in the African region—one specifically for the Southern African affiliates. This acceleration in SAMWU's fulfillment of its international commitments was deeply influenced by changing perceptions about the direction of political transition and the dynamics of local government restructuring. At the same time, due to the union's effort for the ANC's 1994 election campaign, resource constraints were relaxed. This allowed SAMWU to focus on its critique of privatisation and the neoliberal orientation of the new government's economic policy.

In the sphere of municipal service delivery, SAMWU maintains a stance generally opposed to the existing PPPs (SAMWU 1997), accusing them of unilaterally implementing a disguised form of privatisation that violates the intentions stated in the restructuring framework. It also points out that the introduction of profit-making and cost-recovery mechanisms in service provision, coupled with the downsizing of government subsidisation, leads to a greater reliance on user fees in the financing of services and therefore to an increased level of commodification. In this way, SAMWU's discourse links to the strength and rights of its own constituency an awareness of the challenge that municipal restructuring poses. In its policy of international solidarity, the organisation emphasises the deterritorialised nature of capitalist urban restructuring and the role played by MNCs as new subjects of social service management.

However, this innovative intuition has paradoxically been translated into rather traditional patterns of solidarity-building. In the specific field of water policy, SAMWU's response to the commodification of this basic necessity was to demand a lifeline of 50 litres of free potable water per person per day, to be cross-subsidised by luxury and industrial consumption, with an articulated programme of action under the "antiprivatisation campaign" (SAMWU s.d.). This included local community mobilisation and self-organised social services for the community (SAMWU 1998). At the same time, renewed direct pressure was put on the companies involved in PPP deals. To that end, SAMWU's participation in the PSI and the PSI Research Unit (PSIRU) provided important leverage. SAMWU also recognised that important differences existed among PSI affiliates, where opposition to privatisation originated mainly from developing country unions (SAMWU 1998). However, the nature of the proposed pressures to be put on foreign companies, and a definition of actors and movements to be involved, remained unclarified. As a result, SAMWU's emphasis on the deterritorialised nature of commodification and privatisation of basic services was translated into a rather conventional approach to union solidarity.

In February 1999, the PSI demanded from the South African government the nullification of a deal to privatise water services on the Dolphin Coast, after circulating a report accusing the firm involved, SAUR-Bouygues, of anticompetitive practices and documenting various cases of corruption involving the company (*Business Day* 16 February 1999; PSIRU 1999). In addition, an attempt was made to build international pressures for disinvestment on Biwater's shareholders, which include NUON (a Dutch company initiated by various municipalities) that owns 50% of Biwater. Many unions around the world joined the call for pressure on Biwater, which strengthened SAMWU's position in its meeting with NUON executives in March 2000. In the same period, SAMWU, backed by the powerful Netherlands' municipal workers union, ABVA-KABO, was also able to bring pressure on the WB-sponsored "World Water Forum" in The Hague and to call for disinvestment from Biwater. This was coupled with popularisation of the union's vision among local authorities in the Netherlands. However, although innovative in its vision of local authorities as potential oppositional subjects, this attempt to build an alliance between SAMWU, foreign unions and municipalities was unable to prevent the Nelspruit water contract from coming into effect (*Star Business Report* 17 March 2000).

The limited success SAMWU has had in mobilising international solidarity in response to the restructuring of water services reveals trends and practices that have substantially narrowed the range of possible allies and arenas of confrontation. One thing that is striking in this regard is the lack of priority given to joint actions with social movements. Neither SAMWU's resolution on international solidarity adopted at the 1997 congress nor the General Secretary's report mention organisations other than trade unions as sources of solidarity. Although SAMWU's IRO, Victor Mhlongo, defines contacts with other social movements as "desirable", he also recognises that links with overseas organisations have overwhelmingly favoured trade union bodies for the purposes of information gathering and pressure building (Mhlongo 2000). This is usually translated into bilateral visits between SAMWU and similar organisations overseas.

This situation is reflected in SAMWU's implicit approach to transnational social movements. SAMWU's national head office decided to participate with the Campaign Against Neoliberalism in South Africa (CANSA)—a network of civil society, NGOs, unionists, church-based activists and Jubilee 2000 South Africa—in a campaign for the cancellation of foreign debt. However, SAMWU's participation is discontinuous and depends more on Mhlongo's personal availability than on a deep organisational commitment (Mhlongo 2000). From SAMWU's point of view, this form of engagement does not solve the dilemmas posed by the search for new forms of international labour solidarity. In particular, it does not solve the uncomfortable choice between a conventional pattern of nation-based union solidarity (with some political effect but limited prospects relative to the power of transnational capital) and tenuous and indirect links with social movements (which have promising prospects but limited political effect in their present form).

These promising prospects are reinforced by post-Seattle international mobilisations that have strengthened South African voices opposed to privatisation and the commodification of basic needs. A renewed focus on strategies for networking with global social movements seems necessary for SAMWU to be able to valorise these new opportunities. However, this task is also linked to a reconceptualisation and an expansion of the range of social alliances, and the adoption of organising and networking tactics that recognise diversity while converging around common objectives. The old South African labour internationalism, based on foreign support for industrial unions that were mainly expressions of national liberation politics, is by now too narrow to appeal to the wide array of subjects opposing global corporate capital. An entrenched tradition of grassroots control of union structures and the contiguity between union members and their communities could definitely provide assets in the task of renewing tactics and strategies. However, a long-standing, male-dominated ethic of workplace centrality and proneness to institutionalised mediation could be barriers—not to be underestimated—to a discourse of global social movement unionism.

Conclusion

This chapter reveals the limitations of the SAMWU approach to internationalisation of the struggle over privatisation and the commodification of social needs. This struggle has given way to a conventional union internationalism that is able to exercise some degree of pressure on governments and companies, but lacks effective strategies for sustained networking and action. The same problems have faced other unions in the South that have tried to respond by redefining their relations with broader social actors. The response of Brazil's *Central Única dos Trabalhadores* to the challenges of liberalisation posed by the rise of the Common Market of the Southern Cone (MERCOSUR) recognises that:

> With the globalisation of economy, we will not be able to face problems like unemployment through defensive and corporatist actions, confined to a national ambit. On the contrary, it will be by acting in an integrated form with workers of other countries that we will confront the consequences of trade and production liberalisation.… One of the weaknesses of our action has been the nonexistence of joint co-ordination and action with other organisations of the social and popular movement. MERCOSUR affects the sovereignty and the interests of the whole society and a charter of social rights must be a joint demand. (Central Unica dos Trabalhadores 1996:12; see also Jakobsen this issue)

SAMWU's analysis of links with social movements has been framed in terms of future "desirability", rather than addressing current weaknesses and lack of perspectives. As a result, the need to globalise practices of resistance in order to tackle the deterritorialised dimension of capital's domination has ended up reproducing traditional patterns of nation-based international union solidarity. The argument underlying this chapter is that the struggle for the decommodification of basic services provides a potentially important terrain for mobilisation in which trade unions could reinvent themselves in representing their members' demands as workers and as citizens, and relate to global social movements on this basis. At the same time, in the case of SAMWU, this potential has remained largely unexplored and confined to narrow boundaries of interunion solidarity. Factors contributing to this outcome include legacies from the apartheid past, the nature of South Africa's insertion in the world economy and the institutional location of unions. The result of the search for a new internationalism, so far elusive, will greatly depend on the interaction of these contradictory forces.

Endnotes

[1] Today COSATU is by far the largest union federation in the country, with more than 2 million members. This is more than twice the size of the two other main federations, the National Council of Trade Unions (NACTU) and the Federation of Unions of South Africa (FEDUSA), combined.

[2] Good examples can be found on <URL: http://www.cosatu.org.za/samwu>.

[3] In its first years SAMWU developed links with municipal unions from the United States (SEIU and AFSCME), Norway, Sweden, Britain (UNISON), the Netherlands, Finland and Japan.

References

Alvarez S, Dagnino E and Escobar A (eds) (1998) *Cultures of Politics, Politics of Culture. Re-visioning Latin American Social Movements.* Boulder, CO: Westview Press

Barchiesi F (2000) Social citizenship and the collapse of the wage-income nexus in postapartheid South Africa. Paper presented at the Annual Congress of the South African Sociological Association, 2–5 July, University of the Western Cape

Baskin J (1991) *Striking Back: A History of COSATU.* London: Verso

Benner C (2000) Building community-based careers—Labour market intermediaries and flexible employment in Silicon Valley. Paper presented at the Urban Futures Conference, 10–14 July, University of The Witwatersrand, Johannesburg

Bezuidenhout A (2000) *Towards Global Social Movement Unionism? Trade Union Responses to Globalization in South Africa.* Labour and Society Programme. Discussion Paper 115. Geneva: International Labour Organisation

Bond P (2000a) *Elite Transition: From Apartheid to Neoliberalism in South Africa.* London: Pluto Press

Bond P (2000b) *Cities of Gold, Townships of Coal: Essays on South Africa's New Urban Crisis.* Trenton, NJ: Africa World Press

Bond P, Dor G and Reuters G (2000) Transformation in infrastructure policy. From apartheid to democracy. Municipal Services Project Background Research Paper, Public and Development Management Institute Johannesburg: University of the Witwatersrand

Bond P and Mayekiso M (1996) Developing resistance, resisting "development": reflections from the South African struggle. In L Panitch (ed) *Socialist Register 1996* (pp 145–167). New York, NY: Monthly Review Press

Borgers F (2000) The clouds clear—Seattle and beyond. HTML file: <URL: http://www.antenna.nl/~waterman/borgers.html>

Buhlungu S (1997) Flogging a dying horse? COSATU and the alliance. *South African Labour Bulletin* 21(3):15–23

Cashdan B (2000) Local government and poverty in South Africa. Municipal Services Project Background Research Paper, Public and Development Management Institute. Johannesburg: University of the Witwatersrand

Central Unica dos Trabalhadores (1996) *A acao do CUT frente ao Mercosul*. Sao Paulo: CUT

Coates D (1999) Labour power and international competitiveness: A critique of ruling orthodoxies. In L Panitch (ed) *Socialist Register 1996* (pp 56–75). New York, NY: Monthly Review Press

COSATU (2000) *Advancing Social Transformation in the Era of Globalisation*. Political discussion document for the 7th National COSATU Congress. Johannesburg: Congress of South African Trade Unions

Danaher K and Burbach (eds) (2000) *Globalize This! The Battle against the World Trade Organization and Corporate Rule*. Monroe, ME: Common Courage Press

Davis M (2000) *Magical Urbanism: Latinos Reshape the US Big City*. London: Verso

Department of Constitutional Development (1998) *White Paper on Local Government*. Pretoria: Government Printer

Desai A (1999) *South Africa: Still Revolting*. Johannesburg: Impact Africa Publishing

Feagin J and Smith P (1987) Cities and the new international division of labour: An overview. In J Feagin and P Smith (eds) *The Capitalist City* (pp 3–34). Oxford: Blackwell Publishers

Forrest K (1994) *Breaking Boundaries: Building an International Workers Movement*. Johannesburg: Umanyano Publications

Friedman S (1987) *Building Tomorrow Today: African Workers in Trade Unions, 1970–1984*. Johannesburg: Ravan Press

Friedrich Ebert Stiftung (1998) *Restructuring the State and Intergovernmental Fiscal Relations*. Johannesburg: Friedrich Ebert Stiftung and Public and Development Management Graduate School, University of the Witwatersrand

Ghai D (1996) *Structural Adjustment, Global Integration and Social Democracy*. Working Paper. Geneva: UNRISD

Gills B (ed) (2000) *Globalisation and the Politics of Resistance*. New York: St. Martin's Press

Hall D (1999) The water multinationals. Paper presented at the PSI Conference on the Water Industry, Sofia, Bulgaria

Hardt M and Negri A (2000) *Empire*. Cambridge, MA: Harvard University Press

Hirst P and Thompson G (1994) *Globalisation in Question*. Cambridge, UK: Polity Press

Hoogveldt A (1997) *Globalisation and the Postcolonial World: The New Political Economy of Development*. Baltimore, MD: Johns Hopkins University Press

International Confederation of Free Trade Unions (ICFTU) (2000) *Globalising Social Justice: Trade Unionism in the Twenty-First Century*. Report for the 2000 World Congress, Durban, South Africa. Bruxelles: International Confederation of Free Trade Unions

Jonas A (1998) Investigating the local/global paradox: Corporate strategy, union local autonomy and community action in Chicago. In A Herod (ed) *Organising the Landscape: Geographical Perspectives on Labor Unionism* (pp 325–350). Minneapolis, MN: Minnesota University Press

Klein N (2000) *No Logo: Taking Aim at the Brand Bullies*. New York: Picador USA

Lambert R (1998) Globalisation: can unions resist? *South African Labour Bulletin* 22(6):72–77

Lee E (1996) *The Labour Movement and the Internet: The New Internationalism*. London: Pluto Press

Marais H (1998) *South Africa: Limits to Change: The Political Economy of Trans-formation.* London: Zed Books

May J (ed) (2000) *Poverty and Inequality in South Africa: Meeting the Challenge.* London: Zed Books

McKinley D (1997) *The ANC and the Liberation Struggle.* London: Pluto Press

Mittelman J (ed) (1996) *Globalization: Critical Reflections.* Boulder, CO: Lynne Rienner

Mhlongo, Victor (2000) SAMWU International Relations Officer. Interview with author, 19 May, Johannesburg

Moody K (1997) *Workers in a Lean World.* London: Verso

Munck R (1998) Labour dilemmas and labour futures. In R Munck and P Waterman (eds) *Labour Worldwide in the Era of Globalisation: Alternative Union Models in the New World* (pp 1–21). London: Macmillan

National Economic Development and Labour Council (NEDLAC) (2000) *Infrastructure Delivery Report.* Johannesburg: NEDLAC

National Labour and Economic Development Institute (NALEDI) (1999) *Unions in Transition: COSATU into the New Millennium.* Edited by Ravi Naidoo. Johannesburg: NALEDI

Needleman R (1998) Building relationships for the long haul: Unions and community-based groups working together to organise low-wage workers. In K Bronfenbrenner (ed) *Organising to Win: New Research on Union Strategies* (pp 71–86). Ithaca, NY: Cornell University Press

O'Brien R, Goetz A M, Scholte J A and Williams M (eds) (2000) *Contesting Global Governance: Multilateral Economic Institutions and Global Social Movements.* Cambridge, UK: Cambridge University Press

Public Services International Research Unit (PSIRU) (1999) *SAUR and Bouygues, Company Profile.* February. London: PSIRU

Ruiters G and Bond P (1998) *Contradictions in Municipal Transformation from Apartheid to Democracy: The Battle over Local Water Privatisation in South Africa.* Municipal Services Project Background Research Paper, Public and Development Management Institute. Johannesburg: University of the Witwatersrand

Sassen S (1992) *The Global City: London, New York, Tokyo.* Princeton, NJ: Princeton University Press

Sassen S (1996) *Losing Control? Sovereignty in an Age of Globalisation.* New York, NY: Columbia University Press

Sassen S (1998) *Globalisation and Its Discontents.* New York, NY: New Press

Schmitthenner H (1999) Refonder le syndicalisme. *Le Monde Diplomatique* June: 16–17

South African Local Government Association (1998) *A Framework for the Restructuring of Municipal Service Provision.* Pretoria: South African Local Government Association

South African Municipal Workers Union (SAMWU) (s.d.) *The SAMWU Vision for Water Provision.* Johannesburg: South African Municipal Workers Union

South African Municipal Workers Union (SAMWU) *How to Deal with Contracting Out in Local Government.* Working document, May. Johannesburg: South African Municipal Workers Union

South African Municipal Workers Union (SAMWU) (1998) *National Antiprivatisation Campaign Update.* 19 March. Johannesburg: South African Municipal Workers Union

Southall R (1995) *Imperialism or Solidarity? International Labour and the South African Trade Unions.* Cape Town: UCT Press

Standard Bank Economic Division (1999) Dilemma posed by rapid growth of financial sector. Services Sector Report, 2 August

Teeple G (1995) *Globalisation and the Decline of Social Reform.* Atlantic Highlands, NJ: Humanities Press

Thomas H (ed) (1995) *Globalisation and Third World Trade Unions: The Challenge of Rapid Economic Change.* London: Zed Books

Van Driel M (1998) Antiprivatisation for democratic public sector reform. *South African Labour Bulletin* 22(1):7–10

Van Driel M (1999) Mass struggle needed: The municipal services partnership framework agreement. *South African Labour Bulletin* 23(3):12–15

Van Niekerk S, Ruiters G, Mcwabeni L, Kruger V and Grinker R (1999) *Public–Private Partnerships: Lessons and Case Studies from the Eastern Cape.* East London: ECSECC

Waterman P (1991) A new labour internationalism: What content and what form? *South African Labour Bulletin* 16(2):69–75

Waterman P (2000) Labour internationalism in the transition from a national/industrial/colonial capitalism to an informatised/globalised one … and beyond. Paper presented at the Conference on the Past and Future of International Trade Unionism, 19–20 May, Ghent, Belgium

Webster E (1988) The rise of social-movement unionism: The two faces of the black trade union movement in South Africa. In P Frenkel, N Pines and M Swilling (eds) *State, Resistance and Change in South Africa* (pp 247–263). London: Croom Helm

Wills J (2000) Great expectations: Three years in the life of a European Works Council. *European Journal of Industrial Relations* 6(1):85–107

Witheford N (1997) Cycles and circuits of struggle in hightechnology capitalism. In J Davis, T Hirschl and M Stack (eds) *Cutting Edge: Technology, Information, Capitalism and Social Revolution* (pp 195–242). London: Verso

World Bank (2000) *Sourcebook on Community-Driven Development in the African Region.* Washington, DC: World Bank

Franco Barchiesi (Senigallia, Italy, 1968) is a Lecturer in Economic Sociology and Social Policy at the Department of Sociology of the University of the Witwatersrand, Johannesburg. His current research is on social citizenship and welfare in South Africa in relation to changes in forms of employment and economic activity.

6

Labor Internationalism and the Contradictions of Globalization: Or, Why the Local is Sometimes Still Important in a Global Economy

Andrew Herod

In this chapter I examine two case studies of workers fighting against transnationally organized corporations. In the first case, a 1990–1992 dispute between the United Steelworkers of America and the Ravenswood Aluminum Corporation, union workers developed an international campaign to pressure the corporation to rehire them after they had been locked out in a dispute over health and safety issues. In the second case, a 1998 dispute between the United Auto Workers and General Motors, strikes by workers at just two plants in Flint, Michigan over the corporation's plans to introduce new work rules resulted in the virtual shutdown of GM for several weeks. Drawing on these two cases, I suggest that, in challenging transnationally organized employers, workers may on some occasions best achieve their goals through engaging in practices of transnational solidarity aimed at matching the global organization of their employer ("organizing globally"), whereas on other occasions they may be able to do so through highly focused local actions ("organizing locally") against strategic parts of a corporation. Of course, which of these two strategies is most likely to succeed in particular cases will depend on a coterie of contingencies, such as how interconnected the corporation's component parts are. However, the fact that different geographical strategies may be open to workers challenging globally organized capital means at least two things. First, some workers may not have to organize at the same geographical scale (ie globally) as corporations in order to challenge them. Second, through their choices of which strategy to pursue, workers are clearly shaping the very process of globalization itself and the new global geographies which globalization is auguring.

Introduction

Globalization continues to transform the time-space organization of capitalism. The shrinking of relative distances between places and the speeding up of social and economic life that is central to this transformation are having significant implications for workers and union strategy. However, although neoliberal ideologues have often attempted to imply that the globalization of capital is an unstoppable juggernaut to which workers can only submit themselves, there are, in fact, a number of paradoxes and contradictions contained within the temporal and spatial reorganization of capitalism which globalization is auguring. Four are particularly pertinent.

First, despite the neoliberal argument that, under a superfluid "Third Wave" capitalism (Toffler 1980) of "friction-free exchange" and "superconductive" financial markets (see Luke and Ó Tuathail 1998), capital is no longer constrained by geography and can pretty much relocate anywhere in the world almost at the drop of a hat (this is unquestionably the thrust of Ohmae's [1990] "borderless world" metaphor), it is still as true today as it ever was that firms must locate somewhere. More precisely, all firms must continue to negotiate the contradiction between being sufficiently mobile to take advantage of new opportunities that may arise elsewhere, and being sufficiently embedded in a region to allow them to develop the business links with local suppliers or to train particular groups of skilled labor that are necessary for them if they are to engage in profitable production (cf Cox and Mair 1988). As I will argue below, the need to be embedded to various degrees in certain locations—what Mair (1997) has called firms' need for "strategic localization"—can provide significant opportunities for workers and their unions when battling transnational corporations (TNCs).

Second, given that individual capitalists may gain significant advantages which they can exploit in the market place by reorganizing their production and distribution systems temporally so as to speed up the circulation time of their capital (a process which also invariably involves a geographic reorganization), the management and control of space and time can be crucial avenues of conflict between workers and employers.

Third, when thinking about the new time-space organization of capitalism it is necessary to recognize that, because this new organization develops in a spatially and temporally uneven manner, new historical geographies of capitalism impact workers in different parts of the world in different ways. Most importantly for what I will argue below, the fact is that some workers live in a faster, more interconnected, and smaller world than do others, a reality which will undoubtedly affect their organizing strategies.

Fourth, the contemporary speed-up of social life associated with a host of new technologies (such as e-mail and the Internet) and ways of organizing social life and work (such as "just-in-time" production—more about which below), contains an important paradox, at least with regard to the relationship between capital and labor. Specifically, whereas many corporations see the ability to speed up their operations as a way of reducing the turnover time of their capital (thereby increasing profitability), the greater interconnectedness of the global economy in general—and of the separate parts of any individual TNC in particular—that high-speed telecommunications and transportations technologies have augured mean that the consequences of any particular event can be transmitted much further and much faster than ever before. As the speed of communication and interconnectivity has quickened, we have moved closer to what Foucault (1986:22) called the "epoch of simultaneity," wherein information travels around our globe so quickly that there is an increasing synchronicity between the occurrence of an event and our knowledge of it. Paradoxically, as the speed of the spread of social actions' consequences has quickened, so do corporations have concomitantly less time in which to respond to, and to try to manage, crises.

In this chapter, I want to explore some of these paradoxes and contradictions as they relate to the issue of workers' political praxis. More specifically, I seek to question the assumption in much current writing and public proclamation that international labor solidarity is *the* strategy for unions to pursue in an increasingly globalizing international economy—that if they are to successfully challenge TNCs, workers *must* organize transnationally as a matter of course.[1] Specifically, I suggest that, whereas in certain situations the traditional "transnational solidarity" model in which workers attempt to make common cause globally with their confederates who work for the same TNC overseas may be crucial to their success, in other situations a second model may also provide workers with an effective means of challenging TNCs—a model which focuses not upon the global scale of worker organization but, instead, upon the very local scale of organization. At first glance, such a localist strategy may seem somewhat puzzling, given that the impetus for TNCs to "go global" with their operations has often been precisely so that they may play workforces in different parts of the world against each other. Likewise, workers' abilities to develop solidarity across space have typically been seen as a way to limit such whipsawing. Yet, as paradoxical as it might seem, I want to suggest here that, in an increasingly interconnected planetary economy, a locally focused campaign against a TNC may sometimes prove highly effective, particularly if such local disputes target crucial parts of that corporation's global operation.

Certainly, which of these two strategies—what we might call "organizing globally" and "organizing locally"—is more effective in specific cases will depend upon the contingencies of the situation within which workers find themselves. Equally, I do not want to suggest that workers face an "either/or" choice, for organizing at multiple scales simultaneously may be necessary to best serve their goals. The point I wish to make, however, is that rather than simply assuming that workers have to "go global" so as to match the geographic organization of their employers, organizing at other geographic scales such as the local may, in fact, prove to be a more useful strategy in certain circumstances. Such a realization forces us to recognize both that union strategy may be significantly shaped by the geographical realities within which workers find themselves and that the choices workers make concerning which types of strategy to pursue can have significant implications for the ways in which the geography of global capitalism is made (see Herod 2001).

The chapter itself is in three sections. The first two sections outline two case studies reported on in more detail elsewhere (Herod 1995, 2000), which highlight workers' success in "organizing globally" and "organizing locally" against transnationally organized corporations. My purpose in recounting these disputes is twofold. First, I want to show that, contra the pessimistic views of many on the left and the disavowal by many of those on the right, workers *can* in fact organize against a TNC and win. Second, I want to use these two examples to think through a number of issues related to the geography of worker solidarity across space that these different modes and scales of organizing may augur. The final section of the chapter ponders a number of questions related to the geographical implications for worker solidarity of these strikingly different strategies.

Strategy #1—Organizing Globally in a Global Economy: The 1990–1992 RAC-USWA Dispute

In 1989, the Ravenswood Aluminum Corporation (RAC) bought an aluminum smelter in the small town of Ravenswood, West Virginia. During the next 18 months, five workers were killed and several others injured in accidents at the plant. Consequently, officers of the plant's United Steelworkers of America (USWA) Local 5668 determined to make health and safety a key part of any new contract negotiated with RAC. However, when the union's contract with the company expired on October 31, 1990, RAC security officers escorted Local 5668 members out of one end of the plant as they brought nonunion replacement workers in at the other. Thus began one of the most acrimonious disputes between an employer and a union to hit the US economy during the 1990s. As it turned out, the campaign waged by the USWA and its allies to have the locked-out union workers reinstated would also be one of the most imaginative campaigns implemented by a US union against an employer in recent memory.

Initially, the dispute between the USWA and RAC remained largely a local affair, as both sides made a number of vituperative pronouncements in the local media. Two months after the lock-out began, however, the dispute took an unexpected turn as Local 5668 officials received anonymously a copy of an audit of RAC conducted by the Price Waterhouse accounting firm. Among other things, the report detailed a web of corporate ownership that stretched far beyond Ravenswood, nestled on the banks of the Ohio River. In particular, the document showed that the Ravenswood plant appeared to be a small cog in a much larger financial and commodities conglomerate run out of Zug, Switzerland by international commodities trader Marc Rich. At the time, Rich controlled companies estimated to trade in excess of $30 billion per year and had operations in many parts of the world. He was also a fugitive from US justice, having been indicted on a number of charges ranging from illegal avoidance of income taxes to mail fraud to breaking the US embargo on trading in Iranian oil (for more on Rich, see Copetas 1985). Whereas part of the plant was owned by local managers, the bulk appeared to be owned by Rich, although his ownership was through various corporate arrangements designed to hide his involvement.

As the connections between Ravenswood and the Marc Rich group of companies became more apparent, representatives from Local 5668 and from the International union's office in Pittsburgh, Pennsylvania sketched out a five-pronged plan for ensuring that the locked-out union workers would be readmitted to the plant. First, USWA officials pursued the labor law aspects of the dispute with the National Labor Relations Board, arguing that this was an illegal lockout. Second, they worked with federal regulators to investigate a number of health, safety, and environmental violations for which they argued RAC was liable. Third, Local 5668 members and their supporters engaged in a number of morale-boosting solidarity activities, including leafleting at the New York Stock Exchange and several university campuses and state capitols, plus hosting a number of "solidarity caravans" made up of trade unionists from across the country. Fourth, working closely with the AFL-CIO's Strategic Approaches Committee, the USWA International union initiated a consumer boycott to pressure over 300 end-users of RAC aluminum not to buy metal from the plant during the dispute. In the end this proved highly successful, as several major (and many minor) users of RAC aluminum dropped their orders with the corporation, including Anheuser-Busch, the Miller Brewing Company, and the Strohs Brewing Company. Fifth, the USWA initiated an international campaign designed to harass Rich wherever he did business around the world.

The locked-out Ravenswood workers and union and AFL-CIO officials in Pittsburgh and Washington, DC quickly realized that, for Rich, the RAC plant was only one of many within his corporate empire. They surmised that, if they were to be successful in their quest to gain back their jobs, they would have to make connections with workers in those countries around the world in which Rich did business. This they proceeded to do. Making use of the fact that the USWA and the AFL-CIO were both members of a number of international labor organizations—including the International Metalworkers' Federation (IMF), the International Federation of Chemical, Energy and General Workers' Unions (ICEF), and the International Confederation of Free Trade Unions (ICFTU)—union officials in Pittsburgh and Washington, DC began to make contacts with numerous trade unionists and sympathetic politicians around the world.[2] Their principal weapon was the fact that Rich appeared keen to ward off outside interest in his financial dealings for two main reasons (Uehlein 1992). On a personal level, such interest might have undermined any attempt on his part to negotiate a deal with the US Justice Department which would allow him to return to the United States without facing jail time.[3] And on a business level, the USWA's ability to draw attention to Rich's nefarious past might have threatened future deals he was trying to consummate in Eastern Europe, Latin America, and the Caribbean.

After conducting a thorough analysis of Rich's known holdings and how RAC fitted into them, the USWA and staffers at the Industrial Union Department (IUD) at the AFL-CIO in Washington, DC plotted out an international campaign to bring pressure to bear upon Rich. In June 1991, the IUD and the USWA sent representatives to Switzerland to meet with local unionists and several members of the Swiss parliament. Using their IMF and ICEF contacts, the US unionists persuaded their counterparts in the Swiss metalworkers union to stage several press conferences to bring the Ravenswood situation to the attention of the Swiss nation and lawmakers. They also contacted the Dutch bankworkers' union, which subsequently arranged for them a meeting with representatives of the Nederlandsche Middenstandsbank, which had financed part of the loan originally used to buy the Ravenswood plant. This was significant because, after having been apprised of RAC's liability should it be subjected to a negative legal decision concerning violations of US labor, health and safety, and environmental laws, the bank's directors subsequently withdrew support from one of the local RAC managers who was trying to raise more funds.

In October 1991, the US unionists also leafleted the London Metals Exchange, where they learned that Rich had a deal pending to buy an aluminum smelter in Czechoslovakia. Fortuitously, at this time the Geneva office of the International Metalworkers' Federation was beginning to make significant contacts with trade unionists in Eastern Europe and so was able to put the US unionists in touch with the national leadership of the Czechoslovakian Metalworkers' Federation OS KOVO (see Herod 1998a, b for more details on the activities of the IMF and OS KOVO during the early 1990s). Fearing that a corporate operator like Rich would strip the smelter of any assets and then close it down, OS KOVO's national leaders successfully pressured President Vaclav Havel to intervene to prevent the proposed purchase.

By late 1991, the difficulties of organizing sustained anti-Rich actions from across the Atlantic had persuaded the USWA and the IUD that they needed to open a European office to coordinate their activities. After opening such an office in Paris and hiring a coordinator to take on much of the day-to-day tasks of writing press releases and conducting research on Rich's other proposed ventures in Eastern Europe, the US unionists were able to work more closely with their European confederates. The International Union of Food and Allied Workers' Associations (IUF), for example, organized a rally of some 20,000 trade unionists on behalf of the Ravenswood workers in Bucharest, Romania, where Rich had planned to buy the famous Athénée Palace Hotel, a deal that was subsequently thwarted. Events were organized in several other Eastern European countries where Rich had deals pending, including Bulgaria and Russia.

Eastern Europe was not the only region in which USWA and IUD officials were active. In Jamaica, the IUD contacted Prime Minister Michael Manley, who in his youth had worked with the USWA as an organizer in the island's bauxite mines. Manley in turn lobbied the Venezuelan government not to allow Rich to consummate a deal he had pending in that country. Through the IMF and the ICEF, the USWA also lobbied Venezuelan trade unionists and briefed representatives of the Organización Regional Interamericana de Trabajadores, the ICFTU's regional organization for Latin America and the Caribbean. Such pressure was ultimately enough to convince Venezuelan President

Carlos Andres Perez to publicly dismiss Rich from bidding on an aluminum deal.

By April 1992, the USWA, the IUD, and their supporters had organized anti-Rich actions in 28 countries (including the Netherlands, Britain, Canada, France, Venezuela, Romania, Bulgaria, Czechoslovakia, and Switzerland) on five continents, and had plans to conduct additional activities in Australia, Russia, Israel, Hong Kong, and Finland. Combined with the impacts of their other activities, the US unionists and their overseas confederates had managed to bring tremendous pressure to bear upon Marc Rich and his operations. Although Rich continued to deny that he had anything to do with RAC, on April 11 a representative of the largest shareholder in RAC—a long-time Rich associate—seized control of the corporation's board and fired the local plant manager (who was also a part owner of RAC). During the next few weeks a new union contract was worked out, one which included the dismissal of the replacement workers and the return of the locked-out union workers, a strong union successorship clause, and wage and pension increases. In return, the union agreed to the loss of some 200 jobs through attrition. On June 29, 1992, some 20 months after they had been locked out of their plant, Local 5668 members returned to work.

Strategy #2—Organizing Locally in a Global Economy: The 1998 GM-UAW Dispute

During the 1980s and 1990s, auto producers increasingly came to rely upon "just-in-time" (JIT) systems of production and inventory control. Whereas traditionally auto manufacturers have stockpiled components in large warehouses so that the components will be readily at hand, under JIT components are only brought into an assembly plant shortly before they are needed (see Babson 1995; Dohse, Jürgens, and Malsch 1985; Green and Yanarella 1996; Kenney and Florida 1993; Linge 1991). This means that companies do not have to have so much of their capital tied up in components sitting in warehouses waiting to be used, nor do they have to pay for the land and other costs associated with maintaining such warehouses. However, many commentators (eg Moody 1997; Parker and Slaughter 1988) have argued that the implementation of JIT represents an attack upon workers on the shop floor, who must frequently abandon traditional working methods and work at paces determined not by union contract but by the flow of components into the plant. Although in the 1980s the leadership of the United Auto Workers (UAW) tried to develop a "partnership" with management concerning the introduction of new working methods designed to keep the US industry competitive, by the late 1990s UAW leaders were coming under increasing pressure from the union rank and file who were suffering the negative effects of such new work organization.

Within this context, on Friday June 5, 1998, some 3400 members of UAW Local 659 walked off the job at a metal stamping plant in Flint, Michigan in protest over the corporation's efforts to change local work rules to limit workers' abilities to "bank time."[4] For GM, such a change in work organization was important to achieve the flexibility the corporation said it required if the Flint plant were to serve as one of seven in the US, Mexico, and Canada that would provide parts for a new generation of sport utility vehicles and pickup trucks. The impact of the strike at the Flint metal stamping plant was felt almost immediately as the lack of parts led managers at an assembly facility in nearby Orion, Michigan to send 2800 workers home. By the end of June 8, the first full day of the dispute, an additional four assembly plants (including one in Ontario) had sent workers home, and by the end of the first week 50,429 workers at 71 other assembly and components plants had been laid off due to lack of work. Indeed, GM's reliance upon JIT production and inventory control meant that the Flint strikes had a snowballing effect: the inability of assembly plants to get parts from Flint meant that they no longer had need of parts from other components facilities, and this, in turn, led those facilities to send workers home.

The situation was exacerbated for GM when, on June 11, a second plant (also in Flint) was shut down by strike action on the part of 5800 members of UAW Local 651. This plant was a Delphi Automotive Systems facility (at the time Delphi was a GM subsidiary[5]) that provided the corporation with spark plugs, speedometers, and fuel filters. Significantly, it was the only one in North America that made certain crucial components used on GM vehicles. By the end of the second week of the strikes, a total of 121 assembly and components plants had been either partially or totally closed due to lack of work, and 105,514 workers had been laid off. As the dispute continued into July, its effects drew in even more plants and workers. At its height, on July 23, 193,517 workers had been sent home and 27 of GM's 29 North American assembly plants had been closed, while 117 components plants in Canada, the US, Mexico, and even Singapore had been forced either to close completely or to cut back significantly on production.[6] By the time the dispute ended, the corporation saw its market share drop from 31.9% in August 1997 to 21.6% in August 1998. GM also lost production of approximately 500,000 vehicles and posted an after-tax loss of $2.3 billion for the second and third quarters of 1998, while the dispute trimmed almost 1% off the US's gross domestic product (GDP) for 1998 (*Automotive News* 1998:39; *Ward's Auto World* 1998: 37–42).

The principal reason the dispute spread so quickly was the vulnerability GM faced as a result of its adoption of JIT, which left the corporation without large quantities of stockpiled components to ride out any disruptions in the supply chain, while the dispute's wide geographic spread reflected GM's development during the 1980s and 1990s of an increasingly integrated, continent-wide system of production. This temporal and spatial character of the spread of the impacts of the Flint strikes is significant for the argument I am making here for at least three reasons. First, the fact that the impacts of local disputes in a single community were transmitted throughout GM's North American corporate structure and even beyond in a relatively short space of time illustrates how quickly a union may be able to drag into a "local" dispute many more workers and plants. In other words, whereas a corporation may think it is dealing with local issues which may have sparked a strike in a single plant, the fact is that, for corporations operating under JIT, a union may be able to spread a dispute rapidly to other plants, such that it can effectively bring to bear on "local" disputes the weight of its entire membership. Further-more, the inability of a corporation so affected to sustain such a wide-spread shutdown may force it to the bargaining table more quickly, whereas the impacts of such "local" disputes on the wider regional or national economy may bring pressure from government to settle early, perhaps on terms favorable to the union. Thus, the ability of a union to identify and shut down critical parts of a corporation's overall operation through engaging in strategically focused strikes (which may technically be over "local" issues but nevertheless impact the corporation in virtually its entirety) can be a powerful weapon in a union's arsenal. Indeed, this is a strategy that the UAW has employed with some considerable success during the past decade.

Second, the fact that workers from communities far and wide can be affected by such "local" disputes may have important—if sometimes contradictory—implications for union strategy. On the one hand, the ability of a particular local union to spread a dispute in such a manner may allow it to secure support and resources in its struggle with a company from many more workers who might consider the issues at stake to be ones that also affect their own lives. On the other hand, such workers may alternatively feel that they have been dragged into a dispute over issues in a plant which may be hundreds of miles away, and they may resent the fact that they have been laid off—temporarily or even permanently—over matters which they feel do not affect them. In such situations, they may decide to engage not in solidarity across space with their union brothers and sisters working for the same corporation elsewhere but, instead, may criticize workers on strike at other plants for the ways in which such strikes have inconvenienced them. Of course, which of these two responses workers adopt will be conditioned by the contingencies of their location, their attitudes towards their own employers and towards other members of the union, and so forth.[7]

Third, and perhaps most significantly, the ability of workers at just two plants in Flint, Michigan to affect production throughout almost all of GM's North American operations illustrates the power that the local may have in a global economy. As GM has increasingly shifted towards the development of a highly integrated JIT continental production system in which components produced in one part of North America must be whisked as quickly as possible to assembly operations in another part, so has grown the ability of small numbers of auto workers to bring to a grinding halt the corporation's operations through local, strategically focused strikes. To put this in slightly different terms, as GM has sought to shrink the relative distances between the communities in which its plants are located by ensuring speedy delivery of components between them, so, too, has it become easier for workers in certain key plants to spread the impacts of a dispute quickly across large distances. In turn, this has meant that GM has had much less time in which to respond to any disruptions in its production chain, which is giving these workers added political power. Thus, in the case of the 1998 dispute, GM was not able to reorganize its supply chains to restart production at its Silao, Mexico and Bowling Green, Kentucky assembly plants until the end of July. Significantly, this occurred the day before the UAW signed an agreement ending the dispute that committed GM to no substantive changes in work rules in the Flint plants for the immediate future, to investing some $180 million in the stamping plant represented by Local 659 (in exchange for a 15% increase in productivity), to withdrawing its complaint in federal court charging that the strikes were illegal (thereby freeing the UAW from the threat of imposition by the courts of fines which could have ranged in the billions of dollars), and to agreeing not to close several plants for at least a further two years. It took another week or so after the agreement was signed for all of GM's plants to return to production. The ability of just 9200 workers in two plants in a single community to disrupt to such an extent the operations of one of the world's largest TNCs, then, is testimony to the power that locally focused industrial actions on the part of workers may sometimes have in an increasingly integrated global economy.

Discussion: Challenging TNCs in a Global Economy

Throughout this chapter, I have considered what some of the changes to the spatial and temporal relationships between places brought about by processes of globalization mean for workers' abilities to secure their interests against TNCs. In outlining the Ravenswood and the GM disputes, I have tried to show how different groups of workers in very different situations resorted to quite different strategies articulated at very different geographical resolutions to achieve their goals. Of course, there are a number of things that are particular to each of the disputes. However, there are also a number of more general lessons that might be drawn from these two cases, lessons that are worth pondering with regard to the role of workers' political practice in shaping the emergent geography of the global economy.

Perhaps the most obvious thing to emerge out of an analysis of these two cases is that globalization contains within it a number of para-doxes and contradictions for workers. Certainly, the phenomenon of the shrinking globe may lead to greater competition between places and workers as many spatial barriers are dismantled, but it may also facilitate greater contact between workers in different parts of the globe and so bring about increased opportunities for solidarity between them. For instance, while the fact that the Ravenswood plant was part of a TNC whose operations stretched around the world clearly provided the locked-out workers with the not insignificant problem of taking on a huge corporation and a powerful set of opponents, at the same time it also facilitated the USWA's expansion of the dispute beyond the confines of a small West Virginia town. The fact that the USWA and its allies in various international labor organizations were able to "piggy-back" onto the organizational structure of Marc Rich's investments and to use this structure to make contact with workers in different parts of the world allowed them to tap into political, financial, and social resources from sympathetic workers and others which probably would have been unavailable to them had the Ravenswood plant not been part of a larger corporate entity.

Equally, the fact that, as Barber (1995) suggests, globalization appears simultaneously to be stimulating in its wake the rise of intense localisms in many places means that, if they are to be successful, TNCs must frequently pay particular attention to local tastes and desires and to local economic and political constraints.[8] Such localism has implications for workers. On the one hand, it may provide spaces—both material and metaphorical—for workers to challenge TNCs. Having an island of local stability on which to stand in a sea of global change may provide the necessary support and traditions upon which workers can draw to defend their interests. Furthermore, the fact that TNCs frequently have to tailor their operations to local conditions and tastes because consumers may refuse to purchase imported goods or goods that do not conform to local expectations because they have been produced elsewhere means that local workers and governments may be able to exert considerable influence over them. Thus, if corporations are to operate in particular regions or countries, for example, they may have to cut agreements with various national or local labor federations or politicians respecting certain labor rights, local content in final products, and the like.[9] On the other hand, defense of the local to preserve traditions and jobs is often one side of a coin whose obverse is rabid xenophobia, and such localism may thus result in a parochial labor politics designed deliberately to protect particular spaces within the global economy at the expense of workers located elsewhere.

Clearly, the resolution of this dialectic of globalization and localization is a geographically uneven process that plays out differently in different places and times. However, it raises, I would suggest, three sets of important questions concerning how class processes relating to the changing terrain of power between capital and labor intersect with, and play out differently across, space. The first of these questions is: how do particular groups of workers view their relationship to globalization, and how may that be shaped by, among other things, their geographic location? Workers whose jobs are threatened by imports are likely to see things differently than those working in locales with industries that are booming due to growing overseas markets. Globalization, then, is likely to mean different things to different groups of workers, and this in turn will affect their political practices and stance towards labor internationalism. Equally, we should not assume a priori that globalization necessarily undermines the power of every worker. Indeed, globalization can also facilitate the bringing together of workers (Ravenswood, Swiss, and Czech metalworkers, for instance). This point is sometimes not recognized by many on the left, but it was certainly acknowledged by Marx and Engels ([1848] 1948: 28), who alluded to this as a possibility a century and a half ago when they suggested that "national differences and antagonisms between peoples are vanishing gradually day by day, owing to the development of the bourgeoisie, to freedom of commerce, to the world market, to uniformity in the mode of production and in the conditions of life corresponding thereto" and that "the supremacy of the proletariat will cause them to vanish still faster."[10]

The second question concerns the goals of workers who do engage in international solidarity activities and might be summarized as: what kind of internationalism for what kind of globalization? While there is sometimes a tendency to see international solidarity through rose-tinted glasses as a vaunted example of the workers of the world uniting, it is important to ask for what purpose workers are engaging in such activities. Not all international solidarity is necessarily geared towards bringing about "proletarian internationalism." Although determining the precise reasons for why workers engage in certain political practices is a complex issue, Johns (1998) has provided in this regard a useful insight concerning the intersection of spatial and class interests. She argues that some types of solidarity may be designed to protect particular privileged spaces in the global economy (eg communities in the US) by, for example, encouraging overseas workers to organize and thus to reduce their attractiveness to capital looking to relocate from such privileged spaces (what she [1998:256] calls "accommodationist solidarity"). Other types of solidarity actions, however, may be designed to challenge the class relations of capitalism without regard to which particular places within the global economy benefit or are negatively affected by such activities (what she [1998:256] calls "transformatory solidarity"). The fact that workers may engage in different types of solidarity actions that have quite different implications for different places raises, of course, the question of which strategies workers choose to use and how they see one or the other as most useful for their immediate concerns. These decisions are likely to be shaped considerably by the contingencies of place—for example, is a local economy booming or in recession? does it have a history of xenophobia or of militant labor internationalism? and so on.

The third question relates to that of strategy and what should be the geographical focal point of action in any particular conflict with a TNC. In presenting the two cases above, I would suggest that workers may face different sets of political, economic, *and geographic* questions concerning the strategies they should adopt when confronting TNCs. Thus, in some instances they may find it more useful to attempt to develop international actions aimed at linking together workers in different locales across the planet. In other instances, they may decide that engaging in well-articulated, very local campaigns against particular key "control points" in a corporation's structure is more useful for their purposes. In recognizing that the specifics of their particular situation means that different groups of workers may find praxis aimed at different geographical scales—a locally focused campaign versus a global one, for example—more useful in different circumstances, we should not, however, fall into the trap of assuming that one is necessarily a more progressive political stance than the other. Although there is often a tendency to think that transnational labor campaigns are, by their very nature, more politically progressive because they bring together workers across space, as Johns points out, many international solidarity campaigns are, in fact, quite politically regressive in that they are designed precisely to preserve the privileged position of some workers in the global economy (often, those in the global North) at the expense of others (frequently, those in the global South). Equally, we should not assume that local campaigns are necessarily parochial and concerned only with defending local communities' privileged positions within the global economy. They may in fact be designed to challenge directly at key locations in the production process the broader class relations that exist between capital and labor. Indeed, the UAW used this strategy quite effectively during the 1990s to challenge GM's efforts to introduce new work methods (cf Babson 1998). Prohibited from engaging in national strikes during the period of its contract with the auto producer, the national union leadership has used local strikes at high profit plants to pursue its goals across the industry as a whole.

In arguing that in some cases workers may best secure their interests by developing campaigns designed to foster transnational labor solidarity whereas in others implementing targeted local actions against specific key control points of a TNC may be more appropriate, I do not want to present matters in "either/or" terms. In both cases, activities at other scales are often necessary if workers are to be successful—in the Ravenswood case, local solidarity amongst workers in the town was a crucial base upon which to build the international aspect of the campaign, and in the case of the UAW the refusal of workers in other plants to use machinery removed from the Flint plants by GM was an important aspect of worker solidarity during the dispute. Nor am I suggesting that local campaigns are useful for all situations (this is not a "the local trumps all" argument). Rather, what I am trying to suggest is that the primary geographical focus of worker action need not necessarily be at the same geographical scale as that of workers' employers—it is not necessary in all cases for workers to organize transnationally to mirror the scale of organization of their employers if they are to beat TNCs. There is no set "scalar formula" by which workers and their organizations should go about challenging TNCs. Indeed, the very significance of economic, political, geographic, and other contingencies in any particular dispute means that there cannot ever be a single formulaic guide for workers' praxis.

The ability of the two UAW local unions in Flint, then, to so significantly impact GM's production was the specific result of the vulnerability which the corporation has generated for itself by relying upon JIT, which was not the situation with Ravenswood—a contrast which suggests, perhaps, that those workers who live in the more interconnected world of "fast capitalism" (Agger 1989), with its JIT and highly networked production, may have different strategy options open to them than do those who live in what we might call the world of "slower capitalism," where speed and interconnectedness are less crucial aspects of the production process. Furthermore, suggesting that workers *must* or even *ought* to organize transnationally to challenge a TNC may have unintended negative political consequences for unions' efforts to come to grips with the processes and consequences of globalization, for the very difficulties of trying to organize transnationally may set them up to fail. Workers may think that if they cannot organize globally, there is no point in attempting to organize at other scales. In such instances, not only may the rhetoric of "global solidarity at all costs" result in workers and unions having to spend more time and resources developing international links when challenging a TNC than may be necessary if similar results can be achieved by organizing at other scales, but such a rhetoric may also become quite politically paralyzing, particularly if given the right spin by capital.[11]

Finally, the fact that workers may have different options open to them—depending, as ever, on the particularities of their own situations—and that they may choose to exercise different options at different times and in different places is also politically important because it challenges the belief that capital alone is remaking the geography of the global economy (cf Gibson-Graham 1996; Herod 1995, 1997a, b). By choosing to engage in one type of campaign rather than another, workers also affect how the geography of the global economy is made, for different strategies will result in different geographies of capitalism. This is important to continually bear in mind if we are ever to realize the possibilities for a more humane world and its attendant economic landscape.

Acknowledgements

Thanks to Jane Wills, Peter Waterman, and an anonymous reviewer for comments on an earlier version of this chapter. A longer and somewhat different version of this chapter will also appear in *International Trade Unions: Theory and Strategy in the Global Political Economy*, Jeffery Harrod and Robert O'Brien, eds, to be published by Routledge Press as part of its *Review of International Political Economy* series.

Endnotes

[1] For example, Richard Trumka, Secretary-Treasurer of the AFL-CIO (*Labor Notes* 1991:4; emphasis added), has suggested that "[i]f we're going to be able to effectively challenge companies like Shell or Exxon or DuPont and other corporations which operate without regard to national boundaries, *we have to redefine solidarity in global terms …*" In a speech given at the 17th World Congress of the International Confederation of Free Trade Unions on April 4, 2000 in Durban, South Africa, John Sweeney, the President of the AFL-CIO, has suggested that "[t]he global economy that corporations have forged *can only be tamed by the international solidarity* of working families everywhere" (emphasis added). There are myriad other examples of such rhetoric.

[2] The IMF and the ICEF are both International Trade Secretariats with which unions in particular industrial or trade sectors (metalworkers, food workers, journalists, teachers, etc.) may affiliate for the purposes of coordinating cross-border activities. Subsequent to the Ravenswood lockout, the ICEF merged with the Miners' International Federation (MIF) to form the International Federation of Chemical Energy, Mine and General Workers' Unions (ICEM). The ICFTU has several regional organizations.

[3] In January, 2001 any fear of serving time in jail appeared to have been allayed when President Clinton issued Rich a controversial pardon.

[4] Typically, production of parts at the Flint plant had been based upon a quota system: that is, the workforce had to make a certain number of parts per shift. However, many workers would work sufficiently quickly early in their shifts that they might have completed the requisite number of parts before its end, allowing them to "bank" time. In such cases they were entitled to leave the job, though they had to remain within the plant until their shift was over. Whereas UAW members saw this practice of banking time as a legitimate right, the corporation argued that, if workers could complete their work ahead of time, they should remain on the job to produce more components.

[5] Subsequent to the 1998 dispute, GM sold Delphi off, though GM intended to continue using Delphi as its major supplier of components, and Delphi's agreements with the UAW concerning representation, wages, working conditions, and so forth were to be kept the same as before the sell-off, at least for the immediate future.

[6] The two assembly plants that remained open were the Saturn plant in Spring Hill, Tennessee (where production is much more self-contained than at most other GM assembly plants and so less open to disruption in the supply chain) and the Ramos Arizpe, Mexico small car plant (which GM kept operating by using local suppliers).

[7] Examples of both types of reaction were evident during the UAW-GM dispute. Whereas some workers complained that they had been forced to forego much pay over

a dispute which they felt had little to do with their own work situations, in other cases workers in plants not yet affected by the Flint disputes refused to increase production to make up for lost components, while the national leadership of the Canadian Auto Workers refused to accept dies which GM was attempting to remove from the striking stamping plant in Flint and relocate to its Oshawa, Ontario complex.

[8] For an interesting account of how many US TNCs have had to adapt their products to suit European cultural tastes, see Pells (1997:278–324). Some writers (eg Swyngedouw 1997) have termed this process one of "glocalization" (see also Kanter 1995).

[9] On such economic nationalism by US workers in the face of globalization, see Frank (1999).

[10] In this statement, Marx and Engels do not appear to have recognized what Barber (1995) has called the conflict between "McWorld and Jihad," wherein people who feel their local cultures are under threat as globalization erases differences between places resort to rabid defenses of those local cultures. Nevertheless, their point about how (neoliberal) globalization may contain its own contradictions because it may spur some forms of "proletarian internationalism" is well taken, even if they did not quite put it in these terms.

[11] I do not want to suggest by such a comment that workers might not want to engage in transnational contacts with other workers for other reasons, such as developing a greater understanding of their situations and the like. Rather, I am suggesting that for the narrower purposes of challenging a particular TNC on a particular issue it may not always be necessary to develop a transnational campaign.

References

Agger B (1989) *Fast Capitalism*. Urbana: University of Illinois Press

Automotive News (1998) Rivals make hay in August as GM share sinks to 21.6%. 7 September:39

Babson S (ed) (1995) *Lean Work: Empowerment and Exploitation in the Global Auto Industry*. Detroit: Wayne State University

Babson S (1998) Ambiguous mandate: Lean production and labor relations in the United States. In H Juárez Núñez and S Babson (eds) *Confronting Change: Auto Labor and Lean Production in North America [Enfrentando el Cambio: Obreros del Automóvil y Producción Esbelta en América del Norte]* (pp 23–50). Puebla, Mexico: Autonomous University of Puebla

Barber B (1995) *Jihad vs McWorld*. New York: Ballantine

Copetas A C (1985) *Metal Men: Marc Rich and the 10-Billion-Dollar Scam*. New York: G P Putnam's Sons

Cox K R and Mair A (1988) Locality and community in the politics of local economic development. *Annals of the Association of American Geographers* 78:307–325

Dohse K, Jürgens U and Malsch T (1985) From "Fordism" to "Toyotism"? The social organization of the labor process in the Japanese automobile industry. *Politics and Society* 14(2):115–146

Foucault M (1986) Of other spaces. *Diacritics* 16(1):22–27

Frank D (1999) *Buy American: The Untold Story of Economic Nationalism*. Boston: Beacon Press

Gibson-Graham J K (1996) *The End of Capitalism (As We Knew it): A Feminist Critique of Political Economy*. Cambridge, MA: Blackwell

Green W C and Yanarella E J (eds) (1996) *North American Auto Unions in Crisis: Lean Production as Contested Terrain*. Albany, NY: SUNY Press

Herod A (1995) The practice of international labor solidarity and the geography of the global economy. *Economic Geography* 71(4):341–363

Herod A (1997a) From a geography of labor to a labor geography: Labor's spatial fix and the geography of capitalism. *Antipode* 29(1):1–31

Herod A (1997b) Labor as an agent of globalization and as a global agent. In K Cox (ed) *Spaces of Globalization: Reasserting the Power of the Local* (pp 167–200). New York: Guilford

Herod A (1998a) The geostrategics of labor in post-Cold War Eastern Europe: An examination of the activities of the International Metalworkers' Federation. In A Herod (ed) *Organizing the Landscape: Geographical Perspectives on Labor Unionism* (pp 45–74). Minneapolis: University of Minnesota Press

Herod A (1998b) Theorising unions in transition. In J Pickles and A Smith (eds) *Theorising Transition: The Political Economy of Change in Central and Eastern Europe* (pp 197–217). New York: Routledge

Herod A (2000) Implications of just-in-time production for union strategy: Lessons from the 1998 General Motors-United Auto Workers dispute. *Annals of the Association of American Geographers* 90(3):521–547

Herod A (2001) *Labor Geographies: Workers and the Landscapes of Capitalism.* New York: Guilford Press

Johns R (1998) Bridging the gap between class and space: US worker solidarity with Guatemala. *Economic Geography* 74(3):252–271

Kanter R M (1995) *World Class: Thriving Locally in the Global Economy.* New York: Simon and Schuster

Kenney M and Florida R (1993) *Beyond Mass Production: The Japanese System and its Transfer to the US.* New York: Oxford University Press

Labor Notes (1991) Newswatch. November:4

Linge G J R (1991) Just-in-time: More or less flexible? *Economic Geography* 67(4):316–332

Luke T W and Ó Tuathail G (1998) Global flowmations, local fundamentalisms, and fast geopolitics: "America" in an accelerating world order. In A Herod, G Ó Tuathail and S Roberts (eds) *An Unruly World? Globalization, Governance and Geography* (pp 72–94). New York: Routledge

Mair A (1997) Strategic localization: The myth of the postnational enterprise. In K Cox (ed) *Spaces of Globalization: Reasserting the Power of the Local* (pp 64–88). New York: Guilford

Marx K and Engels F ([1848] 1948) *The Communist Manifesto.* 27th printing of 100th Anniversary Edition. New York: International Publishers

Moody K (1997) *Workers in a Lean World: Unions in the International Economy.* New York: Verso

Ohmae K (1990) *The Borderless World.* New York: Harper Business

Parker M and Slaughter J (1988) *Choosing Sides: Unions and the Team Concept.* Boston, MA: South End Press

Pells R (1997) *Not Like Us: How Europeans Have Loved, Hated, and Transformed American Culture since World War II.* New York: Basic Books

Sweeney J (2000) Speech given at the 17th World Congress of the International Confederation of Free Trade Unions, 4 April, Durban, South Africa. HTML file: <URL: http://www.aflcio.org/publ/speech2000/sp0404.htm>, last accessed March 2001

Swyngedouw E (1997) Neither global nor local: "Glocalisation" and the politics of scale. In K Cox (ed) *Spaces of Globalization: Reasserting the Power of the Local* (pp 137–166). New York: Guilford Press

Toffler A (1980) *The Third Wave*. London: Collins
Uehlein J (1992) Director of Special Projects, Industrial Union Department at the AFL-CIO. Interview with author, 10 August, Washington, DC
Ward's Auto World (1998) Picking up the pieces. September:37–42

Andrew Herod is an Associate Professor of Geography at the University of Georgia. His research interests include trying to understand how globalization is impacting organized labor and how, through their activities, workers and unions have shaped the geography of capitalism. He has pursued these questions through work in the United States, Latin America, and Eastern Europe. He is the editor of *Organizing the Landscape: Geographical Perspectives on Labor Unionism* (1998, University of Minnesota Press), which was designated a "breakthrough book" in May 1999 by the critical journal *Lingua Franca*, and is coeditor of *An Unruly World? Globalization, Governance, and Geography* (1998, Routledge). He is also the author of *Labor Geographies: Workers and the Landscapes of Capitalism* (2001, Guilford Press).

7

World Trade and Workers' Rights: In Search of an Internationalist Position

Rohini Hensman

Trade unions and NGOs have been divided sharply over the issue of a workers' rights clause in WTO trade agreements, and have failed to reach a consensus despite heated debate. This appears to be due to elements of protectionism and nationalism in positions on both sides. Arguments against a workers' rights clause can be classified into those opposing (1) globalisation, (2) the WTO, (3) any linkage between workers' rights and trade, and (4) the proposed mechanisms for enforcement. The first three types of objections can be traced to nationalistic considerations, which subordinate the interests of workers to a "national interest" that represents various business groups. The fourth type, however, includes valid criticisms and reveals elements of protectionism in the current proposals for a workers' rights clause. If the proposal is revised to eliminate these elements, it should be possible to arrive at a consensus among progressive labour unions and NGOs. This would be an important step towards an internationalist strategy to fight for minimum labour rights worldwide.

Preliminary Clarifications

The desirability or otherwise of a social clause protecting workers' rights being incorporated into the multilateral trade agreements of the World Trade Organisation (WTO) has been the subject of heated debate within the trade union movement internationally, with in-stitutions like the International Confederation of Free Trade Unions (ICFTU) and the International Trade Secretariats strongly in favour and others—like all the party-affiliated national unions in India, across the political spectrum (Central Trade Union Organisations of India 1995)—just as strongly opposed. The principal reason why no common ground has been established seems to be that arguments on both sides are tainted with what we might call "labour protectionism" —ie the desire to protect employment in one's own country at all costs. This is a disastrous situation from the standpoint of labour internationalism. Not only does it make any global strategy impossible, but it also subordinates the interests of workers in each country to those of some section of capitalists. It is only by identifying and eliminating these nationalistic considerations that a truly internationalist strategy—so essential in this era of unprecedented globalisation —can be achieved.[1]

Globalisation is usually understood to mean the increasing integration of national economies into the world economy through the removal of barriers to international trade and capital movements. Thus, tariff and nontariff barriers to imports and exports, and restrictions on the inflow and outflow of capital, would ideally cease to exist in a fully globalised world economy. Of course, this is very far from being the actual situation today. Most countries in the world protect national industry and agriculture in some way, either by restricting imports or by providing state subsidies to make them more competitive. However, it is the purpose of the World Trade Organisation (WTO), set up in January 1995 by the Uruguay Round of General Agreement on Tariffs and Trade (GATT), to dismantle these restrictions and move towards a situation of "free trade". Thus far, the free movement of labour has not been on the agenda of the WTO, but it can be argued that this too is a necessary element of globalisation; we will return to this point later. The current phase of globalisation is strongly associated with the development of information technology and the electronic media, and the effect of these, along with imports, on culture is also seen as an important aspect of globalisation.

It is important to note at this stage that "globalisation" refers to globalised *capitalism,* just as the opposition to "globalisation" generally seeks a return to a *national capitalism.* This may be called national socialism, or socialism, or state socialism, or may even claim to hark back to a precapitalist past, but it is still a form of capitalism. So the conflict between globalisers and antiglobalisers lies in their advocacy of different forms of capitalism, which do not *necessarily* coincide with the division between capitalism that recognises minimum workers' rights and capitalism that does not. In Hitler's Germany and the Soviet Union under Stalin, to name just two examples, economic nationalism was quite compatible with the systematic violation of labour rights.

The basic argument of trade union bodies demanding a link between world trade and workers' rights is that, in the absence of that link, trade liberalisation *undermines* workers' rights by removing all obstacles to companies shifting production to countries or sectors where workers' rights are weakest, or importing products from them. This in turn puts pressure on countries or sectors that have strong labour legislation to weaken it, so as to attract investment and avoid a flight of capital or to make their products competitive. The result is a "race to the bottom", with the average level of workers' rights falling lower and lower globally. The existence of workers without rights becomes a means of blackmailing those who have them. Hence, some trade unions have seen it as crucial to fix a minimum level below which labour rights will not be allowed to sink.

The proposed workers' rights clause incorporates the International Labour Organisation (ILO) Core Conventions:

1) No 87, the Freedom of Association and Protection of the Right to Organize Convention, 1948, and No 98, the Right to Organize and Collective Bargaining Convention, 1949, dealing with the right to organise and bargain collectively;
2) No 29, the Forced Labour Convention, 1930, and No 105, the Abolition of Forced Labour Convention, 1957, dealing with the elimination of forced labour;
3) No 138, the Minimum Age Convention, 1973, dealing with the abolition of child labour; and
4) No 100, the Equal Remuneration Convention, 1951, and No 111, the Discrimination (Employment and Occupation) Convention, 1958, dealing with equal pay for women and the elimination of discrimination in employment and occupation.

These are called core conventions because governments, unions and employers from the member countries of the ILO—ie virtually all the countries in the world, with developing countries forming the majority—agreed that they were fundamental to the rights of *all* human beings at work, regardless of the level of development of a country, and applicable to all sectors, including the informal sector and Free Trade Zones.

On 18 June 1998, the International Labour Conference adopted the *ILO Declaration on Fundamental Principles and Rights at Work and Its Follow-up,* which declares that *all member states have an obligation to implement the core conventions, even if they have not ratified them.* It was initially proposed that that there should be a linkage between these labour rights and trade agreements of the WTO, and that members violating these rights should be punished by trade sanctions. This proposal has been modified in the course of the subsequent debate, and it remains unclear exactly how the linkage is to be established and how compliance would be enforced.

Objections to the social clause by trade unions and NGOs can be grouped into four main clusters: (1) opposition to globalisation;

(2) opposition to the WTO, which partially overlaps with (1); (3) opposition to any link between workers' rights and world trade; and (4) opposition to the proposed mechanism of enforcement. These objections will be discussed in the next four sections.

Opposition to Globalisation

In India, opposition to globalisation has come from the extreme right as well as the nationalist left. The Hindu nationalist right comprises the Rashtriya Swayamsevak Sangh (RSS) and the "family" of organisations affiliated to it (Sangh Parivar), especially the Swadeshi Jagran Manch (SJM). It opposes globalisation from the standpoint of *"swadeshi"*, which in this context means domestic capital that is not confident of being globally competitive, as well as from that of cultural nationalism that seeks to preserve upper-caste Hindu values (*Business Standard* 1994, 1995). It has not spared even its own affiliate, the Bharatiya Janata Party (BJP), from criticism for its "weak-kneed attitude towards the World Trade Organisation", urging it to withdraw India from the WTO (*Business Standard* 1998b). In January 2000, the SJM and other RSS affiliates organised a protest demonstration against WTO Director-General Mike Moore, proclaiming that "[w]e will not allow a global system" (Open Letter to Mr Mike Moore 2000: 84–85).

Economic and cultural nationalism—hatred of multinationals on one side and minorities and communists on the other—are closely linked in RSS ideology. What unites the two strands is xenophobia, hatred of the foreign, whether it is foreign capital or religions and ideologies like Islam, Christianity, feminism or Marxism that originated outside India. While Guru Golwalkar admired Hitler's extermination of minorities in *We or Our Nationhood Defined*, Deen Dayal Upadhyay advocated the "virtues of small traders and small industry flourishing in a mythical, Hindu-only, pastoral paradise" in his *Integral Humanism* (Barman 1998).[2] At the meeting of the RSS's Pratinidhi Sabha (its highest body) in March 1999, when India was reeling under a series of brutal attacks on Christians, the two themes were linked when senior leader K C Sudarshan said that the RSS would come out with two resolutions. The first would be on conversions which "are damaging the very basic culture of the country ...; the second resolution will review the failure of WTO" (*Economic Times* 1999a).

It is not in India alone that the extreme right opposes globalisation. In the US, racist, anti-Semitic, right-wing politician Pat Buchanan declared that "[w]hat is good for General Motors is no longer good for America if General Motors is shutting down plants in Michigan and opening them in Mexico City" (*Economic Times* 1996b). In Europe, neo-Nazis like Joerg Haider "make opposition to the WTO, global-isation and immigrant workers the main issues in their campaign to 'save' their Aryan way of life" (Sakai 2000). At Seattle, "the NGO … leaders represented in the elite 'think tank' of the International Forum on Globalization … catered to nationalism and accepted neo-Fascists as their allies" and subsequently, "neo-Nazis have come out in public applauding the 'angry white people' who 'shut down the Jew World Order' at Seattle" (Sakai 2000:15, 18, 22).

Nationalist opposition to global capital has been a defining feature of fascism ever since Hitler wrote *Mein Kampf* (1943, quoted in Henwood 1993:303). By contrast, Marx (Marx 1974:350) supported the free trade party of his time, believing that it was creating the material conditions for coordinated action by workers of different countries, which he believed was the only force capable of superseding capitalism—hence the slogan "Workers of the world unite". There seems to be good reason to agree with the Dutch antiracist group De Fabel van de Illegaal when they conclude that "[I]deologically separating or criticising international or foreign capital simply does not fit into left-wing politics" (Krebbers and Schoenmaker 2000:52). One of the most dangerous illusions fostered by liberal and left eco-nomic nationalism is the idea that capitalism can overcome problems of poverty, unemployment and crisis provided it remains national, and that the real enemy is the foreign Other. Although it starts from different premises, this position ends up uncomfortably close to that of the far right, and the rhetoric is often indistinguishable. One dam-aging outcome is that it deprives workers of their most potent weapon against global capitalism: global solidarity. Even more disturbing is the possibility that, with their overriding emphasis on nationalism, in India as in Europe and the US, "[l]eft politics actually tilled the ground for Fascist regrowth" (Sakai 2000:16).

At a more practical level, if we look at this issue from the standpoint of the economies of most developing countries, access to global markets is crucial, and trade liberalisation—which removes barriers to such access—is actually in their interests. The complaint of the gov-ernments of most developing countries is not that they are opposed to free trade, but that they are not getting a fair deal—that developed countries are forcing them to remove barriers to imports even while those countries themselves retain or put up barriers to imports from developing countries. Thus, for example, then-Minister for Commerce and Industry Murasoli Maran said that India "was committed to a strengthened, rule-based, nondiscriminatory multilateral trading system that should be fair and equitable ... He underlined that trade negotiations should concentrate on the core issues of market access ensuring smooth flow of trade ..." (*Business Standard* 1999d).

It is not only domestic business in the Third World that would suffer if globalisation and trade liberalisation were reversed in favour of high levels of protectionism. Millions of workers in export production would at one blow become unemployed and—in the absence of social security systems—destitute. The loss of their purchasing power could in some cases lead to other local industries closing down for lack of demand, creating more unemployment. For nongovernmental organisations (NGOs), trade unions and political parties supposedly defending the interests of developing countries, calling for a reversal of globalisation, which would cause economic devastation and a massive increase in unemployment in Third World countries, makes no sense.

Opposition to the WTO

All those who oppose globalisation would, *a forteriori*, oppose the WTO, whose mandate is to promote free trade, breaking down barriers to the movement of commodities and capital from country to country. There are additional reasons why the WTO is opposed. Many observers have welcomed the WTO as being fairer than the earlier GATT regime. Its first major ruling upheld a complaint made by Venezuela and Brazil that US petrol norms discriminated against imports, and inspired this comment:

> The World Trade Organisation (WTO) has teeth. And it is willing to use them, even against the mighty United States ... Under the GATT, disputes could and did last for years on end. Even if and when the GATT dispute settlement panel did come to a decision, the ruling was practically worthless. GATT worked on the basis of consensus, which meant that a powerful country like the US could hold up the implementation of a ruling for an indefinite period ... The WTO now has the power to insist that the US change trade regulations that are in violation of multilateral rules ... The WTO corrects some of the power imbalance between the rich and poor countries that existed under GATT .... (Ghei 1996)

A subsequent case confirmed this view. India, Malaysia, Pakistan and Thailand won a case against the US, which had attempted to restrict imports of shrimps from these countries on the grounds that the fishing equipment they used did not have Turtle Excluder Devices (TEDs) (*Economic Times* 1998b). The WTO ruling was not that TEDs should not be used, but that unilateral US insistence that countries from which it imported should adopt US norms—as opposed to international or multilaterally or bilaterally negotiated ones—was contrary to the WTO agreement (Chimni 2000). An editorial commented:

> Xenophobes and antitraders would do well to note the victory that has been won by the Indian fishery sector in a dispute at the WTO with the EU and the US. The triumph in these markets, two of the world's biggest, clearly shows that any suggestion of an international conspiracy against Indian exports is baseless. What it shows, too, is the utility of bodies like the WTO … it has acted just as an impartial regulatory body should … Another, earlier triumph for freer trade with the EU was that of unbleached cotton fabric exports to some member countries. Indian exports were allowed, taking the interest of major consumers of the item into consideration. (*Economic Times* 1998a)[3]

The consensus among those who have studied the way in which the WTO functions appears to be that it is an improvement on the earlier GATT regime from the standpoint of developing countries. It is certainly more democratic than the World Bank and IMF, which are quite openly dominated by rich countries, and perhaps even than the UN, where permanent members of the Security Council have veto powers. As Professor T N Srinivasan, chairman of the Department of Economics at Yale University, put it, "Institutions like the WTO are rule-based and they are meant to protect the weak against the strong. Developing countries would be at a disadvantage against the developed countries in the absence of an organisation like the WTO" (*Business Standard* 1999a). According to another comment, "WTO is an international body that functions on a 'one country-one vote' principle. Indeed, there is a standard American complaint that GATT and WTO have been hijacked by the developing countries" (*Business Standard* 1998a). It was this perception that the WTO represents a *loss* of power for the USA that led to Pat Buchanan's call for the US to pull out of it (*Economic Times* 1996a). If the least developed countries (LDCs), which have gained little from trade liberalisation so far,

> are still anxious to gain entry into the WTO, it is because the fragility of their economic conditions makes them long for some

degree of multilateralism and basic ground rules. With all its warts and secretive processes, the WTO is still a better option for most such countries than overt bilateral control by a particular major power, which is the state many of them otherwise find themselves in. (Chandrashekhar and Ghosh 1999)

If these assessments are correct, then WTO director general Mike Moore's charge that "protesters demanding the body be destroyed were working against the poor people and countries they want to protect" (*Economic Times* 1999e), an African delegate's complaint against the protesters that "[y]ou are behaving like racists" (*Business Standard* 1999f) and an Indian NGO's accusation that "the rioters were targeting developing nations" and "almost managed to subvert the legitimate concerns of the Third World" (Centre for Science and Environment 1999) are not entirely baseless. If the WTO is destroyed without a better alternative being set up, it would mean going back to a regime where developed countries could freely discriminate against developing countries without the latter being able to seek redress in any way.

This does not, of course, mean that there are no power imbalances within the WTO. There were many complaints from Third World countries about their exclusion from the deliberations in Seattle. For example:

The Organisation of African Unity ... said there was no transparency in the process and the African countries were being marginalised. (*Economic Times* 1999i)

The developing countries predictably focused on the lack of transparency in the negotiating process ... Their objections took on an angry edge when on Thursday security personnel were used to keep delegates from developing countries out of the Green Room. The Dominican ambassador reflected this anger when he said the failure of the negotiations was "an important lesson in humility for a small group of countries that seem to think that the WTO is a club". (*Economic Times* 1999k)

Developing country diplomats and their ministers at the five-year-old World Trade Organisation's first major test were insulted at the way they were brushed aside by the big powers. "They have been treating us like animals, keeping us out in the cold and telling us nothing", said veteran Egyptian trade negotiator Munir Zahran. (*Sunday Times, Sri Lanka* 1999)

However, the logical response is not a return to a pre-WTO trading system that is even more heavily weighted against the Third World, but to demand a democratisation of the WTO, with transparency, accountability and equal access to decision-making for all countries.

Another criticism has been that the WTO "serves primarily corporate interests" (eg Bond 2000) and not the interests of the mass of the world's population. If this is true, we need to ask why. It is governments, not companies, who are members of the WTO; if they represent only the interests of big business, that demonstrates a failure of democracy on *their* part. This is certainly true of the Indian government, which represented *exclusively* business interests and made no attempt to hide the fact. For example, in the period leading up to the WTO meeting at Seattle in November–December 1999,

> N N Khanna, special secretary in the commerce ministry, ... said India's negotiations at the Seattle round of World Trade Organisation would be corporate-driven and would genuinely reflect the needs of industry. At a seminar on General Agreement on Trade in Services organised by Federation of Indian Chambers of Commerce and Industry ..., Khanna told industry to come out with policy papers which were knowledge-based so as to give inputs to the negotiations. (*Business Standard* 1999b)

Workers and trade unions were not, of course, issued any such invitation. Another headline says it all: "Industry spells out India's strategy for Seattle talks" (*Business Standard* 1999c). One cannot accuse the Indian government of excluding civil society from the WTO negotiations: Indian business was very much involved, both before the Seattle meeting and as part of the official delegation (*Economic Times* 1999l). The problem is that only the minuscule section of civil society constituted by the wealthy and powerful was included. The Indian government was there, not as the representative of its one billion people, but as the representative of Indian capital.

What is required here is a different type of democratisation of the WTO, one that gives a voice in its deliberations and decisions to the mass of people in the world. The problem, of course, is that most of this mass is unorganised and therefore incapable of putting across its demands. However, trade unions comprise one set of organisations consisting of ordinary working people, and some NGOs also represent the interests of nonelite groups. Providing a mechanism for this type of civil society organisation to influence WTO decisions would constitute a democratisation of the organisation's functioning. However, many of the institutions demanding democratisation in terms of greater equality for Third World countries are rigidly opposed to any interests other than business ones being represented. The Indian government, for example, reiterated again and again their opposition to workers' rights receiving any consideration in the WTO (for example, *Business Standard* 1999d, e, g; *Economic Times* 1999h, j; and many more).[4] For trade unions with an internationalist perspective, *both* types of democratisation are crucial. The demand for a workers' rights clause is a demand for the latter type; revising it so that it does not contradict the first type is the challenge facing us.

Opposition to Any Link Between Workers' Rights and the WTO

In preference to the somewhat meaningless and/or misleading terms "social clause" and "labour standards", we will use the more precise term "workers' rights clause", which is increasingly being used by the ICFTU (ICFTU 2000). Opposing the inclusion of workers' rights in trade agreements, some developing country governments—including the Indian government—have put forward several arguments, many of which are supported by the national trade union federations and some NGOs. On the other hand, other NGOs and more radical independent trade unions have been extremely critical of these views. Below are some of the points that have been debated in India. This debate owes much to two consultations organised by the Centre for Education and Communication (CEC Delhi) in 1995, in Delhi (March) and Bangalore (November), as well as discussions in the Trade Union Solidarity Committee (TUSC), a coordination of independent (ie unaffiliated to any party) left unions, in Bombay in April and May 1995 and August 2000.

The government and some NGOs hold that labour is not a trade-related issue and therefore should not be included in trade agreements (eg *Economic Times* 1999f; John 2000). This contention contradicts the almost universal complaint by trade unions, including those in India, that trade liberalisation has had a powerful and negative impact on labour. Indeed, even employers and the government only insist that labour is not a trade-related issue when there is talk of strengthening or enforcing workers' rights. The minute they want to *attack* workers' rights—for example, by revising labour laws to eliminate them (D'Costa 2000)—labour suddenly becomes the *key* trade-related issue, and workers' rights the foremost if not sole reason why they are unable to compete successfully! The self-seeking hypocrisy of such double-speak hardly needs to be laboured.

Another argument is that a workers' rights clause is aimed at wiping out labour cost differences between developed and developing countries, thereby destroying any comparative advantages that poor countries have today. This contention has the most widespread acceptance, ranging from the World Bank (1995:6), through the governments of India and other developing countries (eg *Economic Times* 1999h), to Indian trade union federations (eg Mahendra 1996), and it needs to be examined carefully from all sides.

First, is it true that the intention is protectionist? Not in all cases, surely. When attempts are made to eliminate child labour from carpet production and tea plantations, for example, it is not because these compete with commodities from developed countries, but because there is genuine concern for child workers. Even where the product does compete, as in the case of garments, we cannot assume ulterior motives in all cases. Suppose, however, that in some cases the intention *is* protectionist. Does it follow that it should automatically be rejected? Radical journalist and antinuclear activist Praful Bidwai, as well as unionists in the TUSC, pointed out that much of India's labour legislation was introduced by the British colonial regime under pressure from the Lancashire mill-owners, whose motive was unambiguously protectionist. Yet trade unionists did not reject these measures; on the contrary, they used them to improve employment conditions for workers (see, eg, Vivekanandan 1996:161).

Second, is it true that wage costs will be equalised by a workers' rights clause? There is no proposal for equalising wages and conditions between different countries. Even the issue of a minimum wage is absent from the Core Conventions. The proposal is only that *certain minimum workers' rights that have already been accepted as an international standard should be respected in all countries.* Wages and conditions will continue to be much worse in developing countries, and will improve only as a result of collective bargaining. This argument, therefore, amounts to demanding that workers should be deprived of basic rights in the interests of global competitiveness. Taking it up, labour activist Sujata Gothoskar of Bombay (1996:62) said, "With this argument, every struggle by the workers for a better life may be argued as eroding the competitive advantage of our country. Does this not negate the rationale and existence of the trade unions themselves?"

In fact, the proposition that the lack of minimum workers' rights in some Third World countries is a problem solely or primarily for developed countries needs to be examined. As the ICFTU (2000) has noted, it is a much greater problem for other Third World countries, which are trying to enforce these minimum rights but are undercut by governments attempting to increase exports and attract investment by denying them. This logic can be seen at work even within a relatively homogeneous region like South Asia. Child labour in the carpet industries of India and Pakistan undermines the efforts of Nepal to keep its carpet industry free of child labour, child labour in the garment factories of Bangladesh causes problems for the garment industry of Sri Lanka which is free of child labour, and so on and so forth. A powerful argument for basic workers' rights being enforced in all countries is that it will prevent developing country governments bidding one another down in this way, and prevent multinationals from blackmailing both governments and workers by threatening to shift their investments elsewhere if minimum rights are enforced—which is, no doubt, the reason why the World Bank opposes it!

This brings us directly to the next argument, which is that linking workers' rights to international trade undermines national sovereignty and the national interest (Ganguly 1996). Questioning this definition of "national interest", Srilata Swaminadhan (1996:56–57), an activist of the Rajasthan Kisan Sanghathan working with the rural poor, commented,

> It is being borne home with every action of the government that "national interest" means only the interest of the minority rich who rule this country and control all its wealth and resources ... Is it not the height of hypocrisy that our government should consider linking equal wages to men and women with trade, to be against the interests of the nation? Is it not revealing that it considers giving a guarantee to stop child labour as harmful to our country?

It is true that, if "national interest" is defined narrowly as the interests of the ruling class, linking workers' rights to international trade would undermine it. However, if it is defined more broadly as the interests of the overwhelming majority of the population consisting of working people, it is hard to see how strengthening their rights could undermine their interests! Moreover, as we saw above, such a clause could actually *boost* the sovereignty of Third World nations attempting to protect the rights of their workers against recalcitrant multinationals threatening to pull their investments out if the rights are protected. It would only undermine the sovereignty of those governments that are hand-in-glove with the most brutal employers, those who refuse to recognise even the most basic workers' rights.

Child Labour

This issue merits special attention. It is somewhat different from other fundamental workers' rights in that it is primarily a human rights and ethical argument about the right of a certain class of human beings *not* to be workers, and only secondarily an argument about the effect of child labour on workers' rights. We will only touch on the first argument, since the latter argument is our main focus here.

Anyone who has loved and cared for a child knows how much cruelty is involved in forcing a child to perform the same task for hours on end. This cruelty is compounded where the task is hazardous to health and safety or involves brutal punishments (all too common). Anyone who has cared for a child also knows the inexhaustible curiosity of children, the endless questions that are often a scientific or philosophical challenge to the adult carer. If schooling often does not satisfy this curiosity, that is an argument for changing the educational system, rather than depriving children of the wherewithal to satisfy their thirst for knowledge. Child labour violates the child's right to sufficient rest, play, care and education. There is surely an element of class racism in any justification for allowing poor children in the Third World to be subjected to deprivation and abuse which would be unthinkable for middle- or upper-class children.[5]

Opponents of a workers' rights clause argue that child labour cannot be eliminated without eliminating poverty, and that any attempt to do so will merely result in worsening the condition of the children (eg Grote 2000; Kabeer 2000; Mehta 1999). When we look at these arguments carefully, we notice a slippage, conscious or unconscious, from poverty of the *child or child's family* to poverty of the *country* in which child labour takes place. These are two very different things. To say that only dire necessity can drive a child into wage-labour is obvious, almost banal. The contention that the prevalence of child labour in a country is a function of *its* poverty, however, is not supported by the evidence. A cross-country study of child labour (Ahmed 1999:1820) concluded that "poverty is not even a significant reason for child labour when the influence of other explanatory factors for child labour are simultaneously taken into account, whereas unequal income distribution and lack of access to education are much more important reasons for a high level of child labour".

To the extent that there is a correlation between poverty and child labour, the direction of causality also needs to be examined. In the labour-surplus economies of South Asia which lack any social security, employment of children increases adult unemployment and leads by a vicious circle to more child labour, both in the present (because the children of those unemployed adults might then be forced to work to support the family) and in the future (because children currently employed are virtually unable to work by the time they are in their thirties, and send their own children out to work to support the family). By competing with adult labour, child labour (which is even cheaper) also lowers overall wages and undermines the bargaining power of trade unions. It is thus a *cause* of poverty.

While it is certainly correct to point out that alternative forms of employment available to children—such as domestic service, scavenging or prostitution—may be even worse than industrial labour (Kabeer 2000:373–374; *Labour File* 1998), it does not follow that the garment factories of Bangladesh are suitable places for children. Below-subsistence wages, with women receiving only 60% of a man's wages for the same work (which is an important reason why children have to supplement the wages of adult workers in the industry) (Custers 1997:148–149); up to 14 working hours per day without even the statutory holiday of 30 days per annum (Kabeer 2000:374); hazardous working conditions leading to accidents like the devastating fire at the Chowdhury Knitwear factory, 30 kilometres from Dhaka, in November 2000, in which at least 50 women and children were killed and over 200 injured (BBC World News 27 November 2000; *Business Standard* 2000): these are not acceptable conditions even for adult workers, much less for children. The justification for employing pre-school children is that working mothers would otherwise have nowhere to leave them (Kabeer 2000:373), but the Indian Factories Act of 1934 (which of course covered what are now Pakistan and Bangladesh as well) had already found a more humane solution for this problem: workplace crèches. So what are the reasons for this persistence of the barbaric conditions of the 19th century into the 21st century?

Underlying the arguments justifying child labour are at least two implicit assumptions, which need to be made explicit. One is that employers have a right to continue violating the most fundamental human rights of workers, and that governments must uphold that right. There are valid criticisms of Senator Harkin's Child Labour Deterrence Bill (Custers 1997:148; Kabeer 2000:367), but it does not seem to have wiped out the Bangladeshi garment industry. Indeed, it demonstrated the complete substitutability of adult for child labour. If employers were required to employ adults in place of children, to pay equal wages for work of equal value and to recognise and negotiate with unions so that they could achieve a living wage for their workers, the problem of child labour would arise only in the case of street children (orphans, abandoned children and runaways from family abuse) and children of parents whose disabilities or sickness prevents them from working.

The second assumption is that the state has no responsibility either to support this latter category of children or to provide all children with free, compulsory and relevant education. The plea of poverty can hardly be taken seriously in the case of countries like India and Pakistan, which seem to have billions of dollars to squander on nuclear weapons, whereas Sri Lanka manages to provide its children with this service despite a decades-old civil war. If a country genuinely lacks the resources to educate its children, then a workers' rights clause would entitle them to international assistance for this purpose. In patriarchal societies, a government policy of encouraging child labour instead of providing education has its most damaging impact on female literacy (compare female literacy rates of around 85% in Sri Lanka with around 25% in Bangladesh, for example). Apologists for child labour justify depriving children in general, especially girls, of the power to choose: to go to school, to be literate and to gain the control over one's life that comes with education. NGOs working with child labour in India disagree as to whether a workers' rights clause will be of much use in a context where over 90% of child labour is not in export production, but they do agree on the need to abolish it (Vivekanandan 1996:166–169).

In India, resistance to ideals like universal education, nondiscrimination, freedom from bondage and trade union rights have to be seen in the context of a state and ruling class steeped in a culture of inequality. Untouchability still practised widely, cases of dalit (formerly "untouchable") children barred from schools, dalit graduates forced to clear human excrement for a living and whole villages of dalit agricultural labourers massacred (*Economic and Political Weekly* 1997; *Economic and Political Weekly* 1999; Star TV News Reports 2000); cases of female infanticide and girls allowed to die for lack of nutrition and health care, so that the female to male sex ratio has been falling steadily and at the last census (1991) stood at 927 females per 1000 males (Krishnaji 2000); bonded labour widespread and more than 90% of the labour force denied basic trade union rights—none of this is inevitable. Instead, it is part of a construction of "India" perpetuated by those who argue that "any kind of homogenisation in a heterogeneous world is quite wrong" (Mehta 2000:9) and a workers' rights clause is an attempt to "force ... Western morality on the rest of the world" (Lal 1999). The biggest irony is that the goal of such arguments —securing the preservation of a casteist, sexist and brutally oppressive society—would also ensure that India remains forever a backward, dependent economy in which the mass of the population cannot even dream of possessing the commodities produced for export to developed countries. Needless to say, the contention that the ideals mentioned above are alien to India is a bizarre distortion of the truth. On the contrary, they inspired the Independence Movement, are embodied in the Constitution and continue to inspire millions of ordinary people today. *Real* development—as opposed to the enrichment of a small elite—requires an improvement in the quality of life for everyone.

How Will It Be Implemented?

The last category of criticisms of a workers' rights clause concerns suggested modes of implementation. These deserve serious consideration. We can classify them under three headings: (1) Who will implement the clause? (2) What will the exact linkage be? and (3) What is the mechanism of implementation?

Who will implement a workers' rights clause? Scepticism that the WTO itself—which has no expertise in labour rights and the mandate of which is free trade—would be able to carry out this task is entirely justified. The CEC first considered the ILO, and then rejected it in favour of a UN Labour Rights Convention (John and Chenoy 1996:5) that would have no connection with the WTO. However, this suggestion misses the whole point of the proposal for a workers' rights clause, which is: how can the *WTO* be prevented from undermining core labour rights? Most proposals suggest some combination of the ILO and WTO. One suggestion is that the ILO monitor implementation of the Core Conventions by governments, while the WTO takes action against offenders (Brett 1995). However, this, too, runs up against the objection that the WTO cannot be trusted to recommend and carry out action that will strengthen workers' rights *without* affecting the workers adversely. Given its experience and expertise in this field, the ILO is clearly the most competent body both to monitor the implementation of the Core Conventions and to suggest and carry out remedial action where they are being violated. This will require trade unions to put concerted pressure on the ILO to play a much more activist role in implementing its Core Conventions than it has hitherto played, and on the WTO to fund these activities of the ILO and respect its decisions.

How will workers' rights be linked to trade? A minimum requirement for preventing a "race to the bottom" is that a WTO member country that has implemented the Core Conventions should be able to refuse to import products made in violation of them, or to give preference to those that comply with them over those that do not, and the WTO should not be able to penalise it for following such a policy. This does *not* amount to trade sanctions imposed by the WTO, which would be an enhancement of its power. Rather, it represents a curtailment of the WTO's power to undermine core labour rights. To prevent this provision from being used in a protectionist manner, a country making false allegations of violations against another country can be made to compensate workers, the government and companies in the second country for losses they have suffered as a consequence, and also to pay punitive damages in proportion to its GDP. This provision will, of course, rule out the denial of trade union rights in Free Trade Zones (FTZs) or Export Processing Zones.

However, there are both practical and ethical problems in linking workers' rights *solely* to export production. In countries with long and constantly shifting subcontracting chains, it would be virtually impossible to ascertain whether a particular product has been made in accordance with the Core Conventions. A humanitarian problem also arises, as in the case of the Harkin Bill, if children are expelled from export production in order to comply with WTO rules but are then pushed into even worse alternatives. It would be more practical as well as ethical to require WTO members to implement core labour rights *for all workers,* including those producing for domestic consumption, casual, temporary and part-time workers, contract (agency, despatch) workers, domestic workers, seasonal and migrant workers and homeworkers. As a women workers' workshop in Korea (Statement from International Women Workers Workshop on Globalisation and Informalisation 2000) concluded, a crucial problem for the majority of women workers and an increasing number of men as well is the informalisation of employment. Such informalisation not only allows employers to evade their obligations with respect to benefits and facilities like paid leave and holidays, social security payments and so on, but even allows them to violate basic trade union rights without any possibility of legal redress, because there is no documentary proof that victimised workers were employed in the first place.

If a workers' rights clause is to be at all effective, it must address this problem. One possible demand, put forward by some women home-workers in India, is that all workers should be issued with an identity card specifying the employer for whom they work. Governments could be required to open centres where employers, workers or their organ-isations can register all these categories of informal workers, to implement legislation outlawing the use of "irregular" workers for jobs of a permanent or perennial nature and to insist on the reinstatement of workers who are dismissed for forming or joining a union. Only some such measure will enable billions of workers in the informal sector to obtain organisational and collective bargaining rights in practice.

How would a workers' rights clause be implemented? The mechanism that has received widest publicity is the imposition of trade sanctions against countries that violate the Core Conventions, as Clinton threatened at Seattle (*Economic Times* 1999g). This proposal seems to be motivated by labour protectionism rather than a genuine concern for globalising minimum workers' rights. Trade sanctions could destroy the economy of a country, making labour standards worse rather than better and victimising rather than helping the most vulnerable, as in Iraq. Another objection is that sanctions, by their nature, are weapons of the strong against the weak; one cannot, for example, envisage Bangladesh enforcing sanctions against the US, even though it is well known that many of the Core Conventions are flouted in the US. Sanctions would therefore reinforce rather than subvert inequalities between nations, perpetuating an unequal global order. This inequality is against the interests of workers everywhere, because it means that *even if a workers' rights clause is implemented,* workers in poor countries will still have an extremely low standard of living, while workers in richer countries will constantly be threatened with the prospect of their jobs drifting away to poorer ones.

In addition, trade sanctions may not address the real causes of violations, or may address some but ignore others. For example, the Melzer Report confirmed what critics of the World Bank and IMF had been saying for a long time: that the policies imposed on Third World countries by these institutions often compounded problems of poverty and inequality, and this could result in a degradation of labour standards. Or, powerful companies could blackmail a small country that is attempting to upgrade labour standards by threatening to pull out, as happened when the People's Alliance government in Sri Lanka attempted to make the recognition of trade unions and collective bargaining compulsory in FTZs in 1995. Trade sanctions would hardly remove the main cause of these violations. In fact, according to the Assistant General Secretary of the Public Services International (Waghorne 2000),

> the international trade union movement has made it crystal clear that we see the use of incentives and assistance as the best way to

help countries meet their obligations. The process for getting this done would involve the ILO (after the WTO referred a case to it for advice) using its normal and agreed procedures for investigating a complaint, offering technical and programme advice to a government over a period of years and monitoring progress.

However, even if the emphasis is on assistance and incentives, long experience of the functioning of the ILO shows that, without penalties, large-scale violations will continue.

Solving this problem requires clear thinking, imagination and real dialogue across the labour movement. The ILO would need to be empowered to scrutinise the policies of international institutions like the World Bank and IMF, and veto those that lead to a lowering of labour standards. Putting pressure on offending governments could take the form of fines; for example, if the violations are by a Third World subsidiary of a multinational based in a developed country or a Third World supplier of a West European or North American retailer, both countries could be fined, perhaps in proportion to their GDP. The fines could then be used to implement the Core Conventions (eg take children out of employment and provide for them, set up machinery to deal with cases of bonded labour, union-busting or discrimination, and so on). Governments who wish to implement the Core Conventions but are too weak to do so should welcome measures that would bolster their authority vis-à-vis recalcitrant employers and prevent multinationals threatening to shift their investments to countries which allow violations of the conventions; for governments who collude in or actively perpetrate such violations, this erosion of their "national sovereignty" would be the price they would have to pay if they wanted to be members of the WTO. This would also resolve the question of China's membership, the prospect of which terrifies many developing countries who do not, however, have any rational basis for objecting so long as WTO membership is compatible with violations of the Core Conventions.

It must be emphasised that this would *not* be an intrusion of the WTO onto the territory of labour standards. On the contrary, it would allow the ILO, governments and trade unions to have some control over the impact of world trade on labour rights. Trade unions could use their place in the WTO to insist that the WTO, since it is concerned with globalising commodity and capital markets, should also globalise the labour market. Immigration controls do not stop labour migration; instead, they create a mass of "illegal" and therefore unorganisable and superexploited workers, thus lowering labour standards in general. Open borders would give these workers legal status and enable them to unionise and fight for their rights.

Conclusion

Many of the positions taken in the debate around a workers' rights clause, including some put forward by various trade unions and supposedly progressive NGOs, involve a nationalist element, counter-posing the supposed interests of workers in their own country to those of workers elsewhere in the world. In the long run, all these positions are counterproductive, subordinating the interests of workers to sections of the ruling class. In a situation where labour organising is under attack globally, this is a potentially disastrous situation, frag-menting worker responses to a coordinated employers' assault on fundamental rights. Conversely, if a coordinated strategy to implement the rights embodied in the ILO Core Conventions can be forged, it would mark a new stage of labour internationalism.

In a globalised world economy, only genuinely internationalist strategies that are beneficial to *all* workers—in all countries, for both men and women, in both formal and informal sectors and so forth—can really strengthen the labour movement. This is an attempt to arrive at such a strategy on one particular issue, drawing on criticisms and suggestions made by contributors to both sides of the debate. The proposed solution attempts to accommodate two requirements that have hitherto been seen as conflicting, namely, ensuring equality for developing countries within the WTO *and* protecting basic workers' rights in a globalised economy. It constitutes only a minimum pro-gramme so far as workers are concerned; it does not, for example, take up important issues like health and safety, working hours or social security. These can come later. At the moment, the most important tasks are to establish that development and workers' rights are not contradictory but mutually reinforcing and to initiate a genuine debate within the worldwide labour movement to hammer out a workable scheme whereby both can be achieved.

Endnotes

[1] This paper is part of an ongoing debate. Previous contributions include Hensman (1998, 2000a, b). The opinions expressed are my own, but they draw on both sides of the argument.
[2] It is noteworthy that the RSS hatred of foreign ideologies does not extend to Nazism, perhaps because they share its Aryan supremacism.

[3] See also *Economic Times* (1999d; sample quote:"Ms Esserman pointed out that India had used the dispute settlement mechanisms of the WTO to win three cases on textiles, two against the US and one against the EU") and *Economic Times* (1999b, c).

[4] For example, *Business Standard* (1999d, e, g); *Economic Times* (1999f, h); and many more.

[5] I am *not* ruling out allowing children to work under *all* circumstances. Small children are often eager to participate in household activities, and I have no objection to encouraging girls *and* boys to help with household labour. Nor is it necessary to rule out all paid labour. When a friend and I started a women's cooperative in a *basti* (shanty-town) some 15 years ago, several girls aged 11–14—some of whom were already doing part-time domestic work in nearby apartments—wanted to join. When we finally agreed (mainly because they refused to take *"no"* for an answer!), we found that they treated it as an enjoyable way to earn pocket money, cracking jokes, laughing and singing Hindi film songs while they worked. So I would not object to children working *provided* (1) their health and safety is assured, (2) it does not interfere with their schooling (our cooperative worked for only half a day per week due to marketing problems), and (3) it is *entirely* voluntary and they can quit whenever they please—which means that neither their own livelihood nor that of their families should depend on it.

References

Ahmed I (1999) Getting rid of child labour. *Economic and Political Weekly* 34(27):1815–1822
Anti-Fascist Forum (ed) (2000) *My Enemy's Enemy: Essays on Globalization, Fascism and the Struggle Against Capitalism.* Toronto: Anti-Fascist Forum
Central Trade Union Organisations of India (1995) Appeal from the Central Trade Union Organisations of India to the Fifth Conference of Labour Ministers of Nonaligned and Other Developing Countries. New Delhi, January. Unpublished
Barman A (1998) Integral ignorance. *Economic Times* 9 December
Bond P (2000) "No Time for Reform". *Focus on Trade* 48 (21 May). HTML file: <URL: http://www.focusweb.org/>, last accessed March 2001
Brett B (1995) The ILO and the WTO. *International Union Rights* 2(1):4–5
Business Standard (1994) RSS asks Left to join swadeshi stir. 21 November
Business Standard (1995) RSS to continue attack on globalisation, MNCs. 28 March
Business Standard (1998a) Turtle hawks. 16 October
Business Standard (1998b) RSS plans stir against government today. 30 November
Business Standard (1999a) Anti-dumping is not in India's interests. 1 January
Business Standard (1999b) Industry inputs sought for WTO talks. 4 June
Business Standard (1999c) Industry spells out India's strategy for Seattle talks. 17 September
Business Standard (1999d) Maran opposes labour issues. 2 December
Business Standard (1999e) No secret deal with US, Atal assures Oppn. 2 December
Business Standard (1999f) WTO baiters harming poor, claims Moore. 2 December
Business Standard (1999g) Ministerial group on labour, trade convened. 4–5 December
Business Standard (2000) 50 killed, over 200 injured in Bangladesh factory fire. 27 November
Centre for Science and Environment (1999) HTMl file: <URL: http://www.oneworld. org/cse>, last accessed March 2001

Chandrashekhar C P and Ghosh J (1999) Seattle and the smaller countries. *The Hindu Business Line* 14 December

Chimni B S (2000) WTO and environment: Shrimp-turtle and EC-hormones cases. *Economic and Political Weekly* 35(20):1752–1761

Custers P (1997) *Capital Accumulation and Women's Labour in Asian Economies.* New Delhi: Vistaar Publications

D'Costa B (Hindustan Lever Employees' Union) (2000) Will Maharashtra government turn the clock back? Labour law amendments: Charter for new slavery. *Angdai*, Trade Union Solidarity Committee, Bombay, 15 November. Bombay: Trade Union Solidarity Committee

Economic and Political Weekly (1997) Bihar, more bloodshed. 32(13):622

Economic and Political Weekly (1999) Bihar fractricidal politics. *Economic and Political Weekly* 34(6):308

Economic Times (1996a) US to appeal WTO ruling on gasoline import regulations. 20 January

Economic Times (1996b) Globalisation causes social tension in the north. 2 February

Economic Times (1998a) It works. 15 October

Economic Times (1998b) Shrimp import law is not discriminatory: US. 15 October

Economic Times (1999a) RSS begins paperwork on conversions, WTO pact. 12 March

Economic Times (1999b) WTO rules against Turkey over QRs on Indian textiles. 3 June

Economic Times (1999c) US export subsidies are unfair, says WTO. 28 July

Economic Times (1999d) India used WTO to settle textile disputes. 29 October

Economic Times (1999e) Protesters are acting against the interests of the poor, says WTO chief Moore. 2 December

Economic Times (1999f) WTO must not take up labour norms: Maran. 2 December

Economic Times (1999g) Clinton's labour view stuns ministers. 4 December

Economic Times (1999h) India to sign pact to help China's entry into WTO. 4 December

Economic Times (1999i) Members object to WTO's method of decision making. 4 December

Economic Times (1999j) Working group to study labour-trade link. 4 December

Economic Times (1999k) Seattle round of talks hit by lack of transparency. 5 December

Economic Times (1999l) When the world's an oyster. 12 December

Ganguly P K (Centre of Indian Trade Unions, affiliated to the Communist Party of India Marxist) (1996) Labour rights and national interests. In J John and A Chenoy (eds) *Labour, Environment and Globalisation* (pp 43–46). New Delhi: Centre for Education and Communication

Ghei N (1996) WTO ruling against US gives a ray of hope to Third World. *Economic Times* 21 January

Golwalkar M S (1939) *We or Our Nationhood Defined.* Nagpur: Bharat Publications

Gothoskar S (1996) The social clause—Whose interest is it serving? In J John and A Chenoy (eds) *Labour, Environment and Globalisation* (pp 59–66). New Delhi: Centre for Education and Communication

Grote U (2000) Statement on labour standards at GDN conference of the World Bank, Bonn, 6–8 December. *CUTS-CITEE Communiqué* 1(2):18–22

Hale A (ed) (1998) *Trade Myths and Gender Reality—Trade Liberalisation and Women's Lives.* Sweden: Global Publications Foundation

Hensman R (1998) How to support the rights of women workers in the context of trade liberalisation in India. In A Hale (ed) *Trade Myths and Gender Reality— Trade Liberalisation and Women's Lives* (pp 71–88). Sweden: Global Publications Foundation

Hensman R (2000a) World trade and workers' rights—To link or not to link? *Economic and Political Weekly* 35(15):1247–1254

Hensman R (2000b) Debate: A view from India. *International Union Rights* 7(2):21

Henwood D (1993) *Wall Street.* UK: Verso

International Confederation of Free Trade Unions (ICFTU) (2000) "International Labour Standards and Trade". Congress Statement, 7 April. HTML file: <URL: http://www.icftu.org>, last accessed March 2001

International Labour Organisation (1998) *ILO Declaration on Fundamental Principles and Rights at Work and Its Follow-up.* Geneva: ILO

John J (2000) *Fair Trade and Standard Setting—A Labour Rights Perspective.* Delhi: Centre for Education and Communication

John J and Chenoy A (eds) (1996) *Labour, Environment and Globalisation: Social Clause in Multilateral Trade Agreements—A Southern Response.* New Delhi: Centre for Education and Communication

Kabeer N (2000) *The Power to Choose.* London: Verso

Krebbers E and Schoenmaker M (2000) *De Fabel van de Illegaal* quits Dutch anti-MAI campaign. In Anti-Fascist Forum (ed) *My Enemy's Enemy: Essays on Globalisation, Fascism and the Struggle Against Capitalism* (pp 47–52). Toronto: Anti-Fascist Forum

Krishnaji N (2000) Trends in sex ratio. *Economic and Political Weekly* 35(14): 1161–1163

Labour File (1998) Entire issue: Children Are Dying. 4(8)

Lal D (1999) India urged to resist WTO's social charter. *Economic Times* 6 April

Mahendra K L (All India Trade Union Congress, affiliated to the Communist Party of India) (1996) A protectionist measure. In J John and A Chenoy (eds), *Labour, Environment and Globalisation* (pp 47–48). New Delhi: Centre for Education and Communication

Marx K (1974) Critique of the Gotha Programme. In D Fernbach (ed) *The First International and After* (pp 339–359). London: Penguin Books

Mehta P S (1999) Child labour, social clause and the WTO. *Economic Times* 16 June.

Mehta P S (2000) What next: After Seattle? *CUTS-CITEE Communiqué* 1(2):7–10

Movement in India for Nuclear Disarmament (MIND) (1999) "India's Draft Nuclear Doctrine—A Critique". HTML file: <URL: http://www.angelfire.com/mi/MIND123/DND.html>, last accessed March 2001

Open Letter to Mr Mike Moore. Quoted in full in Singh J (2000) Resisting global capitalism in India. In Anti-Fascist Forum (ed) *My Enemy's Enemy: Essays on Globalisation, Fascism and the Struggle Against Capitalism,* (pp 84–85). Toronto: Anti-Fascist Forum

Sakai J (2000) Aryan politics and fighting the WTO. In Anti-Fascist Forum (ed) *My Enemy's Enemy: Essays on Globalisation, Fascism and the Struggle Against Capitalism* (pp 7–23). Toronto: Anti-Fascist Forum

Statement from International Women Workers Workshop on Globalisation and Informalisation (2001) Korean Women Workers' Associations United, Women Working Worldwide and Committee for Asian Women, 17 October 2000. In *Globalisation and Informalisation* (p 2). Manchester, UK: Women Working Worldwide

Sunday Times, Sri Lanka (1999) Bad planning hits WTO con. 5 December

Upadhyay D D (1965) *Integral Humanism.* New Delhi: Bharatiya Jan Sangh

Vivekanandan V (1996) Outright rejection or strategic use? In J John and A Chenoy (eds) *Labour, Environment and Globalisation* (pp 151–175). New Delhi: Centre for Education and Communication

Waghorne M (2000) "Letter to the Editor". *Focus on Trade* 48 (21 May). HTML file: <URL: http://www.focusweb.org/>, last accessed March 2001
World Bank (1995) *World Development Report.* Washington, DC: World Bank/IBRD

Rohini Hensman is active in the trade union and women's liberation movements. She belongs to the Union Research Group, Bombay, which is a constituent of the Trade Union Solidarity Committee, a coordination of independent unions, and is a member of Women Working Worldwide, a network of women workers' groups in several countries. She has also taken up other human rights issues, especially the persecution of and discrimination against minority communities in India and Sri Lanka. Her publications include numerous articles on all these issues. She is a coauthor of *My Life is One Long Struggle: Women, Work, Organisation and Struggle*, and *Beyond Multinationalism: Management Policy and Bargaining Relationships in International Companies* (1990, Sage), and is the author of *To Do Something Beautiful* (1995, Streelekha), a novel inspired by her work with women and trade unions in Bombay.

8

NAFTA's Labor Side Agreement and International Labor Solidarity

Lance Compa

The North American Free Trade Agreement (NAFTA) and its supplemental labor pact, the North American Agreement on Labor Cooperation (NAALC) reflect the uneven advances of labor rights advocacy in connection with international trade. NAFTA provides extensive rights and protections for multinational firms and investors in such areas as intellectual property rights and investment guarantees. The NAALC only partially addresses labor rights and labor conditions, but within its limits it has shown itself to be a viable tool for cross-border solidarity among key actors in the trade union, human rights, and allied movements. The NAALC's principles and complaint mechanisms create new space for advocates to build coalitions and take concrete action to articulate challenges to the status quo and advance workers' interests. Cooperation, consultation, and collaboration among social actors have brought a qualitative change to transnational labor rights networks in North America.

Introduction
The Rise of Workers' Rights in
Trade Policy Debates

For most of the 20th century, demands to incorporate labor rights and standards like freedom to organize and child labor laws into international trade and investment agreements made policy experts grimace. "That's politics," said government officials, international economists, and multinational executives and investors with dismissive waves. "We don't do that, we do trade," they explained as they laid down free trade rules to roll global commerce forward through Bretton Woods institutions like the World Bank and the International Monetary Fund, global trade groups like the General Agreement on Tariffs and Trade (GATT) and its successor World Trade Organization (WTO), and economic coordinating bodies like the Organization for Economic Cooperation and Development (OECD). Trade expansion brought an international rule of law for such matters as intellectual property rights, investment guarantees, government procurement, free transit across borders for multinational lawyers, bankers, and executives, and other corporate interests. Meanwhile, workers' calls for social justice in new trade regimes were mostly ignored.

Global commerce and trade agreements had profound accumulating effects on working people around the world in the last decades of the 20th century. International trade is inherently social and political. Workers have to struggle for justice, power, and protection against labor rights violations in the new global economy. Their struggles are still rooted locally in the places where they work, in the communities where they live, and under the laws of their local, state, and national governments. However, the link to the global economy and the growing importance of international rules cannot be denied.

The Labor Rights-Trade Link in NAFTA and the NAALC

Negotiated in 1993 by Canada, Mexico, and the United States, the North American Free Trade Agreement (NAFTA)'s supplemental labor pact, the North American Agreement on Labor Cooperation (NAALC), sets forth eleven "Labor Principles" that the three signatory countries commit themselves to promote:

1) freedom of association and protection of the right to organize
2) the right to bargain collectively
3) the right to strike
4) the abolition of forced labor
5) the abolition of child labor
6) minimum wage, hours of work, and other labor standards
7) nondiscrimination
8) equal pay for equal work
9) occupational safety and health
10) workers' compensation
11) migrant worker protection

The signers of the NAALC pledged to effectively enforce their national labor laws in these eleven subject areas, and agreed to open themselves to critical reviews of their performance by the other countries. It is worth noting that these subjects range far beyond the "core labor standards" recently elaborated by the International Labor Organization (ILO). The ILO's definition is limited to organizing and bargaining rights, forced labor, child labor, and discrimination (ILO

1998). Nonetheless, the NAALC failed to address critical issues of development assistance or worker migration, for example, and did not develop a strategy for upward harmonization of labor standards, emphasizing instead effective enforcement of national law.

Complaint Mechanism

Trade unionists and their allies can file complaints on one or more of these labor principles in a new institutional structure that provides for investigations, public hearings, written reports, government-to-government consultations, independent evaluations, nonbinding recommendations, and other "soft law" measures common to most international agreements. At each stage, advocates can intervene to press for favorable outcomes.

A "hard law" edge can be applied for three labor principles, those covering minimum wage, child labor, and occupational safety and health. An independent arbitral panel is empowered to fine an offending government for a "persistent pattern of failure to effectively enforce" domestic labor law. If the fine is not paid, the panel can apply trade sanctions on the firm, industry, or sector in which workers' rights violations occurred.

Experience under the NAALC

For labor rights advocates with the patience and willingness to put it to the test, the NAALC has emerged as a viable new arena for creative transnational action. With its unusual "cross-border" complaint mechanism, the agreement provides an opportunity for workers, trade unions, and their allies in the United States, Mexico and Canada to work together concretely to defend workers' rights against abuses by corporations and governments.

The NAALC is not a full-fledged international enforcement mechanism. It is not intended to resolve specific complaints or to issue orders to reinstate workers unjustly discharged, orders to recognize and bargain with trade unions, orders to remove children from unlawful labor, orders to adjust pay for women to equal that of men, orders to install air filters to reduce health hazards, orders to provide compensation to injured workers, or other remedies associated with labor law enforcement. These matters are left to national legislation and national enforcement mechanisms. Instead, the NAALC is intended as a review mechanism by which member countries open themselves up to investigation, reports, evaluations, recommendations, and other measures so that, over time, such enhanced oversight and scrutiny will generate more effective labor law enforcement. To the extent that legislative responses can be fashioned within national systems, rather than imposed by a supranational power, oversight under the NAALC can also change the climate for labor law reform in each country to achieve greater adherence to NAALC principles and obligations.

Advocates need to be practical about how far governments are prepared to go to hand over traditional sovereignty on labor issues to new international tribunals. Even the European Union, with extensive labor rights provisions that can be enforced by the European Court of Justice, leaves issues of salaries, union organizing and collective bargaining, and the right to strike untouched by EU directives. Single member countries hold veto power over EU policy on social security and social protection, redundancies, and other key matters.

In the six years since it took effect, NAFTA's labor side agreement has given rise to a varied, rich experience of international labor rights advocacy. As of 1 January 2001, nearly 25 complaints had been filed under the NAALC. Some observers have called this number distressingly low considering the volume of workers' rights violations in North America. However, the NAALC aims to get at systemic problems, not specific worker grievances. Cases so far embrace workers' organizing and bargaining efforts, occupational safety and health, migrant worker protection, minimum employment standards, discrimination against women, compensation for workplace injuries, and other critically important issues. Until now such cases were hidden in the bureaucratic interstices of each country's national labor law system, with no international scrutiny or accountability. The NAALC is beginning to change that.

A rapid summary of just a few cases—and a more detailed look at one—suggests the ways in which advocates get results. Gains are not made through direct enforcement by an international tribunal. They come obliquely, through indirect action, by exploiting the spaces created by this new labor rights instrument to strengthen cross-border ties among labor rights advocates and to generate unexpected pressures on governments and on transnational enterprises. To be effective, labor rights advocates using the NAALC must seek help from their counterparts across the borders. NAALC complaints must be filed with an agency called the National Administrative Office (NAO), set up under the agreement, in the labor department of *another* country—not the country where workers' rights violations occurred.

- In 1996, the provincial government of Alberta, Canada announced plans to privatize workplace health and safety enforcement. Labor inspectors would be sacked and become independent contractors. The public employees' union declared it would file a NAALC complaint charging Alberta with not just failure but a complete abdication of its responsibility to effectively enforce health and safety laws. The government dropped the plan (Chambers 1996a, b).

- In 1996, Mexican labor authorities dissolved a small democratic trade union in the fisheries ministry when that agency was merged into the larger environmental ministry, where a bigger progovernment union held bargaining rights. Together with US human rights groups, the dissident union filed a NAALC complaint in the US charging failure to enforce Mexican constitutional guarantees of freedom of association. At a public hearing in Washington, DC, Mexican government officials and leaders of both Mexican unions, labor law experts from both countries, and US labor and human rights advocates testified, generating wide publicity in both countries and a US NAO report that detailed abuses in a government-mandated trade union monopoly. The smaller union regained its registration and has continued its activity in the democratic union movement (UNAM 1999).
- In 1997, Mexican and US telephone workers' unions filed a complaint with the US NAO when workers at the Maxi-Switch electronics factory in Sonora, Mexico tried to form an independent union but were denied registration. Two days before a scheduled public hearing in Tuscon, AZ (near the Sonora plant), the Mexican government and the Mexican union agreed to settle the complaint and cancel the hearing. Registration was granted to the independent union (Resource Center of the Americas 1997).
- A 1997 complaint by a coalition of US and Mexican labor and human rights groups challenged the widespread practice of pregnancy testing in the *maquiladora* factories. A public hearing in Texas near the border area exposed the involvement of well-known US companies like General Motors and Zenith and led to a US NAO report confirming the abuses. Several US multinational firms announced they would halt the practice, and advocacy groups in Mexico launched new efforts for reform legislation to halt pregnancy testing in employment (Dillon 1998).
- In 1997, US and Mexican labor, human rights, and local community advocacy groups filed a NAALC complaint with the US NAO against interference with an independent union

organizing effort and health and safety violations at a Hyundai Motors supplier called Han Young. A 1998 public hearing in San Diego, CA and follow-up governmental consultations and public forums made the case an international incident. The Mexican labor department applied the first substantial fines against any company for health and safety violations. The independent union gained bargaining rights and has maintained an active, high profile campaign with international support for securing a collective agreement (Dibble 1999).

- More than twenty trade union and allied organizations filed NAALC complaints in 1997 with the US NAO and in 1998 with the Canadian NAO on violations of workers' organizing rights and health and safety laws at a US-owned auto parts factory called ITAPSA in Mexico City. The coalition mounted broad-based activity in connection with public hearings in both countries, as well as protests at corporate shareholder meetings. International support has allowed the union to maintain its struggle for recognition (McBrearty 1998).

- A 1999 complaint to the US NAO by flight attendants' unions in the US and Mexico charged Mexico with failing to enforce freedom of association by denying flight attendants represented by a "wall-to-wall" progovernment union at the TAESA airline the right to form an independent union. A March 2000 public hearing in Washington, DC buttressed workers' claims and demonstrated international support for Mexican flight attendants, who undertook protest actions in major airports. Later in 2000, in a parallel situation at another airline, the Mexican government reversed its stance and allowed flight attendants to vote separately on union representation to avoid a new round of international scrutiny.[1]

- Canadian and US unions filed a NAALC complaint with the US NAO in 1998 after McDonald's closed a Montreal restaurant where workers had formed a union. The complaint targeted flaws in Quebec's labor law that allowed companies to close work sites for antiunion motivation. When the US NAO accepted the complaint and scheduled public hearings, Quebec trade unions, employer federations, and labor department officials agreed to take up the matter in a labor code reform bill rather than have Quebec's "dirty laundry" aired in a US public hearing. The unions withdrew the complaint, and the hearing was cancelled (Associated Press 1998; Ginsbach 1999).

- Twenty-five unions, health and safety advocacy groups, human rights organizations, and allied community support networks filed a major new complaint with the US NAO in 2000 for workers suffering egregious health and safety violations at two Auto-Trim manufacturing plants in the maquiladora region. The 100-page complaint reflects long and careful collaboration among the filing organizations, a high level of technical competency and legal argument, and a powerful indictment of the government's failure to enforce health and safety laws. A public hearing was set for early 2001 (NAFTA 2000).

In each of these cases, new alliances were built among groups that had hardly ever communicated until the NAALC complaint gave them a concrete venue for working together. For leaders and activists of independent Mexican trade unions, in particular, access to international allies and to a mechanism for scrutiny of repressive tactics long hidden from international public view provided strength and protection to build their movement.

This accounting is not meant to overstate the agreement's impact. Each of the cases noted here is more complicated than these capsule summaries can convey, and the advantages gained are uneven. Using the NAALC does not mean going from triumph to triumph. However, the nature of trade union work during the current neoliberal offensive, both in the national context and in the context of globalization, is anything but a triumphant march forward. It is more of a hard slog through rocks and mud, usually with more backsliding and side-slipping than progress.

Any request of workers to turn to the NAALC to air their grievances must be joined by honest cautions that it cannot directly result in regained jobs, union recognition, or back pay for violations. When a specific payoff in new members or new collective agreements cannot be promised, unions and allied groups have to weigh the value of using the agreement in light of staff time, energy, and resources that might be allocated elsewhere. Gains come obliquely, over time, by pressing companies and governments to change their behavior, by sensitizing public opinion, by building ties of solidarity, and by taking other steps to change the climate for workers' rights advances in North America. Perhaps, in time, even direct gains can be achieved as the NAALC system elaborates a kind of labor law jurisprudence for North America that informs decisions by national bodies. That goal is still to be met.

The Problem of Sovereignty

It could hardly be otherwise at this stage of regional integration among such diverse countries. Take one of the early NAALC cases, for example, involving the Sprint Corporation, the US telecommunications giant. In 1994, Sprint closed a San Francisco facility shortly before more than 200 workers there were to vote for union representation. In national legal proceedings, the highest US federal court authorities ruled in the company's favor, saying the evidence showed the closing was a lawful one motivated by business considerations, not anti-unionism. On a separate track, a NAALC complaint on the situation led to widely noted public hearings in San Francisco that gave an international platform to affected workers and union leaders from the United States, Mexico, and Europe, who exposed Sprint's antiunion actions and challenged the company's joint ventures in Mexico and other countries. The NAALC's permanent secretariat published a 250-page study comparing each country's legal regime for anti-union plant closures, a report that highlighted widespread abuses in the US system. Nonetheless, trade unionists involved in the Sprint case denounced the NAALC as worthless because it did not overturn the federal court's decision and order the company to reopen the plant, rehire the workers with back pay, and recognize the union.

Tactically, such denunciations are fair enough as a way to attack Sprint. However, to expect the agreement to create an international labor tribunal empowered to independently take evidence and overrule national courts is completely unrealistic. The agreement was negotiated by countries with highly developed and highly divergent labor law and labor relations systems, each a product of unique time, space, and language-bound social histories. The result was inevitably a compromised hybrid. The states opened themselves to a cross-border oversight mechanism with limited enforcement powers, while guarding sovereignty over key elements of their national systems. It is not the agreement trade unionists and workers' rights advocates would have written were it left to them, but it was not left to them. The challenge is to exploit what was written, and to change it over time to strengthen workers' rights. In some cases unwittingly, NAALC negotiators created new space for advocates to communicate, collaborate, strategize, and act together, seizing opportunities that had never existed.

A Transnational Advocacy Perspective
NAALC "Platforms"

Metaphorically, the NAALC can be seen creating a series of sliding platforms crossing the space of one, two, or three countries. From these platforms, trade unionists and their allies can direct fire at their own and the others' governments, their own and the others' national and multinational corporations, and even their own and the others' corrupted trade unions.

The platforms can cross borders in equal proportion or be anchored mostly in one country. They rest first on the agreement's unique, accessible cross-border complaint mechanism. Workers who suffer abuses, and their defenders, have to file a complaint with the government of *another* country, not the country where violations occurred. Under the agreement, any person can file such complaints. There are no citizenship requirements or requirements that a complainant be an injured party or have a material stake in a case. As a result, social actors who use the NAALC seek partners in the country or country where they intend to file complaints. Indeed, most of the more than twenty cases filed so far have involved transnational coalitions of unions and allied human rights and community groups, who find in the agreement's institutional mechanisms new opportunities to develop relationships and joint action.

Before the NAALC was created, cross-border trade union relationships mostly consisted of thin contacts at two levels. One was between high-level union leaders who attended conferences and conventions and agreed on resolutions of support without much follow-up. The other consisted of sporadic local-union-to-local-union contacts and occasional worker-to-worker delegations usually aimed at helping the poor Mexicans. These links paled in comparison with the business-to-business contacts and boss-to-boss delegations that occur every day in North American commerce.

The new NAALC platforms allow transnational social actors to demand investigations, public hearings, and government consultations on workers' rights violations. Advocates now have the opportunity to strategize and plan together in a sustained fashion, gathering evidence for drafting a complaint, crafting its elements, setting priorities, defining demands, launching media campaigns, meeting with government officials to set the agenda for a hearing and to press them for thorough reviews and follow-up, preparing to testify in public hearings, engaging technical experts to buttress a case with scientific elements (a health and safety case, for example), influencing the composition of independent experts' panels and the terms of reference of their

investigation, and performing other concrete tasks that go far beyond
adopting resolutions or arranging serial worker-to-worker meetings.

Why Bother?
The criticism can be fairly made that this is staff work, not rank-and-
file mobilization. It occupies lawyers, researchers, publicists, and
other union and nongovernmental organization (NGO) professionals
without engaging workers. Worse, it can create false illusions of relief
through bureaucratic legal mechanisms instead of workers' own power.
It looks for help from the same governments that are chiefly interested in protecting capital, not labor. For labor radicals, why bother?

Bother for the same reasons workers have to bother with national
legal systems: because those are the mechanisms workers have gained
after long political organizing and bargaining struggles in a system
that is stacked against them. Legal work, media advocacy, lobbying,
and other "inside game" moves are deeply compromised, flawed,
and frustrating. They are poor, pale, anemic substitutes for rich, red,
robust worker mobilization and struggle against corporate power.
However, the balance of power in a capitalist society—or rather the
imbalance of power, accentuated now by globalization of production
and investment flows—constricts the space for worker action and
makes all the more precious the spaces that become available.

Of course workers must take up struggle through organizing, strikes,
demonstrations, protests, and other forms of direct action. However,
they cannot do it all the time, every day, in every dispute. There are
inherent limits to time, space, energy, resources, and other factors
affecting capacity for workers' struggle. More fundamentally, the
balance of power is unfavorable. Workers are not now in a position to
vanquish the capitalist class or the capitalist state. Their agenda is
necessarily a "Plan B" involving selective struggle, incremental gains
through politics and legislation, and creative exploitation of national
legal institutions as well as new international mechanisms like the
NAALC to advance their interests.

Transnational advocacy networks have to work around the lack
of "hard law" features that create accountability through trials of
evidence, findings of guilt, and enforcement by state power—putting
lawbreakers in jail, or seizing their assets to satisfy a financial judg-
ment. Instead, they must exploit the potential for "soft law" mechanisms typical of the NAALC and other international instruments and
mechanisms. Soft law is marked by investigations, reviews, research,
reports, information exchanges, public hearings (as distinct from trials

of evidence), consultations, evaluations, recommendations, declarations, publicity, and exposés—the "mobilization of shame," as it is sometimes put, to enforce judgments in the court of public opinion. These measures should not be scorned or boycotted by social actors, least of all by transnational actors looking for openings, spaces, platforms, or other bases for creative intervention and exploitation. The challenge is to integrate involvement in institutional settings with action in extrainstitutional settings.

This is not meant as a wide-eyed endorsement of using the NAALC at every opportunity. Choices about resource allocation and measurement of potential gains have to be made. Actors face unavoidable compromises using instruments and procedures created by governments more attuned to corporate concerns than to workers' interests. If advocates become so enamored of international labor rights instruments like the NAALC that they devalue struggle against the neoliberal agenda, like that in the streets of Seattle, it is just a short step to cooptation.

Given the structurally defensive position of workers in a corporate-dominated system, sole reliance on denunciation, confrontation, and rejection, while scorning involvement in efforts to link workers' rights to trade or to use the inevitably flawed agreements that follow, is a self-limiting strategy. Putting all the energy of the international movement against corporate power into protesting WTO and international bankers' conclaves, or launching ad hoc media campaigns against Wal-Mart's latest sale of products made by child labor, is only one side of a strategic whole. Both sides are needed, and both sides need each other. One is a sharp "no" to the corporate agenda and related mobilization that denounces, exposes, protests, and even shuts down—if only for a few hours—the gears of global trade and investment. The other is a savvy, strategic exploitation of pressure points found in international human rights and labor rights instruments, however flawed they may be compared with what labor rights advocates would create on their own without governments or transnational enterprises to contend with.

In contrast to the scornful dismissal of the NAALC by skeptics and critics on the left, fear and loathing mark the views of government and corporate officials at the opposite pole. Former Mexican government officials who made light of the agreement when it was negotiated in 1993 later condemned it for the scrutiny and condemnation it brought to Mexican labor practices under the spotlight of complaints, public hearings, public reports, and government-to-government consultations. One denounced "indiscriminate acceptance" of complaints and warned

that the NAALC served "the tactical interests of US unions and
so-called 'independent trade unions' in Mexico" (Medina 1999). US
corporate executives and attorneys thought the agreement had been
hijacked by trade union radicals to attack company conduct throughout North America, and demanded an end to contentious complaint
procedures where unions and their allies brand companies as workers'
rights violators. An executive of the Washington state apple industry
said "unions on both sides of the border are abusing the NAFTA
process in an effort to expand their power ... NAFTA's labor side agreement is an open invitation for specific labor disputes to be raised into
an international question ... and could open the door to a host of costly
and frivolous complaints against US employers" (Iritani 1998:D1).

The Washington Apple Case
The Washington state apple case serves as a rich example of
"platform-building" through strategic use of the NAALC, and of how
it can foster new ties of solidarity and sustained work among labor
rights advocates in the US and Mexico. More than 50,000 Mexican
workers labor in the orchards and processing plants of the largest
apple-growing region in the US. Employers crushed these workers'
efforts throughout the 1990s to form trade unions, to bargain collectively, to have job health and safety protection, to end discrimination,
and to make other workplace gains.

In 1997 the Teamsters union and the United Farm Workers agreed
to develop a NAALC case on these issues. They reached out for
support to Mexican unions, farmworker advocacy groups, and human
rights organizations. A complaint was drafted, translated, and
redrafted to the satisfaction of the newly formed network. In May
1998 the question was then posed: who should sign the complaint,
which would be filed with the Mexican labor department? Put another
way, who would be publicly identified as the parties that triggered
international scrutiny of labor abuses in Washington State that might
result in sanctions against apple exports to Mexico? Mexico is the
largest single export market for Washington apples, and since the
complaint addressed health and safety violations among many others,
it was susceptible to sanctions. The two US unions were each trying to
organize apple workers, one in the orchards and one in the processing
plants. They wanted to avoid employers' countercharges that they
were out to destroy apple workers' jobs. On the Mexican side, the independent union allies in the Unión Nacional de Trabajadores (UNT),
the Frente Auténtico del Trabajo (FAT), the Frente Democrático de

Campesinos (FDC), and other groups working with their US counter-parts were sensitive to government and official union accusations that they were "puppets" of protectionist US unions. At the same time, from an inside-Mexico competitive standpoint, they wanted to be seen as frontline defenders of migrant workers in the United States, ahead of the official unions and ahead of the PRI government.

After careful consultations through personal visits, telephone conference calls, e-mail exchanges, and other communications among key leaders and staffers of all these organizations, the complaint was officially signed by just the Mexican organizations, not by any US groups. An American NGO, the International Labor Rights Fund, became the public face of the media campaign in the United States, issuing press releases and sending an investigator to the apple-growing region to meet with workers about the cases and to interview potential witnesses for a hearing to be held in Mexico, with behind-the-scenes help from the unions. An experienced organizer from the FAT came to Washington to help the unions in their organizing efforts. The AFL-CIO's Solidarity Center pledged financial support to send Washington apple workers to Mexico for the hearings. Less than one month after the Washington State apple complaint was filed in Mexico, the Mexican Workers Confederation (CTM)—the official, progovernment union federation in Mexico—filed its own first-ever NAALC complaint, over treatment of migrant Mexican workers at an opposite corner of the US in the easternmost state of Maine.

In December 1998 a hearing in the apple case was held in Mexico City. Advocates faced another strategic decision: Should worker witnesses be Mexican migrants alone, which would obviate the need for translation and allow more workers to testify? Or should non-Mexican, English-speaking workers also participate (many Anglo workers are employed in the processing plants, not in the orchards, which are entirely Mexican migrants), at the cost of a bumpier hearing process? US advocates first suggested an all-Mexican, Spanish-only project. However, Mexican advocates thought the effort would be strengthened by presenting united interests of both Mexican and American workers. Longtime Anglo workers joined the delegation; the unions provided interpretation for them during press conferences, during meetings with Mexican workers and trade unionists, and at the hearing at the Mexican labor department. Their shoulder-to-shoulder stance with Mexican coworkers lent a powerful image of solidarity to the public face of the campaign.

The hearing in Mexico City itself was a dramatic example of the reach of the NAALC "platform" and the leaping of spatial, language, and cultural boundaries in the North American context. Half a dozen officials from an agency of the Mexican government heard, in their own language, accounts of labor rights abuses by a delegation of Mexican workers employed in the United States thousands of miles to the north in an industry for which Mexico is a major consumer market. The hearing was prompted by a complaint initiated by US trade unionists in the state of Washington, Washington, DC, and California,[2] then filed by allies in Mexican labor and human rights organizations in Mexico City after lengthy cross-border planning. At the hearing, the Mexican workers were joined by Spanish-speaking US trade union representatives and human rights attorneys, by Mexican independent union and farmworker advocates, and by English-speaking co-workers who deliver their own duly interpreted testimony in English.

The Mexican labor department later issued a report demanding consultations between the labor secretaries of the two countries. They agreed on a program, due to be implemented in early 2001, of public outreach and public hearings chaired by US and Mexican officials from the two federal governments and from the state government. The forums were to take place in the apple-growing region of Washington, where large numbers of workers are prepared to testify in both Spanish and English about conditions.

In succession in this example, labor advocates used the NAALC to build multiple, accumulating pressure on corporations, governments, and unions. The NAALC provided concrete means of pressing the apple-growing industry to improve conditions or risk losing the Mexican market, and of pressing the government of Mexico to conduct a thorough review of the complaint, to hold public hearings for workers from the US, and to issue a strong report seeking ministerial consultations. Using the NAALC led to the *officialista* Mexican labor unions taking their own action on behalf of Mexican migrants in the US by filing the NAALC complaint on events in Maine. It also served to pressure the US government to agree to public events in the state of Washington, to devote its own energies to seeking improved conditions for migrant workers, and to pressure the state government to take steps in matters of state competence to improve these conditions, especially with regard to worker housing, safety, and health. While the process cycled from national to transnational arenas, every step was accompanied by a media campaign that kept the dispute in the public eye and shaped a new, rights-based discourse linked to North American economic integration.

Conclusion

The Washington apple case shows how expanding coalitions of trade union, human rights, migrant worker, women's rights, and other progressive communities involved in using the NAALC are adding new chapters to stories already known of transnational advocacy networks, using new international instruments and institutions to promote their goals (Helfer and Slaughter 1997; Keck and Sikkink 1998; Koh 1991; Mitchell 1998; Smith, Chatfield, and Pagnucco 1997).[3] Until now, admittedly, the new networks have mostly engaged trade union and NGO leaders, organizers, lawyers, researchers, publicists, and other cadres, not masses of workers in a genuine transnational social movement. However, constructing and strengthening ties among these cadres is a precondition to a new global solidarity unionism that is the longer-term goal (Waterman 2000).

The new instruments and institutions of international labor rights advocacy reflected in the NAALC are flawed. Nonetheless, they create spaces, terrains, platforms, and other metaphorical foundations on which advocates can unite across frontiers and plant their feet to promote new norms, mobilize actors, call to account governments and corporations, disseminate research findings, launch media campaigns, educate each other and the public, challenge traditional notions of sovereignty, and give legitimacy to their cause by invoking human rights and labor rights principles—in sum, on which they can redefine debates and discourse by breaking up old frameworks and shaping new ones.[4]

Endnotes

[1] I have personal knowledge of this development, as I serve as legal counsel to the Mexican and US flight attendants' unions in the case.
[2] California is the site of the United Farm Workers union headquarters; the Teamsters union headquarters are in Washington, DC.
[3] I am indebted to Jonathan Graubart, a PhD candidate at the University of Wisconsin, for pointing to these sources in his forthcoming doctoral dissertation. Sidney Tarrow (1999) elaborates the distinction between a transnational social movement and a transnational advocacy network.
[4] One useful description is that of "transnational norm entrepreneurs" (Finnemore and Sikkink 1998:14).

References

Associated Press (1998) US labor body probes antiunion move in Quebec. *The Toronto Star* 21 December:D3
Chambers A (1996a) Privatization of labor rules raises fears: Law may face NAFTA challenge. *Edmonton Journal* 6 September 6:1

Chambers A (1996b) Province's halt of privatization plan ends looming NAFTA complaint. *Inside NAFTA* 25 December 25:14

Dibble S (1999) Strikers shut S Korean-owned maquiladora. *San Diego Union-Tribune* 8 May:C2

Dillon S (1998) Sex bias at border plants in Mexico reported by US. *The Washington Post* 13 January:A8

Finnemore M and Sikkink K (1998) International norm dynamics and political change. *International Organization* 52:887–891

Ginsbach P (1999) US NAO ends review of complaint in organizing at Canadian McDonald's store. *BNA Daily Labor Report* 22 April:A12

Graubart J (forthcoming) Mining the symbolic and political resources of soft international law [working title]. PhD dissertation (in progress), University of Wisconsin

Helfer L and Slaughter A-M (1997) Toward a theory of effective supranational adjudication. *Yale Law Journal* 107:273–341

International Labour Organisation (1998) Declaration of fundamental principles and rights at work. HTML file: <URL: http://www.ilo.org>

Iritani E (1998) Mexico charges upset apple cart in US. *The Los Angeles Times* 20 August:D1

Keck M and Sikkink K (1998) *Activists beyond Borders: Advocacy Networks in International Politics.* Ithaca, NY: Cornell University Press

Koh H (1991) Transnational public law litigation. *Yale Law Journal* 100:2347–2379

McBrearty L (1998) NAFTA hearings reveal abuses. *The Toronto Star* 7 December:1

Medina L (1999) Review of the North American Agreement on Labor Cooperation. Public comments on file with Secretariat of the Commission for Labor Cooperation, Dallas, Texas, and available on the commission's Web site at HTML file <URL: http://www.naalc.org/english/publications/review.htm>

Mitchell R (1998) Sources of transparency: Informational systems in international regimes. *International Studies Quarterly* 42:109–130

North American Free Trade Agreement (NAFTA) (2000) US NAO will review complaint regarding Mexican worker safety. *BNA Daily Labor Report* 7 September:A1

Resource Center of the Americas (1997) Mexico recognizes independent *maquila* union. *Working Together: Labor Report on the Americas* May-June:8

Smith J Chatfield C and Pagnucco R (eds) (1997) *Transnational Social Movements and Global Politics: Solidarity Beyond the State.* Syracuse, NY: Syracuse University Press.

Tarrow S (1999) Does internationalization make agents freer—or weaker? International institutions and transnational contention. Agenda paper, Workshop on European Institutions and Transnational Contention, 5–6 February, Cornell University, Ithaca, NY

Universidad Nacional Autonoma de Mexico (UNAM) (1999) Caso en materia de la SEMARNAP/Secretaria de Pesca. In A Bouzas and E de la Garza (eds.) *Encuentro Trinacional de Laboralistas Democráticos* (pp 33–35). Mexico City: UNAM

Waterman P (2000) Capitalist trade privileges and social labor rights in the light of a global solidarity unionism. Paper for workshop on "How to Promote Labor Standards without Undermining International Labor Solidarity," 4 November, Wellsley College, Wellesley, MA

Lance Compa is a Senior Lecturer at Cornell University's School of Industrial and Labor Relations in Ithaca, NY, where he teaches US labor law and international labor rights. He is the author of the Human Rights Watch report *Unfair Advantage: Workers' Freedom of*

Association in the United States under International Human Rights Standards (2000, Human Rights Watch). Prior to a 1995 appointment to the NAFTA labor commission, Compa taught labor law, employment law, and international labor rights as a Visiting Lecturer at Yale Law School and the Yale School of Management. He also practiced international labor law for unions and human rights organizations in Washington, DC. Before turning to international labor law practice and teaching, Compa worked for many years as a trade union organizer and negotiator, principally for the United Electrical Workers (UE) and the Newspaper Guild.

9

European Integration and Industrial Relations: A Case of Variable Geometry?

Richard Hyman

This contribution considers the implications for industrial relations of European economic integration, and possible trade union responses. We can understand industrial relations as institutions and processes of social regulation of work and employment, whether by law, collective bargaining or more diffuse norms and standards (often, a combination of all three). These systems of worker protection became consolidated at national level; their foundations are eroded by increasing economic international-isation (to which the European single market was a response, but which it further reinforced). Through the dynamic of "regime competition", multinational capital can play off national governments and national trade unions against one another, while norms of worker protection are subverted by growing insistence on "shareholder value". Effective regulation of work and employment must be reconstructed transnationally; but most trade union energy has been devoted to a vain pursuit of European analogues of national legislation and collective agreements within a bureaucratic elite process of "social dialogue". What is needed is, first, effective articulation between European-level trade union action and the day-to-day realities of national and workplace trade unionism, and second, a struggle to create a European civil society within which the protection of workers' rights can win popular support and which can sustain effective collective mobilisation.

Introduction

I begin my contribution with two quotations from Manuel Castells' (1996, 1997, 1998) breathtaking, if contentious, overview of global society at the end of the millennium. In the first volume of his trilogy, he (1996:475–476) argues that modern information technology has disconnected capital from fixity of spatial location, while labour—in other words, existing workers—necessarily inhabits a locale from which it can escape only with difficulty, if at all.

> At its core, capital is global. As a rule, labor is local…. So while capitalist relationships of production still persist (indeed, in many

economies the dominant logic is more capitalist than ever before), capital and labor tend to exist in different spaces and time: the space of flows and the space of places, instant time of computerized networks versus clock time of everyday life.

This has obvious implications for what we term, in the banal Anglo-Saxon phrase, "industrial relations": "under the conditions of the network society, capital is globally coordinated, labor is individualized. The struggle between diverse capitalists and miscellaneous working classes is subsumed into the more fundamental opposition between the bare logic of capital flows and the cultural values of human experience" (Castells 1996:475–476).

In his final volume, Castells (1998) analyses the process of European integration as both a reaction against and a regional reinforcement of economic internationalisation. A project that arose out of political idealism—the institutionalisation of cooperation among European states in place of the centuries of rivalry and war, the diffusion of humane standards of social protection and social welfare—achieved its lowest common denominator as a common market. Shaped primarily to constitute an economic bloc capable of competing with the US and Japan, united Europe acquired its efficacy primarily as one actor within the dynamic of intensified global competition: a process that imposed severe costs on ordinary European workers and citizens, resulting in disenchantment and resistance. "Widespread citizen hostility to the process of unification is reinforced by the discourse of most political leaders presenting the European Union as the necessary adaptation to globalization, with the corollary of economic adjustment, flexibility of labor markets and shrinkage of the welfare state" (Castells 1998:326).

These comments provide an apt entry to my topic. To what extent is "Europe" an arena in which trade unions can effectively coordinate their actions to respond to the dynamics of a capitalism that has increasingly escaped the constraints of national regulation? How far are "the cultural values of human experience" a resource that unions can adopt, and adapt, to win a popular legitimacy that in most countries they have manifestly lost? And how far can this provide a basis for a different style of European engagement, one which might allow the European trade union movement to reinvent itself as an effective protagonist of a genuine "people's Europe"?

The ideal of a "real Social Union", adopted as the goal of the European Trade Union Confederation (ETUC) at its ninth congress, is a challenge to the deregulation of industrial relations, which has been a theme of academic analysts and a project of policy makers in much of Europe for over a decade. In this chapter, I examine critically both the theory and the practice of deregulation. Before doing so, however, it is necessary to clarify what we understand by regulation. This also provides a basis for considering whether the weakening of the established system—or complex of systems—of employment regulation at national level can provide a stimulus to the creation of a new industrial relations order at European level. If so, how can we characterise such a new order?

Industrial Relations: The Architecture of Regulation

We may define industrial relations as the regulation of work and employment, provided that we understand regulation (control by rule, according to the dictionary) in its broadest sense as encompassing a complex web of social processes and a terrain of actual or potential resistance and struggle. It is useful to analyse them in terms of three sets of distinctions, social processes and structures of relations, which may be complementary but are often contradictory.

First of all, industrial relations involves various forms of social regulation which refract and transmute the purely economic dynamics of the employment relationship. In every national regime, there is always some type of interaction (though rarely an equilibrium) between "social" and "economic" regulation. It should be well understood that labour markets are not markets in the normal sense of the word, since labour is not a commodity like any other; and that "normal" markets are themselves social constructs and mechanisms of social power (Polanyi 1952). A productive system resting solely on a cash nexus is inconceivable, as the efforts to invent a "pure" market economy in Eastern Europe clearly demonstrate. Nevertheless, the degree to which forces of supply and demand shape employment relationships varies substantially according to time and place. Historically, the effort to construct national industrial relations systems, certainly in Western Europe, has typically involved the strengthening of social regulation, subjecting market forces to collectively determined rules.

Second, industrial relations involves an interaction between substantive and procedural regulation. National systems may function primarily by specifying at least basic standards in the employment relationship (minimum wages, maximum working time and so on) or by identifying actors and defining processes of interaction though which substantive rules are to be constructed. The former may result in relatively standardised and encompassing regulation, the latter in relatively differentiated and uneven outcomes. Traditionally the British system has been marked by the priority of procedural over substantive regulation (Flanders 1970); in most other European countries the traditional balance has been very different.

Third, we may distinguish three different modes of social regulation. The first rests on legislation and other types of state intervention, the second on agreements (or contracts) negotiated through collective bargaining. The contrast between statutory and "voluntary" regulation is familiar, though somewhat misleading. "Free collective bargaining" more often than not rests on statutory definitions of representativity, of rights of collective organisation and action and of the contractual status of agreements (where this exists). Conversely, legal regulation is usually of limited practical effect unless embedded in some degree of internalisation by the industrial relations actors; in a sense, its application is always negotiated. A third, more diffuse source of social regulation is less frequently discussed: the norms, beliefs and values prevailing within civil society—what Regini (1995:5) calls "communitarian regulation". An example would be the traditional acceptance by a substantial proportion of German employers of an obligation, not mandated by law or collective agreement, to take on new apprentices in order to sustain the pool of workforce skills and supply high-quality job opportunities to school-leavers. This complex of norms, beliefs and values, it should be emphasised, is not necessarily a consensual ideology, as in the Dunlop (1958) model of an industrial relations system; rather, it is commonly a terrain of ideological struggle. The outcome of such normative struggle can help shape both law and collective bargaining.

The Erosion of National Industrial Relations Systems and the Ideology of Deregulation

Industrial relations in most countries emerged initially on a local or sectoral basis, reflecting the contours of labour markets, but in the 20th century became consolidated within a national institutional framework. Each such industrial relations system acquired unique characteristics, reflecting the distinctiveness of economic structure, political traditions and social practice in each country. This is reflected in the diversity of industrial relations models in Europe. Viewed from the outside, there are important common features to the conduct of industrial relations: in most countries it is accepted that the labour market must be socially regulated; that collective bargaining is a desirable mechanism for giving employees a "voice" (Freeman and Medoff

1984); and that collective representative bodies (trade unions and employers' associations) are legitimate institutions with a public status. Yet there are substantial differences, in particular in: the degree to which employment conditions and collective bargaining are legally regulated; the existence or absence of workplace representative structures separate from trade unions; and the relative weight of antagonistic relations or "social partnership".

The national embeddedness of industrial relations systems was for a long period, at least in many cases, a source of resilience and strength. However, it can increasingly be regarded as a weakness. Industrial relations, as we understand the term today, was an invention of the era of the pre-eminent nation-state. In most Western European countries, "modern" systems of industrial relations became consolidated around the middle of this century in a context of relative job security—at least for a substantial core of primarily male manufacturing workers in larger firms—under macroeconomic conditions of "full" employment, often buttressed by legal supports. This was in turn facilitated by stable or expanding demand in key product markets and by institutional and other constraints on destructive market competition. The organised capitalism that achieved its high point in the 1950s and 1960s helped establish trade unions as central actors in a variety of national systems of employment regulation. The relative autonomy of the national polity and economy was the context of the distinctive national systems of employment regulation. Has this autonomy been dissipated, and if so, can national industrial relations systems persist?

The "social market economy" that in different forms characterised postwar Western Europe has been challenged by the intensified competitive restructuring of national economies. One feature of what is commonly described as globalisation—a concept which some analysts (eg Hirst and Thompson 1996; see also Hyman 1999) have criticised, but which certainly identifies real and important changes in the context of industrial relations—is the transnational concentration and centralisation of capital. In Europe, this has been reflected (as was indeed one of the aims of the Single Market project) in an acceleration of foreign direct investment between EU countries and a rapid process of corporate consolidation through mergers, takeovers and joint ventures.

In previous decades, the "problem of the multinationals" for European trade unions was relatively narrow and specific: how to contain foreign-owned (primarily American) multinational corporations (MNCs) within the regulatory frameworks of national industrial relations systems. In the 1990s, the problem became broader and more serious: the internationalisation of significant segments of "national capital" and the potential abandonment by key companies of their traditional role within a national system of "social partnership". Perhaps the most dramatic instance is the case of Sweden, in which the major employers in effect "joined" the EU long before the country's formal accession and demolished the classic centralised "Swedish model" of industrial relations the better to pursue more company-specific and internationalised employment policies. In most other European countries, analogous pressures are apparent.

The growing importance of the "Euro-company" (Marginson and Sisson 1994) threatens established forms of national cross-company standardisation, of which the sectoral collective agreement has been the principal instrument. Hence the fear of "social dumping": that companies will shift production from countries with high wages and rigorous labour standards to those where labour costs and regulations are lower. Whether or not "social dumping" is a serious reality, there is certainly evidence that many MNCs use the *threat* of relocation as a disciplining factor in collective bargaining. A different challenge stems from the fact that while MNCs typically devolve significant operational autonomy to local units, they normally establish a competitive internal regime, seeking to diffuse "best practice" across all subsidiaries (Ferner 1998). This has reinforced the shift towards "flexible" forms of work organisation, working time, task allocation and payment system, all of which have been core elements in the standardised rules defined by national law and collective bargaining. In addition, MNCs typically circulate senior managers internationally, partly to detach then from nationally embedded understandings of "good employer behaviour" and to strengthen their commitment to abstract priorities of "shareholder value".

The visible hand of the MNCs interacts with the increasingly coercive invisible hand of finance capital. The last two decades have seen a radical transformation involving: the liberalisation and deregulation of international capital and currency markets; the acceleration of transactions (to the point of virtual instantaneity) as a result of advances in information and telecommunications technologies; and the breakdown of the American-dominated postwar system of international monetary stabilisation. The result is a highly volatile pattern of capital flows. Unpredictable (speculative) fluctuations in the paper values of company shares or national currencies are translated into disruptive instability in the physical economy.

It was in part in response to this volatility that the EU adopted the project of economic and monetary union (EMU). This requires that all participating governments adopt a similar fiscal and monetary regime, and the "convergence criteria" defined at Maastricht are highly deflationary in their implications. To meet the requirements of monetary union, governments across Europe have therefore imposed new disciplines on public employment and restrictions on the "social wage". The consequence has been a phase of increased industrial conflict and social protest, threatening the principles of "social part-nership" typical of most European industrial relations systems.

The institutions established in the formative period of European industrialisation and the various Keynesian-influenced systems of postwar macroeconomic management depended on the regulatory capacity of the nation-state. It is indeed true that, in most European economies, the key importance of the export sector ensured that industrial relations policies were consistent with international com-petitiveness. Nevertheless, the national state and the parties to collective bargaining could address the labour market as a more or less closed system. The diversity of industrial relations systems exists precisely because all such systems involve *national* relationships between *national* actors.

The consequence of cross-national economic integration is that market dynamics are increasingly subject to external determination. Heightened international competitiveness in product markets, the ex-ternal imposition of policy constraints on governments and the locational decisions of MNCs all impose new, onerous and often unpredictable constraints on the agenda of national industrial relations. Across Europe the question is increasingly heard: can the institutions and practices of national industrial relations survive?

It is in this context that deregulation has become a point of reference for academic analysts and policy makers alike. As with the notion of globalisation itself, that of deregulation is heavily imbued with ideological bias (Standing 1997). Typically, it implies that "liberating" market forces is an alternative—a superior alternative— to social regulation. In fact, however, the "free market" is not an alternative to regulation but rather an alternative *form* of regulation. As dramatically evidenced in Pinochet's Chile and Thatcher's Britain, market liberalism could be imposed only by a massive increase in the coercive powers of the state.

Moreover, the outcome of intensified market pressures has not been to establish an impersonal economic regime but rather to recon-figure the balance of social (and class) forces. First, "deregulation" actually consecrates new rules: intensifying the law of value, with effects that empower some economic actors while disempowering others (the majority). Second, the process enhances the capacity of MNCs to establish company-specific regimes, cutting across and potentially undermining the regulatory capacity of national industrial relations systems. Third, deregulation denotes the rule of central banks and other financial institutions, imposing disciplines that are inherently antagonistic to the principles of social protection and social partnership that underlie most European industrial relations systems.

The notion of deregulation has to be deconstructed, taking account of the differing connotations of regulation itself. In some cases it may indeed mean little else but market liberalism. In others, however, it denotes a shift *within* the configuration of social regulation. It may imply (as in Belgium and Italy, for example) a relaxation of legal pre-scription conditional on a strengthening of collective bargaining, by permitting derogation from statutory norms where alternative regulations are collectively agreed. Or it may entail enhanced procedural regulation to compensate for more flexible substantive rules, as seems to be the case—so far, at least—with the softening of sectoral agreements in Germany. Neither of these trends can reasonably be equated with deregulation *à l'anglaise*.

It would be dangerous and wrong to embrace too economic-determinist a reading of current tendencies, which contain ambiguities and contradictions. The transnational intensification of market forces has real and important implications, which challenge the regulatory capacity of industrial relations regimes at national level; but ideological deployment of ideas of deregulation (as, more generally, that of globalisation) helps create a fatalistic and self-fulfilling presumption that "there is no alternative". On the contrary, the proper task of industrial relations analysis is discovering alternatives.

Towards a New European (Dis)order?

Among criticisms of the globalisation thesis is the argument that economic integration is geographically bounded, primarily involving intensified interdependence within specific world-areas or regions. In particular, such integration has proceeded both through the logic of corporate expansionism and through intergovernmental agreement in North America, the Asian-Pacific and Western Europe—hence the notion of tertiarisation of the global economy (Ohmae 1991; Ruigkrok and van Tulder 1995).

Europe represents the paradigm case. The original creation of a "common market" now dates back over four decades. The removal of tariff barriers inherent in the original European Economic

Community—extended to cover the majority of the countries of Western Europe—was merely the first stage of a developing process. With the Single European Market, nontariff obstacles to free competition were comprehensively dismantled, with the aim of consolidating an integrated European economic area large enough to respond effectively to competition from Japan and North America. Economic unification has been based on the principle of "negative integration" (Streeck 1995): the dismantling of nation-specific restrictions on the free movement of goods, services, capital and labour, without construction of equivalent forms of European-wide protections for employee interests. This route to economic integration was not inevitable; it reflected political choices, sometimes justified by the insistence that market liberalism was an unavoidable response to "globalisation". Yet this is simply untrue. Over 90% of cross-national trade in the EU takes place between member states; the EU economy is no more open than that of the US—and far less so than those of, say, Austria and Sweden when they established their highly regulated industrial relations models.

One paradox of the single market initiative was that the boost to inter-state competition was also an incentive to intra-European concentration of capital, and hence to an increasing tendency to monopoly and oligopoly. As noted above, the past decade has been marked by a rapid growth in cross-national corporate mergers, takeovers and joint ventures, resulting in the rise of the Euro-company. This trend has been particularly significant because, with the notable exception of the UK, most European economies have in the past been little affected by either inward or outward foreign investment.

One clear feature of the operation of Euro-companies is their sensitivity to differences in national industrial relations regimes. This is not primarily a simple question of preference for low-wage sites of production, but rather one of a "benchmarking" of performance across locations according to variety of criteria, with unit labour costs assuming major importance. "Flexibility" in the organisation of production is an important element in such assessments, which in turn inform company decisions on investment and divestment. This inevitably imposes pressures on national systems of employment regulation.

In different ways, the moves towards monetary union have a similar impact. EMU can be regarded as a logical response to the increasing volatility of global financial markets, a means of protecting individual national currencies from the damaging consequences of speculative pressures. However, the basis of monetary union—as defined in the Maastricht convergence criteria—has severe implications for industrial relations. The tight restrictions on budgetary deficits require curbs on public expenditure that challenge established national connections between work and welfare and threaten established systems of public employment and associated institutions of cooperative collective bargaining. To the extent that national trade union movements have acquired significant strength from favourable recruitment opportunities in public employment, these developments represent a systematic threat to their organisational status.

What Is To Be Done?

Can effective employment regulation, under challenge at national level, be reconstituted supranationally? There are no easy answers to this question, and academic observers possess no privileged insights. Yet there are two possible elements of an answer. The ideal of social Europe, rescued from current evasive obfuscations and given concrete, intelligible meaning, could be one starting point. If national regulatory capacity, though by no means eclipsed, is increasingly constrained, the search for supranational regulation must be a major part of the trade union agenda. Though the European Union is far from constituting a supranational state, or indeed a supranational industrial relations arena, there are emergent elements of a possible industrial relations regime, if unions can cross-nationally fashion a common project and pursue it against powerful resistance from those who benefit from labour's disarray.

The debate on the possibility of an effective industrial relations regime at EU level ("social Europe") has persisted for a decade or more and has generated a polarisation of views. One position is deeply pessimistic. On this view, a liberal economic regime provides a terrain on which transnational capital can divide and rule. Investment flows to those national labour market regimes that offer the best prospects for accumulation, encouraging a competitive undercutting of national collective bargaining and national welfare states. An effective EU structure of employment regulation might limit such pressures, but seems scarcely attainable precisely because some national governments perceive advantages in regime competition. There is thus a powerful, if usually tacit, coalition between some (many?) national governments and key agents of capital. European labour is itself divided, and even if united would be the weaker party fighting against the inbuilt bias to market liberalism that underpins European integration.

An alternative position, while not necessarily optimistic, is less dismissive. On this view, the achievements of the social dimension are modest but not insignificant. "Subsidiarity" has obstructed the process of comprehensive employment regulation but has also encouraged the development of a strong regional dimension within the EU, creating new space for labour movement intervention. In addition, the various programmes covered by the EU structural funds have an important redistributive role, doing something to offset the dynamic of uneven development. Most recently, the pursuit of an employment strategy has resulted in decisions which could be dismissed as tokenistic but could equally be acclaimed as the foundations of a new counter-deflationary European dynamic (Goetschy 1999).

This brings us back to the earlier schematic discussion of different modes of regulation in industrial relations. A European industrial relations order, if such a thing is to emerge, will certainly not replicate the prescriptive substantive regulation of national law or centralised collective agreements (which even at national level, some would argue, were dependent on a matching regime of "Fordist" accumulation). It is necessary to emphasise that, if a European industrial relations system is to be created, this should not be seen simply as a transnational version of national systems. As Streeck (1998:11) has insisted, "the emerging European institutions of industrial relations are not about to develop into a replica of a national industrial relations system on a larger scale". Rather, the best that can be expected is less binding and more flexible norms, often of a procedural rather than a substantive character. What becomes increasingly important, then, is whether supranational regulation can complement and reinforce collective pressure by workers and their unions at national and company level, and, in particular, whether European-level trade union institutions can build effective complementary links with worker representatives and activists at every level, down to the shop and office floor.

A key issue, rarely considered in current debates, is the possibility of evolving employment-related norms within civil society at the cross-national level. At the national level, unions in many countries have long derived their influence in large measure from their status as key actors within civil society, or, more recently, have recognised that they can sustain or recapture a significant role only by forging effective links with the other components of civil society.

It seems clear that part of the problem is an erosion of credible mobilising rhetorics, of visions of a better future, of *utopias*. Building collective solidarity is in part a question of organisational capacity, but just as fundamentally it is part of a battle of ideas. The crisis of traditional trade unionism is reflected not only in the more obvious indicators of loss of strength and efficacy, but also in the exhaustion of a traditional discourse and a failure to respond to new ideological challenges. It is those whose projects are hostile to what unions stand for who have set the agenda of the past decades. Unions have to recapture the ideological initiative. To remain significant agents of social and economic mobilisation, unions need new utopias, and these are unlikely to have much purchase if their focus is solely at national level.

In a world—and a Europe—marked both by differentiation and by interdependence, there is a need for a trade unionism which can recognise and respect such differentiations of circumstances and interests: within the constituencies of individual trade unions, between unions within national labour movements, between workers in different countries. To adopt a piece of much-used EU jargon, European integration involves intersecting processes with different rhythms that constitute a process of "variable geometry". Building effective trade union solidarity at European level will certainly entail its own form of "variable geometry". The alignment and integration of diverse interests is a complex and difficult task that requires continuous processes of negotiation; real solidarity cannot be imposed by administrative fiat, or even by majority vote. This is an argument of key importance in assessing perhaps the most significant of all achievements in European social legislation: the 1994 directive on European Works Councils. A sceptical evaluation would emphasise the limited capacity of such bodies, required to convene only once a year, primarily to receive reports from management and with no right to constrain corporate decision making. Yet a different perspective might stress the potential for such fora to facilitate mutual exchange of information, understanding and aspiration among worker representatives, which in the longer term could enable genuine solidarity.

This links to issues of strategic leadership and democratic activism. It is easy to recognise that urgent current needs exist for new models of transnational solidarity and for enhanced capacity for transnational intervention. However, neither can be manufactured from above. The dual challenge is to formulate more effective processes of strategic direction while sustaining and enhancing the scope for initiative and mobilisation at the base—to develop *both* stronger centralised structures *and* the mechanisms for more vigorous grassroots participation. This entails new kinds of articulation between the various levels of union organisation, representation and action.

Within the European Union, one of the more fatuous of recent rhetorical devices is the idea of "social dialogue". Representatives of European labour spend much time and energy in discussion with their counterparts on the employer side. Very exceptionally indeed this results in an agreement, couched in such general terms and with such limited content as to contain little of practical significance. Rather more frequently, discussions result in a "joint opinion". It may indeed be comforting (or perhaps not!) to know that union representatives can at times align their opinions with those of employers, but the effect in the real world is imperceptible. *Within* and *between* trade unions themselves, however, the pursuit of dialogue and the search for common opinion are vital requirements. Hence the task of European trade unions today may be encapsulated in the slogan: *develop the internal social dialogue!* Enhanced organisational capacity and solidarity demand a high level of multidirectional discussion, communication and understanding. To be effective at international level, above all else, trade unionism must draw on the experience at national level of efforts to reconstitute unions as bodies that foster interactive internal relationships and serve more as networks than as hierarchies.

One problem for those seeking to create a European industrial relations system (a possible translation of that elusive term, *espace social*) is an implausible specification of the objective. Typically, a European industrial relations system is seen as essentially a transnational version of national systems. However, there is little prospect of creating direct analogues of national collective bargaining and "political exchange" cross-nationally since, as already argued, the EU is in key respects *not* a supranational state, nor are the European "social partners" authoritative national trade unions and employers' organisations writ large. The risk is that much energy and many resources are invested in the pursuit of elaborate form with minimal substance.

The underlying flaw in the pursuit of European-level regulation by supranational equivalents of collective bargaining or legal enactment is that such processes and the resulting instruments lack the support of the more diffuse shared perspectives and normative commitments which give them much of their effectiveness at national level. The search for a European industrial relations system has in the main been an elite project, bureaucratically conducted. Without engaging with popular concerns and aspirations, the whole elaborate repertoire of commission communications, joint opinions, drafts and redrafts of directives and the rest is little more than a sideshow, with minimal relevance for the real world of work and employment. What is lacking is a moral economy at European level, beyond the traditional abstract commitment to a "social market" on the part of both social and Christian democrats, a commitment that was always ambiguous and has been increasingly undermined by the marketising pressures of the last decades.

The goal of effective European regulation must remain a chimera unless popular commitment can be mobilised in its support. Yet to the extent that there is a dominant "public opinion" in most European countries it is suspicious of, if not downright antagonistic to, the idea of European integration. All too often, the representatives of European labour have embraced too uncritically the process of unification as marketisation, unwittingly fuelling disenchantment with their own representative status. This might be reversed if it were possible to formulate, and propagate, unambiguous standards of moral economy with an appeal across countries and languages that could inspire enthusiasm in place of alienation. How could a meaningful European moral economy be constructed? Ideas, ideals and identities typically emerge through contestation and struggle; sometimes they represent accommodations between conflicting interests, but often also they are the points of reference whereby oppressed majorities can challenge imperious minorities. They are both the product and the foundation of civil society, which I understand as a sphere of social relations distinct from both state power and market dominance. At national level, unions in many countries have long derived their influence in large measure from their status as key actors within civil society; or more recently have recognised that they can sustain or recapture a significant role only by forging effective links with the other components of civil society. By contrast, the weakness of a European civil society is a major obstacle to the creation of a genuine European system of industrial relations.

Notionally, a European civil society already exists. The European Commission has declared its desire to foster a European "civil dialogue", and provides material support for a wide variety of NGOs that can function as interlocutors, just as it subsidises employee representation within the longer-established routines of social dialogue. But this is window-dressing. Organisations licensed from above cannot realistically be regarded as thereby representatives of popular will. Without widespread consciousness of European citizenship, it is fatuous to speak of European civil society.

Yet real intimations of a European civil society are not altogether absent. To take one obvious example, the struggle from the 1960s for women's rights created a climate of opinion that formed the basis for the innovative decisions of the European Court of Justice and the interventionist policies of the European Commission in the field of equal opportunities. Another instance is the outrage caused by

Renault's closure of its Vilvoorde plant, reinforcing demands for an effective European employment policy. The consolidation of this emergent European civil society should be seen as an important task for trade unions and for other supporters of effective social regulation in employment. One problem is that the concept of civil society has itself been appropriated and devalued by enthusiasts of a deeply ambiguous "third way", often to give a human face to neoliberal policy. To recapture a progressive meaning, it is necessary to embrace Standing's (1999:387) argument that "a *network* of citizenship associations is needed to give voice to *all* those faced by insecurity".

If trade unions are to reassert their relevance as representatives of labour and as actors at European level, there has to be a radical shift of emphasis that embraces such a concept. While engaged with the process of European integration, they must become far more vocal and forceful as opponents of the dehumanising advance of market forces. It will be a difficult struggle, but the goal must be to construct new social controls over market processes at European level and hence a new defence for the status of employees, particularly of those most vulnerably placed within the emerging peripheral labour market. Concerned scholars have a duty to assist such a struggle, which should be at the heart of a conflict of perspectives on the meaning and future of Europe.

References
Castells M (1996) *The Rise of the Network Society*. Oxford: Blackwell
Castells M (1997) *The Power of Identity*. Oxford: Blackwell
Castells M (1998) *End of Millennium*. Oxford: Blackwell
Dunlop J T (1958) *Industrial Relations Systems*. New York: Holt
Ferner A (1998) Multinationals, "relocation" and employment in Europe. In J Gual (ed) *Job Creation: The Role of Labour Market Institutions* (pp 165–196). Cheltenham: Edward Elgar
Flanders A (1970) *Management and Unions*. London: Faber
Freeman R B and Medoff J L (1984) *What Do Unions Do?* New York: Basic Books
Goetschy J (1999) The European employment strategy: genesis and development. *European Journal of Industrial Relations* 5(2):117–137
Hirst, P and Thompson G (1996) *Globalization in Question: The International Economy and the Possibilities of Governance*. Cambridge, UK: Polity Press
Hyman R (1999) National industrial relations systems and transnational challenges. *European Journal of Industrial Relations* 5(1):89–110
Marginson P and Sisson K (1994) The structure of transnational capital in Europe. In R Hyman and A Ferner (eds) *New Frontiers in European Industrial Relations* (pp 15–51). Oxford: Blackwell
Ohmae K (1991) *The Borderless World: Power and Strategy in the Interlinked Economy*. New York: Harper

Polanyi K (1957) *The Great Transformation*. Boston: Beacon

Regini M (1995) *Uncertain Boundaries.* Cambridge, UK: Cambridge University Press

Ruigkrok W. and van Tulder R (1995) *The Logic of International Restructuring.* London: Routledge

Standing G (1997) Globalization, labour flexibility and insecurity: The era of market regulation. *European Journal of Industrial Relations* 3(1):7–37

Standing G (1999) *Global Labour Flexibility: Seeking Distributive Justice*. London: Macmillan

Streeck W (1995) From market-making to state-building? In S Leibfried and P Pierson (eds) *European Social Policy* (pp 389–431). Washington: Brookings

Streeck W (1998) *The Internationalization of Industrial Relations in Europe: Prospects and Problems*. MPIfG Discussion Paper 98/2. Cologne: Max Planck Institut für Gesellschaftforschung

Richard Hyman (Reading 1942) has recently moved to the London School of Economics after 33 years at the University of Warwick. He is the founding editor of the *European Journal of Industrial Relations*. His latest book, entitled *Understanding European Trade Unionism: Between Market, Class and Society*, was published by Sage in April 2001.

10

Uneven Geographies of Capital and Labour: The Lessons of European Works Councils

Jane Wills

This contribution explores the ways in which trade unions have sought to organise workers in transnational corporations (TNCs) before looking at the pitfalls and possibilities of European Works Councils in more detail. The EWC directive covers an estimated 1400 companies across Europe, employing at least 15 million workers, and there are now more than 500 EWCs in existence. These new institutions are designed to allow employee representatives from across Europe to meet together for the purposes of information exchange and consultation with the senior managers from the TNC concerned. EWCs thus provide new horizontal networks of employee representatives across Europe and create new opportunities for information exchange, the formulation of transnational trade union responses and strategy and even active solidarity across national divides. This contribution draws upon original empirical evidence that highlights the difficulties of making EWCs work in this way. It is argued that there are at least four areas in which trade union intervention would make a difference to the operation of EWCs: (1) building active networks within and beyond any EWC; (2) sharing corporate intelligence; (3) formulating strategy at the level of the EWC; and (4) fostering identification with colleagues in other parts of the corporate network.

Introduction

The growing power of transnational corporations (TNCs) is recasting the map of contemporary political-economy. In 1998, there were more than 60,000 multinational companies in the world, which—together with 500,000 local partners—controlled nearly a quarter of global output, with sales in excess of $11 trillion (UNCTAD 1999). The concentrated wealth, power and influence of the largest of these corporations allows them to operate at global dimensions, taking advantage of local opportunities for more profitable production, improved trade, more effective marketing and higher sales. The geographical reach of such TNCs both reflects and enhances their power, affording these corporations increased leverage over governments, workers and communities. Geographical mobility (real and imagined) is central to the emerging power relations of contemporary capitalism (see Bauman 1998; Bourdieu 1998; Harvey 1989).

A number of commentators have highlighted the negative impact of capital mobility on labour, as Castells (1996:475) explains (see also Hobsbawm 1995; Peck 1996; Tilly 1995):

At its core, capital is global. As a rule, labour is local. Informationalism, in its historical reality, leads to the concentration and globalization of capital, precisely by using the decentralizing power of networks. Labour is disaggregated in its performance, fragmented in its organization, diversified in its existence, divided in its collective action. Networks converge toward a metanetwork of capital that integrates capitalist interests at the global level and across sectors and realms of activity: not without conflict, but under the same overarching logic. Labour loses its collective identity, becomes increasingly individualized in its capacities, in its working conditions and in its interests and projects.

Such analysis is now largely taken for granted, and it is clear that the new power-geometry of networked capitalism has left its mark on trade unions and their members. Workers generally accept the news of capital relocation, plant closure and/or faltering investment with resignation, and there is little appetite or enthusiasm for any collective response. Indeed, the established repertoires of workplace-based collective action—including strikes, demonstrations and community campaigns—are usually insufficient to force TNCs to reverse their decisions. As Haworth and Ramsay (1986) explain in their overview of labour internationalism, workplace-based trade unionism is dependent upon the viability of any plant or operation (see also Lazes and Savage 1997; Vogler 1985). When closures are announced, the union has no mechanism to reverse the decision being made:[1]

The [union] responses to minor management tactics may appear quite successful while their plant remains viable in management's strategy, but the impulse to build international defences is weak … Confronted by a major restructuring or closure proposal from management, the union strategy is exposed, since particularly in an MNC [multinational corporation] it is likely to find its line of defence utterly outflanked. It is too late to build an offensive strategy to divert the enemy, or seek alliances where others may see short-term benefits from the management plan, or resent lack of earlier support when they were in need in turn. Meanwhile, the union reaction to management is likely to be hasty and confused, often retreating still further into the false security of traditional forms of defence. (Haworth and Ramsay 1986:63)

In what should be their finest hour, trade unions have usually proved themselves impotent to reverse anything beyond the terms of redundancy and the scale of retraining on offer.

In a globalised economy, trade unions have left a vacuum at the heart of their organisation. Unless unions can devise new mechanisms to respond to the contemporary political-economic reality in which workers are vulnerable to the relocation of investment along the arteries of large corporations and their chains of suppliers and sub-contractors, they are unlikely to renew their authority. In this context, trade unions have recently begun to rethink their organisational structures, strategy and activity. The twin models of social partnership and social movementism have come to prominence as solutions across the Anglo-American-Antipodean economies, but each remains largely unproven (Heery 2000; Peetz 1998; Wever 1997, 1998). The partnership agenda formally acknowledges the dependence of unions on corporate competitiveness and argues that mutual (management-labour) gains are possible through employee involvement at work (Kochan and Osterman 1994; Nissen 1997; Towers 1997; TUC 1997a; Weiler 1990; Wever 1995; see also Wills and Lincoln 1999). In contrast, the social movement agenda suggests that unions should liberate themselves from complete dependency on the workplace and build radical social movements around workers' interests in the community (Bronfenbrenner et al 1999; Moody 1997; Tillman and Cummings 1999; Waterman 2001).

In practice, both models have to address the importance of globalisation. If trade unions are to successfully respond to TNCs, trade unionists need to devise new ways of organising at local, national and transnational scales. As a strategy document of the International Federation of Chemical, Energy, Mine and General Workers' Unions (ICEM 1996:55) suggests, "To reassert their ability to control change in the interests of workers and the communities in which they live, modern trade unions will have to develop the necessary power relationship to the real decision networks of the global economy—the transnational corporations".

This chapter explores the contemporary challenges facing trade unions as they seek to develop international strategy and practice. Taking a historical overview, the chapter highlights the need to rethink the theory of internationalism and to devise new ways to foster an ethic of solidarity between workers and activists in different locations. Through the lens of European Works Councils (EWCs), the chapter then goes on to highlight the limitations of much international contact between worker representatives and to posit a new agenda for trade union strategy at this scale.

Networks of Capital and Labour

Transnational corporations necessarily implant networks of production and sales across the world. These networks, although dynamic, are characterised by common corporate ownership and often by strong central control. In addition, however, TNCs are linked to complex webs of connection with small and medium firms (SMEs) that produce and supply goods and provide services and support. Networks of suppliers, subcontractors, franchisers and homeworkers have allowed major companies to increase their flexibility while also broadening the scale of production and distribution, without incurring the risks and rigidities associated with direct control. Companies can thus combine strong central control with dispersed production. Yet such networks also create new relationships between workers, and between workers and consumers, across the globe (Gereffi and Korzeniewicz 1994). Unions could turn these networks of interconnection laid by capital into sources of power for organised labour (as was attempted during a previous wave of financial internationalisation at the end of the nineteenth and the beginning of the twentieth centuries, see Lenin 1934 [1917]; Lorwin 1929; see also Wills, 1998). The same technology, communication and transport systems that have allowed corporations to straddle borders are also available to trade unions in their international work (for an excellent discussion of the internet and labour internationalism, see Lee 1997). By using TNCs as key nodes in the cartography of international employment, unions can use the infrastructure and connections laid by corporations to forge networks of solidarity between workers across space. As Moody (1997:280) highlights, workers in TNCs are in a unique position with regard to the emerging power geometry of contemporary capitalism:

> While only a minority of workers are employed directly by TNCs, their potential impact at the heart of the world economy gives these workers a uniquely strategic position. Clearly, the TNCs dominate many nominally independent employers, set the worldwide trends in working conditions and preserve the unequal wage

levels that perpetuate competition among workers even in the same TNC. These giant corporations have deep pockets to resist strikes or other forms of action, but they are also vulnerable at many points of their cross-border production chains.

Yet the history of attempts to organise workers within TNCs—let alone to forge links between workers along chains of suppliers and subcontractors—illustrates the complexities of such work. Ever since the growth of TNCs in the 1950s, the various International Trade Secretariats (ITSs) have sought to coordinate world company councils (WCCs) where trade unionists can share information, develop a common strategy with regard to the employer and build solidarity across space (Bendiner 1987; Cox with Sinclair 1996; Flanagan and Weber 1974; Kujawa 1975; Levinson 1972; Litvak and Maule 1972; Olle and Schoeller 1977; Treckel 1972). By the 1960s a large number of such councils had been established, particularly in the motor vehicle, chemical and electrical industries (see Table 1 for a list of those formed before 1974).

In the early days it was often assumed that the councils would be able to foster the rescaling of trade union organisation and that transnational collective bargaining would result. As Piehl wrote in 1974, "Just as the national organisation of capitalism has led to the national organisation of those dependent on it for employment, so the MNC as the modern form of the international capitalist economy will bring about the internationalism of the trade union movement" (quoted in Olle and Schoeller 1977:72). In practice, however, almost 40 years after such initiatives began, workers in TNCs are still no nearer transnational trade union organisation, multinational collective bargaining or vibrant international solidarity. Company councils and organisations such as Transnationals Information Exchange (TIE; see Moody 1997) have facilitated valuable information exchange, but they have had a very limited impact on labour relations within TNCs. Indeed, managerial policy to decentralise collective bargaining while stepping up investment abroad has increased the geographical isolation and the diversity of conditions faced by workers within TNCs.

Such difficulties reflect the persistent tension between local and/or national interests and transnational sentiment among workers. Even as far back as 1864, at the founding meeting of the International Working Men's Association (the First International), it was national interests that motivated British trade union leaders to take part (Braunthal 1980; Lorwin 1929; Milner 1990). In what Waterman (2001) refers to as "national internationalisms", trade unionists have

Table 1: World Company Councils Formed before 1974

Year/Place of Foundation	Corporation	Instigating Body
1966 Detroit	General Motors	IMF
1966 Detroit	Ford	IMF
1966 Detroit	Chrysler-Simca-Rootes	IMF
1966 Wolfsburg	VW/Daimler-Benz	IMF
1967 Geneva	International Harvester	IMF
1967 Brussels	Philips	EMB
1969 Geneva	Saint Gobain	ICF
1969 Brussels	Fokker/VFW	EMB
1971 London	BLMC, Fiat/Citroen, Renault-Peugeot, Nissan-Toyota	IMF
1971 Geneva	Rhone-Poulenc	ICF
1971 Geneva	Kimberley Clark Corp.	ICF
1971 Geneva	Michelin	ICF
1971 Geneva	Dunlop-Pirelli	ICF
1971 Istanbul	Shell, Gulf Oil	IFPCW
1972 Geneva	W.R. Grace and Co.	ICF/IUF
1972 Geneva	Nestle	IUF
1972 Bielefeld	Oetker	IUF
1972 Geneva	Ciba-Geigy	ICF
1972 Geneva	Hoffman-La Roche	ICF
1972 Geneva	Akzo	ICF
1972 London	Shell	ICF
1972 London	BP	ICF
1972 Geneva	Pilkington	ICF
1973 Paris	Goodyear	ICF
1973 Paris	Firestone	ICF
1973 Geneva	Unilever	ICF
1973 Geneva	St. Regis	ICF
1973 Gothenburg	Volvo-Saab	IMF
1974 Geneva	Du Pont	ICF

Source: Olle and Schoeller (1977:65–6). Note: EMB=European Federation of
Metalworkers; ICF=International Federation of Chemical and General Workers' Unions;
IMF=International Metalworkers' Federation; IUF=International Union of Food and
Allied Workers' Associations; IFPCW=International Federation of Petroleum and
Chemical Workers.

tended to focus on making international contacts only when the local
and national arenas have proved inadequate to their tasks (see also
Johns 1998; Logue 1980; Nairn 1980; Vogler 1985). During the years
after World War II, when the nation-state proved to be fertile ground
for supportive legislation and intervention, trade unions focused their
attention (and their political commitments) at that level, leaving
international affairs on the back burner. Indeed, in some instances,

labour internationalism effectively became part of state foreign policy, destroying independent trade unions in the developing world in order to further the ideological and economic battles of the cold war (see Herod 1997; Thomson and Larson 1978).

In this vein, Olle and Schoeller (1977:67–68) suggest that trade union participation in WCCs since the 1950s has been motivated by a desire to protect working conditions and jobs in the affluent world in the face of competition from less developed nations. As workers in industrialised capitalist economies are threatened by the new international division of labour and the opportunities for profitable investment available in places with cheap labour and poor working conditions, they have coalesced around the defence of their interests. Rather than being launched in the spirit of solidarity and openness to the needs of their comrades abroad, then, labour internationalism has often been motivated by local and national concerns. Moreover, when labour internationalism has been forged in this context, it has proven difficult to formulate common agendas and shared activity through WCCs (Bendiner 1987:185). Diverse institutional frameworks, complex trade union cultures and a weak commitment to internationalism have conspired against the creation of strong relations of solidarity between workers in different locations (Haworth and Ramsay 1986; Ramsay 1997a). Even at a national level, the experience of combine committees within large companies has illustrated how difficult it is to foster solidarity between workers in different plants across the UK (Terry 1985).

In practice, WCCs have proven rather more successful in establishing new relationships between officials from national and international trade unions and senior management in TNCs. In this context, the development of negotiated International Framework Agreements that endorse some or all of the International Labour Organisation (ILO) Conventions against forced labour (Conventions 29 and 105), to uphold the right to free association and collective bargaining (Conventions 87 and 98), to prevent discrimination and support equal pay for work of equal value (Conventions 100 and 111) and to outlaw child labour (Convention 138) are an important step forward (Breitenfellner 1997; European Works Councils Bulletin 2000a, b). Companies such as IKEA, Nestlé, Danone, Accor and Statoil have signed written agreements with various ITSs in recent years, giving trade unionists a mechanism to defend and extend their rights and organisation across national divides. Such agreements provide unions with a negotiated mechanism to monitor activities along the corporate chain, acquire information and secure union organisation (Gallin 1999a; Wills

2001a).[2] However, unless these documents are used as tools for union, community, consumer and NGO mobilisation, they are unlikely to foster grassroots activity that stretches beyond national divides.

Historical experience of WCCs would suggest that contact between workers who are employed by the same company does not automatically lead to new relations of trust, mutual concern and solidarity (Baldry et al 1983; Haworth and Ramsay 1986; Terry 1985). Just as the labour process and the division of labour tend to reinforce strong sectional interests among different groups of workers within any workplace, even greater differences exist between workers from different plants, cultures and political traditions (Hyman 1975). History illustrates that the promotion of genuine labour internationalism has occurred when individual political commitments to an abstract notion of working class unity and solidarity override local and particular concerns. As Waterman (2001:26) notes in relation to the 20th century, "Internationalism would seem to have been most firmly adhered to by certain socialist organisers and theorists, attempting to graft the universalism, cosmopolitanism and democratic internationalism of European radical traditions onto the more locally-rooted discontents of the working class". These socialist organisers and theorists often successfully used the notion of solidarity to inspire action, and in certain cases, to secure real gains from working class organisation. Yet, as discussed, the abstract notion of working class solidarity (based on Marx's famous dictum, "Workers of the world unite, you have nothing to lose but your chains!") has not been strongly embedded amongst the troops of the labour movement in the 20th century. Trade unionism has tended to be pragmatic, anti-intellectual and inspired by short-term, workplace-based goals. Material circumstances and political affiliations have tended to conspire against the adoption of genuine labour internationalism. In today's economy, there is a desperate need to reimagine and reconstruct the notion of solidarity in ways that incorporate networks of trade unionists beyond the national arena.

Unions could intervene to shape workers' perceived interests and shared ideas in ways that might foster new strategies for dealing with TNCs and their networks of suppliers, subcontractors, franchisers and homeworkers. As Streeck (1995, quoted in Platzer 1998:91) remarks in relation to European integration, unions have choices about the interventions they make, which in turn have implications for the affiliations and alliances workers adopt:

> In pursuit of their interests, capital and labour have a choice in principle between building cross-national alliances within classes

or national alliances between classes. How group interests align themselves with each other and with national states is affected by the opportunities offered by national and international institutions. In the process, political resources are generated and distributed in a way that favours some interests over others, thereby conditioning the outcome of multilevel policy-making.

Yet despite the importance of trade union intervention in the institutions of industrial relations, there is remarkably little debate about how new forms of labour internationalism might be constructed (for further material about the formation of workers' interests see Kelly 1999; Offe and Wiesenthal 1985). Labour internationalism is undertheorised as both tradition and practice, and in the contemporary economy there is a pressing need to redress this lacuna. As MacShane (1992:144) puts it in his call for new intellectual intervention in the field of labour internationalism, "Far too much of the debate about what to do internationally is muted, disguised, deflected or simply silenced because of labor diplomatic rules of speak, hear and try not to see mistakes, stupidities, cupidities by organisations bearing the title 'labour union'".

In tandem with others engaged in the project of rethinking labour internationalism, this contribution seeks to explore the ways in which new strategy might be developed (Gallin 1994, 1999b; Hyman 1999; Moody 1997; Munck and Waterman 1999; Waterman 2001). Echoing Harvey's (2000) plea to move beyond the militant particularism of place-based politics to negotiated universal principles, Hyman (1999:107) has suggested that the reinvention of solidarity must

> recognise and respect differentiations of circumstances and interests: within the constituencies of individual trade unions, between unions within national labour movements, between workers in different countries. The alignment and integration of diverse interests is a complex and difficult task which requires continuous processes of negotiation; real solidarity cannot be imposed by administrative fiat, or even by majority vote.

The challenge is to put this approach into practice. As will be seen in the case of European Works Councils, there is still a long way to go.

The Experience of European Works Councils

The European Works Councils Directive (Number 94/95) was adopted on 22 September 1994. This directive requires that all companies with more than 1000 employees and with at least 150 employees in each of two member states of the European Union (EU) set up a forum or procedure for information and consultation with employees (for more information on the background to this development, see Gold and Hall 1994; Hall 1992, 1994; Hall et al 1994; Marginson et al 1998; Rivest 1996). It is estimated that this directive covers 1400 large and medium-sized companies across Europe, employing at least 15 million workers and eventually involving something like 40,000 EWC representatives across the EU.[3] This is the first time that multinational companies have been legally obliged to establish transnational institutions for the conduct of employee relations. By late 2000 there were at least 500 EWCs in existence.[4]

EWCs are designed to bridge the information and representation gap for employees in TNCs. The brief of EWC meetings is focused on sharing information with employee-representatives, covering matters such as the financial performance of the group, corporate strategies and employment. For the most part, trade unions have welcomed the development of EWCs. Indeed, in many ways they represent the pinnacle achievement of years of campaigning to foster the transnational participation and representation of workers in the decision-making of TNCs (Knutsen 1997; Streeck 1997a). The British Trades Union Congress (TUC) has explicitly linked the development of EWCs to globalisation, arguing that they will allow trade unionists to strengthen "the foundations of international co-operation which is becoming increasingly important in a global economy" (Monks in TUC 1997b: inside front cover; see also ETUC undated). The development of EWCs has propelled Europe to the forefront of discussions about trade union organisation in the global economy; as Breitenfellner (1997:545) remarks: "Europe promises to become the chief laboratory for experiments in global unionism".

In the context of the global economy, in which TNCs are nodes at the hub of networked economic and social relations stretching across huge geographical distances, EWCs might prove to be vital instruments through which trade unionists can develop their own networks. Trade union and employee representatives from the key European operations of each TNC are elected or appointed to sit on EWCs, meeting at least once a year. These meetings allow rank and file trade union representatives to meet the senior board members of their company (creating *vertical networks* between workers and managers); they also create new opportunities to forge *horizontal networks* between workers across the EU. Such networks might facilitate independent information exchange, the formulation of strategy in relation to the company and active solidarity between the trade unionists involved. Just as was envisaged in the development of WCCs, such channels could allow workers to check management information, to anticipate managerial decision-making and to plan for change in advance (see Marginson 1998; Weston and Martinez-Lucio 1997, 1998). Building new relationships beyond the annual formal meeting of the EWC is central to this endeavour. In the long term, it may prove possible to build a new kind of European community amongst workers through EWCs (see Lecher 1998; Turner 1996).

Seizing these opportunities is less than straightforward, however, as EWCs only allow employee representatives to meet each other once a year in circumstances when, with the assistance of simultaneous translation services, they can exchange experiences, developments and ideas.[5] There is no automatic resource provision to stimulate contact outside these meetings; any such activity largely depends upon the representatives taking the initiative, or doing so in conjunction with their trade union organisations. To date, research evidence reveals a rather mixed picture of employee-led communication outside the formal EWC meetings. While there are positive examples of independent networks emerging from EWCs (see Lecher, Platzer and Nagel 1999; Lecher and Rüb 1999; Müller 1998; Weston and Martinez-Lucio 1997, 1998; Whittall 2000), it is clear that there are also many EWCs where workers have not been able to make the EWC work in this way (Hancké 2000; Wills 2000, 2001b). In practice, experience has proven very varied; each EWC has a different written agreement, based on divergent expectations and varied national, corporate and trade union cultures (Fitzgerald, Miller and Stirling 1999; Marginson et al 1998; Marginson 2000; Pedersini 1998).

In order to explore the operation and outcomes of EWCs in more depth, I conducted a variety of research projects between 1996 and 1999. In brief, this work involved a questionnaire survey of managers in UK-owned firms that were in scope of the directive; longitudinal qualitative research at a number of case study firms; and interviews with representatives from British, European and international trade union organisations (see Wills 1998, 1999a, b, 2000, 2001). Unexpectedly, the survey research highlighted the benefits that EWCs brought to managers in TNCs. Survey respondents found their EWC advantageous in terms of two-way communication (88% of respondents), getting management views over to employees (63% of respondents), hearing the voice of employees (50% of respondents) and involving employees in the business (50% of respondents).[6] While half of the respondents cited the dangers of transnational trade unionism as a chief concern, the managerial respondents were also using the EWC to develop nonunion channels of workplace representation and to foster new relationships with trade union representatives. In short, managers appeared to be devising effective strategies to manage EWCs, using these new institutions as an additional arm in their corporate communications, and there was little evidence that employee-representatives were intervening decisively in the life of EWCs (see also Ramsay 1997b; Sadler 2000; Schulten 1996; Streeck 1997a, b). Such findings were reinforced by the case study research conducted in three UK-owned TNCs, a summary of which is presented in Table 2.[7]

Research at these EWCs highlighted the lack of genuine consultation taking place in these new institutions. While trade unionists expected the EWC to give them an opportunity to discuss corporate change and to effect corporate decisions, managers used the EWC solely for information purposes, reporting decisions that had already been made. For this employee representative from Company B, the meetings were something to sit through rather than get involved in:

> You go to a big long session where you get blasted with facts and figures and business strategy. When they've told you everything there's not a lot of interest in what's coming from our side. What we think. I just sit through the process at the moment. There's not time for us to say very much.

In the absence of real consultation, the employee representatives grew increasingly disillusioned with their EWCs and put little effort into making them work. In practice, managers dominated the agenda at the EWC meetings, using them to reinforce the message that workers needed to keep costs down and remain competitive if they were to retain jobs. When workers were already feeling vulnerable to possible closure, downsizing, internal competition and investment elsewhere, these meetings probably increased tensions between employee representatives from different locations. As this Italian representative put it to the senior managers at the 1999 EWC meeting in Company B:

> We need assurances. We want to leave feeling secure about our jobs and the future. But today I have felt ill. I don't have confidence. It's the same every year. I get alarmed. I want to know that something is being done to reverse trends.

Although the employee representatives valued the chance to find out more about the company for which they worked and to establish contact with each other, there was little sign of independent networking between them after the meetings. The vast majority of representatives in the case study firms had no contact with each other outside formal events. The only exception was amongst the representatives in the largest financial services subsidiary in Company C, who published their own bulletin from September 1997. Produced at the initiative of one of the two representatives from the staff union in the UK (who also happened to have excellent language skills), this bulletin included articles by the Spanish, Portuguese, French and British representatives about ongoing change in their part of the group. This bulletin appeared only twice, in English, before the company demerged (and then merged again; see Table 2), and it is the only evidence of any systematic independent information exchange between employee representatives at any of the case study EWCs.

At each of the case study EWCs—particularly amongst the representatives from manufacturing operations—the relocation (or possible relocation) of production and the choice of sites for new investment caused tensions between local and national groups. In some cases the EWC heightened fear of redundancies and factory closure: the employee representatives were understandably concerned with defending their local and national interests before pursuing international ones. In Company A, production work was relocated from Wales to Belgium after a factory closure during 1999; a similar process took place in Company B during 1996, when work was shifted from Germany to Portugal. In Company C, factories were also closed in a number of European locations during the lifetime of the EWC, although it was less clear than in other situations whether the work was being moved across borders within Europe or relocating further afield.

Such economic insecurity made it difficult to establish relations of trust between employee representatives from different parts of the European operations in each EWC. As demonstrated by these comments from representatives in Companies A and B, the urge for survival precluded any interest in forging solidarity between plants across the EU:

Personally, I don't feel European at all. I've always been … uninterested. The people that elected me want me to look after them. They are my first concern obviously, and we compete with everyone else. It's difficult to tie in Europe with my members.

At the end of the day, we need to feed ourselves and clothe ourselves and our families. I suppose it's survival of the fittest—

Table 2: Summary of the Case Study Research Firms

	Activities	Emps. (date)	EEA Countries	EWC Signed	EWC Size (UK Seats)	UK Seats Union/ Nonunion	Admin Cttee?	Experts?	Annual Meetings	Special Meetings
A*	Manufacturing and merchanting high value product	14,410 (12/95)	14	9/96	24 (4)	2/2	Yes	France & UK union official	^ Paris 97 ^ Ashford UK 98 ^ Paris 99	^ Paris 97 Ashford UK 99 Heathrow UK 99
B**	Production of supplies for industry	6850 (1995)	16	8/95	29 (6)	5 union/ 1 consult. cttee	No	Full-time union official from UK	Germany 96 ^ Slough UK 97 Barcelona 98 ^ Heathrow UK 99 ^ Amsterdam 00	
C***	Manufacturing one product and financial services	20,000 (1996)	10	9/96	27 (16)	Variable— most nonunion	Yes	EIF rep.	London 96 London 97 London 98	London 97 London 98 (sectoral mtgs)

* In 1999 the company split up into three semiautonomous divisions, one of which was to be sold off.

**Company B only refers to one division of a larger multinational, which has divisional EWCs.

***In September 1998 this company demerged into two parts and the financial services section merged with another large MNC in the same sector. Research stopped at this point, as the representatives were split into two different EWCs, one of which had to negotiate a merger with an existing EWC.

^ Meetings attended by researcher.

or maybe that should be the cheapest! At the end of the day everybody is just trying to work, to have a home and a roof over their head. That must be prominent in everybody's mind all over Europe.

While employee representatives reported greater understanding of the geography of their firm and felt for others losing their jobs, there was no sense in which common action or strategy was possible to prevent such things or ameliorate their effects.

Making EWCs Work for Workers

This research has highlighted the desperate need for additional trade union intervention in the operation of EWCs if they are to provide new mechanisms for the development of transnational solidarity between workers. As already discussed, labour internationalism and solidarity are not automatic. Conscious intervention on the part of labour leaders, backed up by their institutions, could help to create such sentiment between workers. Pleas for this have been made elsewhere, but they have yet to be really heard (see also Hancké 2000; Lecher 1998; Lecher, Platzer and Nagel 1999). There are at least four areas in which trade union intervention would make a real difference to the operation of EWCs:

(1) Building Active Networks within and beyond the EWC

Only one of the EWCs studied had established any firm infrastructure to facilitate communication between representatives outside annual meetings and this was a newsletter covering only a subsection of the EWC. Surprisingly, e-mail systems, the Internet and translation software were not even discussed in detail at any of the EWCs under review. Where it did take place, communication outside the annual meeting was largely haphazard. If EWCs are to function effectively, they have to have means of independent communication during the year. Unions could play a fundamental role in establishing—with or without management support—a basic e-mail infrastructure and providing the training to use it. The Internet could also be used as a repository of information about local terms, conditions and developments that could be updated on a regular basis. Translation software would allow employee representatives to read this material in their own languages and to translate messages between each other. By facilitating fast and efficient communication and information exchange in this way, EWCs would be much better integrated into everyday trade union activities and would provide an important source of independent information to assist negotiations, campaigns and policy at all levels. Without such networking facilities, it is difficult to imagine EWCs ever playing a more effective long-term role in trade union organisation.

(2) Sharing Corporate Intelligence

All the companies studied were undergoing major change and restructuring, often involving acquisitions, mergers and closures. An annual meeting, at which senior managers present their view of developments, does not allow employee representatives to grasp the full scale of the changes and their implications. While some representatives do have access to more regular information through their national works councils, British representatives are left in the dark. The case studies showed how workplace-based shop stewards and employee representatives from the UK were catapulted straight into the European arena with little ongoing support or information provision. Trade unions could provide an extremely important service by collecting corporate intelligence from the media and specialist sources and sending it out to EWC representatives. Matters covered in the *Financial Times* may have acute bearing on the lives of trade union members, yet these workers often have no detailed knowledge of the plans being discussed. If EWC members were better informed, they could attend the annual meetings with sharper questions for the board members, an improved ability to unpack the figures and arguments presented and a clearer idea of the key issues they need to address.

If employee representatives—with the support of their national unions and the ITSs—could develop an understanding of the structure and composition of corporate ownership, they might be able to find new means of influence over board members. Pension and investment funds or key shareholders might prove to be important sources of political influence in the event of a trade union campaign. Tracing the webs of ownership and decision-making across national borders would give EWC members a better understanding of the firm, while also requiring that representatives pool the knowledge of fellow members and their national trade union organisations. As MacShane (1999:173) has argued:

> Unions will have to relearn the techniques of the collective organisation of knowledge. They have to become new centres of

knowledge. When trade unions are organizing their collective knowledge so that they out-knowledge the investment funds, the City analysts and the media policy-shapers, then they may return to a position of influence. To achieve that, they are going to have to start not *thinking* internationally, but *acting* internationally. Forget the old slogan, think global, act local, it's the other way round now ... unions have to think local but act globally.

The collation of knowledge is a central prerequisite for strategic intervention in the networks of TNCs.

(3) Formulating Strategy at the Level of the EWC

Managers dominated the agenda of all the EWC meetings covered in the research; there was never any opportunity for the employee side to lead the debate. Even the employee-side meetings were spent catching up on recent developments and reporting job losses. There was no time or space for the employee representatives to set their own agenda, or to raise their concerns in a more professional way. As these British representatives from the EWC in a UK-owned financial services company explained:[8]

> Our problem is that we spend so little time in discussions with each other that formulating goals is a problem. I would like the European Works Council to take the initiative more and challenge the employers to take a less short-term view of the business.

> I believe that as a forum we have to have a very clear idea of what we are trying to get out of the EWC. I have raised this as an issue and we need to discuss it, we need to have an agenda, we need to have a clear picture. At the moment, we all come at it from different angles and we are never going to achieve anything like that ... That is our problem as a forum, we don't have a strategy, we don't have a clear agenda of what we want, of what we can all buy into.

> If we are going to make the annual meeting work then the employees need a meeting, not the day before because it is too late then, we need a meeting earlier on ... If you can't meet it's difficult to forge a strategy ... I think we should be allowed meetings for the whole forum at least once or twice a year, outside of the annual meetings.

While such comments illustrate the importance of formulating employee-side strategy at EWCs, the workers involved have typically had neither the time nor the means to develop a coherent approach. Focused trade union intervention to provide the support and facilities necessary for the employee-representatives to share ideas outside meetings would help to free up their face-to-face meetings for strategic discussion. In addition, resources could be deployed in holding extra meetings, workshops or training events in order to develop strategy for the long term (on the importance of training, see Miller and Stirling 1998). Activities might involve small task groups collecting information, formulating agenda items and writing policy documents for the EWC; in time, the brief might widen to include corporate campaigning and the mobilisation of trade union members across national divides. Moreover, by avoiding the thorny—and potentially divisive—issues of jobs and investment, employee representatives could develop relations of trust, friendship and co-operation on a more "neutral" agenda. Issues such as health and safety, equal opportunities, training, corporate ownership and new management practices are likely to yield interesting developments as workers share their knowledge and experiences with each other (see Müller 1998).

(4) Fostering Identification with Colleagues in Other Parts of the Corporate Network

Fostering a strong European trade union network through an EWC provides a bedrock from which to launch a wider set of relations beyond the EU. The gathering of corporate intelligence to trace the global webs of interconnection spun by each TNC could be coordinated by each EWC. In conjunction with the relevant ITSs, EWC representatives could conduct a social audit of the links in each chain of investment, production, supplies and subcontractors, identifying the presence of trade union organisation and highlighting poor working conditions and/or violations of human rights. Rather than being seen as another dimension of "Fortress Europe", EWCs could thus become key nodes of corporate and trade union intelligence, facilitating new forms of practical solidarity between workers along the arteries of TNC networks. In this way, EWCs would be central to the negotiation and monitoring of corporate codes of conduct and International Framework Agreements with the largest TNCs in the world.

By strengthening EWCs to be active networks, able to collect corporate intelligence, develop strategy and spread connections worldwide, employee representatives could make EWCs into catalysts of new

forms of labour internationalism and new ways of responding to
TNCs. Such intervention would make EWCs more effective, increase
their appeal and foster new interest in internationalism amongst
ordinary workers. In this model, networked trade unionists might
campaign for access to training, education and even employee ownership for workers facing redundancy in one country, while lobbying
for trade union rights in other locations. Strategy would be locally
determined, but conceived and co-ordinated from a transnational
perspective. A network that embraced the chain of corporate control
and influence to all corners of the globe would allow trade unionists
to grapple with the TNC as a whole, to consider the situation of
workers at each node of the network and determine local activity in
light of the whole. The existence of EWCs makes such intervention
possible. However, there is still a vacuum at the heart of these
important new institutions.

Concluding Remarks

As indicated in the previous section, EWCs illustrate the real potential for fostering new forms of labour internationalism today. The
European trade unions are amongst the most powerful in the world.
They operate in the most favourable political and regulatory climate,
they have the right to demand that TNCs establish a network of
employee-representatives across the EU, and yet EWCs are not proving
to be active vehicles for labour internationalism. The trade unions
have been slow to grasp the opportunities proffered by EWCs. Such
activity need not involve high-profile campaigns or militancy, but
it does depend upon supporting an active network of trade unionists,
the careful collation and exchange of information and ideas, the
development of strategy and the focused intervention that might
foster solidarity in the long term. Although there are some signs that
EWCs are developing a life of their own, there is no clear indication
that the European trade unions are developing the type of intervention necessary to support EWCs in this way (see Hancké 2000; Lecher
1998; Lecher, Platzer and Nagel 1999). An opportunity to integrate
the international dimension into everyday trade union activities is
being lost. Workers in TNCs are being rendered largely powerless in
the face of capital relocation, real and imagined.

The 73 million people who are employed by TNCs—more when
indirect employment is taken into account—are the most unionised
workers world-wide (Gallin 1999b). The ability to build links between
these workers, in the context of a strong trade union movement reaching

across borders, is critical to fostering a more humane model of globalisation. While the traditional structures of trade union organisation are ill suited to the present economic and political order, EWCs could provide an important vehicle to demonstrate the value of transnational trade union organisation. EWCs could be important nodes in a network of labour organisation along the chains of TNCs and beyond. There are signs that such new developments have been possible in the Americas; the same could be true of EWCs (see Alexander and Gilmore 1999; Armbruster 1995; Nissen 1999).

In their overview of the contemporary order of things, Hardt and Negri (2000) highlight the historical importance of labour internationalism. Labour internationalism, they suggest, has historically been all about a common agenda being translated from one situation to another, as workers recognise their common interests across divides of nationality and particularity. In contrast, they argue, one of the key political dilemmas of our age is the lack of real communication between those engaging in struggle in one place and those in another. While protest in any particular place can speak with great intensity to global concerns (Hardt and Negri cite incidents such as the Palestinian intifada, Tiananmen Square, the Zapatista uprising in Chiapas, the riots in Los Angeles and the French and Korean workers' protest as examples), they argue that such mobilisation has not crossed national divides. So although there are real connections between those employed by the same corporations and those who consume the goods and services they produce, economic globalisation has not yet given new life and substance to labour internationalism that builds on common challenges and experience across space.

There is a political challenge to trade unions to foster an ethic of solidarity based on the real connections between workers in different locations. Experience at EWCs points to the importance of networking, sharing corporate intelligence, developing strategy and looking at the global corporate chain in this process. In so doing, trade unions can reimagine and reinvent labour internationalism for the 21st century.

Acknowledgements
I am grateful to David Sadler, Peter Waterman and Dan Gallin for their thoughtful comments on an earlier draft of this contribution. The research documented here was funded by the ESRC, grant number R000221873. I am extremely grateful to all those who participated in this research, particularly Mark Carley and Linda Ryan from the European Works Councils Bulletin who worked with me on the

questionnaire survey; managers, trade union officials and employee-representatives from the case study firms; and representatives from the European Trade Union Institute, a number of European Industry Federations and some of the International Trade Secretariats where I conducted interviews during 1997 and 1998.

Endnotes

[1] This argument still resonates almost 20 years after Haworth and Ramsay put pen to paper. In March 2000, BMW announced that they were to sell and effectively close their operations at Longbridge, Birmingham (UK), with the loss of almost 10,000 production jobs and many more among the suppliers, subcontractors and service providers in the region. The unions had no effective response to this action and appeared impotent in the face of the decision. Calls for a boycott sounded hollow when the factory was losing money and the management had determined to sell. The unions had no leverage to alter the decision: partnership agreements and increased productivity had not secured the jobs for the long term, and the trade unions fuelled nationalism in response to the closure. In the event, part of the company was sold to an ex-manager-led bid, and production and some of the jobs were saved.

[2] These negotiated framework agreements are similar to the non-union-led corporate codes of conduct and ethical trading initiatives discussed by Hale and Shaw in this volume, the main difference being that they are negotiated with international trade unions. This gives the unions greater scope for using the agreements to intervene in corporate practices.

[3] The figure of 40,000 representatives arises from the assumption that each of the 1400 EWCs will have 30 members.

[4] About 430 voluntary, or "article 13", agreements were made before 22 September 1996; since that date, at least 110 such agreements have been made in European-based firms *(European Works Councils Bulletin* 1999:10).

[5] Although most EWCs meet once a year, there are a number that allow more regular meetings (for the case of the British Steel EWC, see Wills 1999b). The majority allow emergency meetings to be held when an issue of transnational significance arises during the year (see Marginson et al 1998).

[6] The figures presented here relate to the 18 survey respondents from firms with EWCs. Questionnaires were sent to all 240 UK-owned firms said to be in scope of the directive, although only 34 responses were received (14% of those sampled). These firms employed more than half a million employees in the UK and many more overseas, covering all sectors of the economy. For more information, see Wills (1999a).

[7] This research involved observation of EWC meetings where possible and interviewing the managers and employee-representatives involved in them between 1996 and 1999. The companies are anonymised to protect the identities of those participating.

[8] This research was generated through a special project with the trade union representing UK workers in a major financial services company. The trade union commissioned research to explore what the EWC representatives thought of their EWC and how it could be improved.

References

Alexander R and Gilmore P (1999) A strategic organizing alliance across borders. In R M Tillman and M S Cummings (eds) *The Transformation of US Unions: Voices, Visions and Strategies from the Grassroots* (pp 255–266). Boulder: Lynne Rienner Publishers

Armbruster R (1995) Cross-national labor organizing strategies. *Critical Sociology* 22:75–89

Baldry C, Haworth N, Henderson S and Ramsay H (1983) Fighting multinational power: Possibilities, limitations and contradictions. *Capital and Class* 20:157–166

Bauman Z (1998) *Globalization: The Human Consequences*. Oxford: Polity Press

Bendiner B (1987) *International Labour Affairs: The World Trade Unions and the Multinational Companies*. Oxford: Clarendon Press

Bourdieu P (1998) *Acts of Resistance: Against the New Myths of Our Time*. Oxford: Polity Press

Braunthal J (1980) *History of the International*. Vol 3:*1943–1968*. London: Victor Gollancz

Breitenfellner A (1997) Global unionism: A potential player. *International Labour Review* 136:531–555

Bronfenbrenner K, Freidman S, Hurd R, Oswald R A and Seeber R L (eds) (1998) *Organizing to Win: New Research on Union Strategies*. Ithaca, NY: ILR Press

Castells M (1996) *The Information Age: Economy, Society and Culture*. Vol I, *The Rise of the Network Society*. Oxford: Blackwell

Cox R W (with Sinclair T J) (1996) *Approaches to World Order*. Cambridge, UK: Cambridge University Press

European Trade Union Confederation (ETUC) (undated) *European Works Councils*. Brussels: European Trade Union Confederation

European Works Councils Bulletin (1999) Article 6: State of play. *European Works Councils Bulletin* 22 (July/August):10–14

European Works Councils Bulletin (2000a) Codes of corporate conduct and industrial relations—Part 1. *European Works Councils Bulletin* 27(May/June):11–16

European Works Councils Bulletin (2000b) Codes of corporate conduct and industrial relations–Part 2. *European Works Councils Bulletin* 28(July/August):7–16

Fitzgerald I, Miller D and Stirling J (1999) Representing the global outpost: European Works Councils in the Northeast. *Northern Economic Review* 29(Autumn):46–62

Flanagan R J and Weber A R (1974) *Bargaining without Borders: The Multinational Corporation and International Labor Relations*. Chicago: University of Chicago Press

Gallin D (1994) Inside the new world order: Drawing the battle lines. *New Politics* Summer:107–132

Gallin D (1999a) Trade Unions and NGOs in Social Development: a Necessary Partnership. Paper prepared for the United Nations Research Institute for Social Development (UNRISD). Geneva: Global Labour Institute

Gallin D (1999b) Organized labor as a global social force. Paper presented at an Industrial Relations Workshop, 20 February, Washington, DC

Gereffi G and Korzeniewicz M (eds) (1994) *Commodity Chains and Global Capitalism*. Westport, CT: Greenwood Press

Gold M and Hall M (1994) Statutory Works Councils: The final countdown? *Industrial Relations Journal* 25:177–186

Hall M (1992) Behind the European Works Councils Directive: The European Commission's legislative strategy. *British Journal of Industrial Relations* 30: 547–566

Hall M (1994) Industrial relations and the social dimension of European integration: Before and after Maastricht. In R Hyman and A Ferner (eds) *New Frontiers in European Industrial Relations* (pp 281–311). Oxford: Blackwell

Hall M, Carley M, Gold M, Marginson K and Sisson K (1994) *European Works Councils: Planning for the Directive*. London: Industrial Relations Services

Hancké B (2000) European Works Councils and industrial restructuring in the European motor industry. *European Journal of Industrial Relations* 6:35–60

Hardt M. and Negri A. (2000) *Empire*. Cambridge, MA: Harvard University Press

Harvey D (1989) *The Condition of Postmodernity*. Oxford: Blackwell

Harvey D (2000) *Spaces of Hope*. Edinburgh: Edinburgh University Press

Haworth N and Ramsay H (1986) Matching the multinationals: Obstacles to international trade unionism. *International Journal of Sociology and Social Policy* 6: 55–82

Heery E (2000) Social movement or social partner? Alternative futures for British labour. Paper presented at the European Trade Unions in the Millennium Conference, March, University of the West of England, Bristol

Herod A (1997) Labor as an agent of globalization and as a global agent. In K Cox (ed) *Spaces of Globalization: Reasserting the Power of the Local* (pp 167–200). London: Guilford Press

Hobsbawm E (1995) Guessing about global change. *International Labor and Working Class History* 47:39–44

Hyman R (1975) *Industrial Relations: A Marxist Introduction*. London: Macmillan

Hyman R (1999) Imagined solidarities: Can trade unions resist globalization? In P Leisink (ed) *Globalization and Labour Relations* (pp 94–115). Cheltenham, UK: Edward Elgar

International Federation of Chemical, Energy, Mine and General Workers' Unions (ICEM) (1996) *Power and Counterpower: The Union Response to Global Capital*. London: Pluto Press

Johns R (1998) Bridging the gap between class and space: US worker solidarity with Guatemala. *Economic Geography* 74:252–271

Kelly J (1999) *Rethinking Industrial Relations: Mobilization, Collectivism and Long Waves*. London: Routledge

Kochan T A and Osterman P (1994) *The Mutual Gains Enterprise: Forging a Winning Partnership Among Labor, Management and Government*. Boston: Harvard Business School

Knutsen P (1997) Corporate tendencies in the Euro-polity: The European Union Directive of 22 September 1994 on European Works Councils. *Economic and Industrial Democracy* 18:289–323

Kujawa D (ed) (1975) *International Labor and the Multinational Enterprise*. New York: Praeger

Lazes P and Savage J (1997) New unionism and the workplace of the future. In B Nissen (ed) *Unions and Workplace Reorganization* (pp 181–207). Detroit: Wayne State University Press

Lecher W (1998) European Works Councils; experiences and perspectives. In W Lecher and H-W Platzer (eds) *European Union-European Industrial Relations: Global Challenges, National Developments and Transnational Dynamics* (pp 234–251). London: Routledge

Lecher W and Platzer H-W (eds) (1998) *European Union-European Industrial Relations: Global Challenges, National Developments and Transnational Dynamics*. London: Routledge

Lecher W, Platzer H-W and Nagel B (1999) *The Establishment of European Works Councils: From Information Committee to Social Actor*. Aldershot: Ashgate

Lecher W and Rüb S (1999) The constitution of European Works Councils: From information forum to social actor? *European Journal of Industrial Relations* 5:7–25

Lee E (1997) *The Labour Movement and the Internet: The New Internationalism*. London: Pluto

Lenin V I ([1917] 1934) *Imperialism: The Highest Stage of Capitalism*. London: Lawrence and Wishart

Levinson C (1972) *International Trade Unionism*. London: Allen Unwin

Litvak I A and Maule C J (1972) The union response to international corporations. *Industrial Relations* 11:62–71

Logue J (1980) *Toward a Theory of Trade Union Internationalism*. Kent, OH: Kent Popular Press

Lorwin L (1929) *Labor and Internationalism*. New York: Macmillan

MacShane D (1992) The new international working class and its organizations. *New Politics* Summer:134–148

MacShane D (1996) *Global Business, Global Rights*. Fabian Pamphlet no 575. London: Fabian Society

MacShane D (1999) Adieu to trade unions? *Critical Quarterly* 41:165–173

Marginson P (1998) EWCS: The role of the negotiated option. In W Lecher and H-W Platzer (eds) *European Union-European Industrial Relations: Global Challenges, National Developments and Transnational Dynamics* (pp 223–233). London: Routledge

Marginson P (2000) The Eurocompany and Euro industrial relations. *European Journal of Industrial Relations* 6:9–34

Marginson P, Gilman M, Jacobi O and Krieger H (1998) *Negotiating European Works Councils: An Analysis of Agreements Under Article 13*. Luxembourg: Office of Official Publications of the European Community

Miller D and Stirling J (1998) European Works Council training: An opportunity missed? *European Journal of Industrial Relations* 4:35–56

Milner S (1990) *The Dilemmas of Internationalism: French Syndicalism and the International Labour Movement, 1900–1914*. Oxford: Berg

Moody K (1997) *Workers in a Lean World: Unions in the International Economy*. London: Verso

Müller T (1998) Employee strategies for realising EWC's potential. *European Works Councils Bulletin* 15:13–16

Munck R and Waterman P (eds) (1999) *Labour Worldwide in the Era of Globalization: Alternative Union Models in the New World Order*. London: Macmillan

Nairn T (1980) Internationalism: A critique. *Bulletin of Scottish Politics* 1:101–125

Nissen B (ed) (1997) *Unions and Workplace Reorganization*. Detroit: Wayne State University Press

Nissen B (1999) Cross-border alliances in the era of globalization. In R M Tillman and M S Cummings (eds) *The Transformation of U S Unions: Voices, Visions and Strategies from the Grassroots* (pp 239–253). Boulder, CO: Lynne Rienner Publishers

Offe C and Wiesenthal H (1985) Two logics of collective action. In C Offe (ed) *Disorganized Capitalism* (pp 170–220). Oxford: Polity Press

Olle W and Schoeller W (1977) World market competition and restrictions upon international trade union policies. *Capital and Class* 2:56–75

Peck J (1996) *Work-Place: The Social Regulation of Local Labour Markets*. London: Guilford

Pedersini R (1998) The Impact of European Works Councils. Eironline HTML file: <URL: http://www.eiro.eurofound.ie/1998/07/study/>, last accessed March 2001

Peetz, D (1998) *Unions in a Contrary World: The Future of the Australian Trade Union Movement*. Cambridge, UK: Cambridge University Press

Platzer H-W (1998) Industrial relations and European integration: Patterns, dynamics and limits of transnationalism. In W Lecher and H-W Platzer (eds) *European Union-European Industrial Relations: Global Challenges, National Developments and Transnational Dynamics* (pp 81–117). London: Routledge

Ramsay H (1995) *Le défi Européen*: Multinational restructuring, labour and EU policy. In A Amin and J Tomaney (eds) *Behind the Myth of the EU: Prospects for Cohesion* (pp 174–200). London: Routledge

Ramsay H (1997a) Solidarity at last? *Economic and Industrial Democracy* 18:503–537

Ramsay H (1997b) Fool's gold? European Works Councils and workplace democracy. *Industrial Relations Journal* 28:314–322

Rivest C (1996) Voluntary European Works Councils. *European Journal of Industrial Relations* 2:235–253

Sadler D (2000) Organising European labour: Governance, production, trade unions and the question of scale. *Transactions of the Institute of British Geographers* 25: 135–152

Schulten T (1996) European Works Councils: Prospects for a new system of European industrial relations. *European Journal of Industrial Relations* 2:303–324

Streeck W (1997a) Industrial citizenship under regime competition: The case of the European Works Councils. *Journal of European Public Policy* 4:643–664

Streeck W (1997b) Neither European nor Works Councils: A reply to Paul Knutsen. *Economic and Industrial Democracy* 18:325–327

Tarrow S (1998) *Power in Movement: Social Movements and Contentious Politics*. Cambridge, UK: Cambridge University Press

Terry M (1985) Combine committees: Developments of the 1970s. *British Journal of Industrial Relations* 23:359–378

Thompson E P (1978) *The Poverty of Theory and Other Essays*. London: Merlin

Thomson D and Larson R (1978) *Where Were You Brother? An Account of Trade Union Imperialism*. London: War on Want

Tillman R M and Cummings M S (eds) (1999) *The Transformation of US Unions: Voices, Visions and Strategies from the Grassroots*. Boulder, CO: Lynne Rienner Publishers

Tilly C (1978) *From Mobilisation to Revolution*. New York: McGraw-Hill

Tilly C (1995) Globalization threats labors' rights. *International Labor and Working Class History* 47:1–23

Towers B (1997) *The Representation Gap: Change and Reform in the British and American Workplace*. Oxford: Oxford University Press

Treckel K F (1972) The World Auto Councils and collective bargaining. *Industrial Relations* 11:72–79

Trades Union Congress (TUC) (1997a) *Partners for Progress: Next Steps for the New Trade Unionism*. London: TUC

Trades Union Congress (TUC) (1997b) *European Works Councils: A TUC Guide for Trade Unionists*. London: Labour Research Department

Turner L (1996) The Europeanization of labour: Structure before action. *European Journal of Industrial Relations* 2:325–344

United Nations Conference on Trade and Development (UNCTAD) (1999) *World Investment Report 1999*. New York: United Nations

Vogler C (1985) *The Nation-State: The Neglected Dimension of Class*. Aldershot: Gower
Waterman P (2001) *Globalization, Social Movements and the New Internationalisms*. London: Continuum
Weiler P (1990) *Governing the Workplace: The Future of Labor and Employment Law*. Boston: Harvard Business School Press
Weston S and Martinez-Lucio M (1997) Trade unions, management and European Works Councils: Opening Pandora's box? *International Journal of Human Resource Management* 8:764–779
Weston S and Martinez-Lucio M (1998) In and beyond European Works Councils: Limits and possibilities for trade union influence. *Employee Relations* 20:551–564
Wever K (1995) *Negotiating Competitiveness: Employment Relations and Organizational Innovation in Germany and the US*. Boston: Harvard Business School
Wever K (1997) Unions adding value: Addressing market and social failure in the advanced industrial economies. *ILR* 136:449–468
Wever K (1998) International labor revitalisation: enlarging the playing field. *Industrial Relations* 37:388–407
Whittall M (2000) The BMW European Works Council: A cause for European industrial relations optimism? *European Journal of Industrial Relations* 6:61–83
Wills J (1998) Taking on the cosmocorps: Experiments in transnational labor organization. *Economic Geography* 74:111–130
Wills J (1999a) Managing European Works Councils in British firms. *Human Resource Management Journal* 9:19–38
Wills J (1999b) Time well spent? The lessons of the British Steel EWC. *European Works Councils Bulletin* 20(March/April):8–11
Wills J (2000) Great expectations: Three years in the life of a European Works Council. *European Journal of Industrial Relations* 6:83–105
Wills J (2001a) Bargaining for the space to organise in the global economy: a review of the ACCOR-IVF trade union rights agreement. *Review of International Political Economy* 8 (forthcoming).
Wills J (2001b) Rescaling trade union organisation: Lessons from the European frontline. In R Munck (ed) *Labour and Globalisation: Results and Prospects*. Liverpool: Liverpool University Press (forthcoming)
Wills J and Lincoln A (1999) Filling the vacuum in "new" management practice? Lessons from American employee-owned firms. *Environment and Planning A* 31:1497–1512

Jane Wills is a Lecturer in Geography at Queen Mary, University of London. She is currently a coeditor of *Antipode: A Radical Journal of Geography* and coordinator of the London Union Research Network. Recent publications include *Union Retreat and the Regions: The Shrinking Landscape of Organised Labour* (written with Ron Martin and Peter Sunley, 1996, Jessica Kingsley), *Geographies of Economies* (edited with Roger Lee, 1997, Arnold) and *Dissident Geographies: An Introduction to Radical Ideas and Practice* (written with Alison Blunt, 2000, Longman). Jane is currently an ESRC fellow, researching the changing geography of the trade union movement in the UK. This research incorporates internationalist responses to globalisation, new organising initiatives, partnership agreements and community unionism.

11

Women Workers and the Promise of Ethical Trade in the Globalised Garment Industry: A Serious Beginning?

Angela Hale and Linda M Shaw

The chapter gives an overview of the recent development within the Ethical Trade Initiative (ETI), especially the development of corporate codes of conduct, and considers the prospects they offer for improving labour conditions for workers in the international garments industry. It argues that two specific features of the industry— competitive production systems based on international subcontracting and the use of predominantly female production workers—are likely to undermine the effective development of a codes-based strategy. Nevertheless, the labour rights agenda at the centre of ETI does provide a space for labour activists, whether operating in or out of formal union structures, to build campaigns and connections around global production networks.

The protests at Seattle showed how challenges to the international trade regime have become a central plank of international policies and strategies, not only for unions but also for a wide range of social activists and campaigners from around the world. In the context of trade, international union strategies have focused on pressing for a linkage between trade and labour standards. At the same time, they have also been drawn into a series of labour rights-based campaigns and initiatives derived from consumer actions and organising.

Consumer-led strategies in Europe and the US have been central to the development of an ethical trade movement seeking to promote respect for and compliance with international labour standards. This chapter will draw on the authors' own experience as activists and researchers on the international garment industry during the past five years and their involvement in the ethical trade movement. The chapter will outline some of the key developments in the garment industry as they impact workers' conditions. We will also review some of the key initiatives and debates in the emerging ethical trade agenda and explore whether the "promise" of improvements for labour, especially for women workers, can be translated into tangible gains through the development of codes of conduct.

Since the growth of ethical trade is very recent phenomenon, it is difficult at this stage to develop any firm conclusions about its long-term implications and impacts. Similarly the specific nature and history of the garment industry may also preclude any general and substantive cross-sectoral comparisons. Nonetheless, many of the developments and discussions outlined below can contribute to ongoing debates not only over the future of ethical trade but also the development of trade unionism at the international level.

As one of the earliest and most globalised industries, the garment industry has long been a focus for research on global shifts in manufacturing industries (Dicken 1998) and more recently on the role of global commodity and production chains in the global economy (Gereffi and Korzeniewicz 1994). The garment sector has also been one of the first industries to develop an agenda for corporate responsibility that included labour standards. This is often referred to as the "triple bottom line", in which companies now face scrutiny over their financial, environmental and social performance. This phenomenon has tended to receive more attention in the US than in Europe, particularly in the media (Klein 2000; Ross 1997), but this situation is now beginning to change (Blowfield 1999). This chapter seeks to develop a further contribution situated within a European context and to focus specifically on the development of the UK-based Ethical Trading Initiative (ETI).

The growing public concern for the triple bottom line in the garment industry was one of the starting points of the ETI. The seal of substantial corporate involvement was confirmed when the largest garment retailer in the UK, Marks and Spencer, finally joined in the autumn of 1999. Membership in the ETI represents a public commitment by companies to the promotion of minimum labour standards throughout their global supply chains. Yet, at the same time that companies were joining the ETI, a huge wave of redundancies began in the UK textile and garment sector—a total of over 40,000 in the 12 months leading up to September 1999 (Hetherington 2000). UK garment retailers, alongside their European counterparts, are switching their supply base to cheaper producers in Asia and Eastern Europe where companies know that minimum labour standards are scarcely complied with (ILO 2000). The apparent contradiction between this strategy and membership of the ETI is avoided by the fact that membership represents, not an immediate guarantee of acceptable standards, but rather the progressive implementation of an agreed code of conduct.

This chapter will discuss whether the promises of improving labour conditions for workers in the international garment industry articulated through the adoption of such ethical trade policies are well founded or likely to prove illusory. Will the "logic" of the industry prove too ruthless for anything more than small and localised improvements in specific factories/supply chains? What bearing does the fact that women are the main production workers have on strategies for improvement? What do workers themselves see as the value of company codes in the context of complex international subcontracting chains?

The Emergence of Ethical Trade

Ethical trade is an umbrella term increasingly used to cover different approaches to improving labour, social and environment conditions along international supply chains. The public presence of ethical trade has emerged very recently, largely within the past five years, in both Europe and North America. The process of defining and analysing ethical trade is still at an early stage, with different and sometimes contradictory approaches across different sectors (Blowfield 1999; Diller 1999; Seyfang 1999). There is no space here to analyse the different academic perspectives. Rather, in relation to the situation in the garment industry, it was deemed appropriate to use the definition most commonly used by activists in the UK: "Ethical trade aims to ensure that conditions within mainstream production chains meet basic minimum standards and to eradicate the most exploitative forms of labour such as child and bonded labour and 'sweatshops'" (Zadek 1998:i–ii).

During the 1990s, public concern grew as the media revealed that reputable companies were selling everyday consumer goods made by exploited workers. Demands for change and for improvements in working conditions have been framed within widespread actions and campaigns throughout North America and Europe. These have occurred on such a scale that they can be seen as one of the significant social movements of the 1990s. Retailers in the garment and sports shoe industries have been particular targets for campaigners (Klein 2000; Ross 1997). In Europe, for example, Dutch groups began campaigning against the clothing retailer C&A over ten years ago. The major, and often underrated, achievement of these campaigns was to push companies—especially garment retailers—to accept some responsibility for working conditions in the factories that supplied them and not just in the factories which they owned directly (Shaw 1997).

A common reaction by many of the companies targeted has been to produce a public statement to the effect that the company is committed to ensuring that its products were made in reasonable working conditions. Often known as "Company Codes of Conduct", these statements have increasingly covered labour standards. One of the first came in 1992 when a report appeared in the *Washington Post* about the production of Levi jeans by Chinese prison labour in the Island of Saipan. Levi Strauss immediately reacted by drawing up a code on labour standards for all its overseas suppliers. Walmart, the US's biggest retailer, drew up a code in 1993, and soon almost all leading US garment retailers followed suit (Ross 1997). European companies were slower to respond, but many are now publishing codes. In the UK, the adoption of labour-based codes has spread rapidly, and all major garment retailers are now publishing a code.

The proliferation of such codes has been rapid. In a recent survey by the International Labour Organisation (ILO), over 200 labour-related codes were found in 22 industry and service sectors, and they were most common in enterprises that dealt directly with consumer products such as garments. The survey revealed wide discrepancies in content and operation. Occupational health and safety was the most frequently addressed issue in codes, with freedom of association/rights to collective bargaining present in only 15% of the codes surveyed (Diller 1999).

As more and more companies proclaimed their new and supposedly labour-friendly codes, these developments generated intense and ongoing debates along a broad spectrum of labour activists. For many, the crucial question was whether these company codes were an indication of real commitment or merely public relations exercises. Questions of autonomy arose as campaigners considered whether to sit down and work with the companies on the implementation of these codes. Would this lead to co-option and suppression of criticism? The relationship between the campaigners, other nongovernment organisations (NGOs) and trade unions raised many issues, not the least debate over whose role it was to negotiate with companies on these issues. The campaigns that brought the companies to the table have been led by NGOs. However, some trade unionists maintain that labour rights and actions that claim to be in the interest of workers should remain solely the province of unions. There is also a fear that codes will become a way of privatising international labour standards (Kearney 1999). Nevertheless, new labour alliances have developed in response to company codes, alliances that have included both NGOs and trade unions. They do have considerable potential despite these "boundary" problems, as similar coalitions between garment unions and community organisations at the local level in the US have illustrated (Needleman 1998).

One of the problems facing these new alliances is the speed and pace of innovations by companies. Not only has there been a huge increase in the number of codes with labour provisions, there has also been a growth in the number of approaches to the vexed question of how to ensure effective monitoring and implementation of codes. Some companies are hiring existing external auditors, often large accountancy firms, who simply add labour standards to their existing portfolio of services. There has also been a growth in the number of not-for-profit organisations offering an auditing service focussing on labour standards, eg Verité. A similarly US-based NGO, the Council on Economic Priorities, has developed an international standard for labour and human rights known as SA 8000. Its advisory board contains corporate, NGO and union representatives. There have also been calls for the ILO itself to be engaged in this process, but at the moment there appears to be no consensus within the organisation over this. In Europe, specifically the UK (ETI) and the Netherlands (Fair Wear Charter Foundation), a multistakeholder approach involving all sectors has been developed.

In the UK, the ETI initially developed out of an attempt by NGOs to try to formulate collectively agreed procedures for ensuring the implementation, monitoring and verification of company codes. Membership includes NGOs and unions as well as companies. The nature of company membership reflects the contours of the NGO-led campaigns, with a predominance of companies in either garments or food retailing. Significantly, government involvement has been from the Department for International Development. This reflects the fact that the key NGOs involved originally were those concerned primarily with "development" issues, eg Christian Aid, Oxfam and the World Development Movement. Debates have continued to be framed within a "development" paradigm. Union membership has also reflected this, with representatives from the International Trade Secretariats and from the International Department of the Trades Union Congress (TUC) rather than from individual UK unions based in the relevant sectors (ETI 2000).

The approach of the ETI to the issue of ensuring effective monitoring and implementation of codes has been centred on the development of a base code. In many respects, this is similar to the model code produced by the International Confederation of Free Trade Unions (ICFTU), as both use ILO Conventions as reference points.

ETI Base Code—Main Provisions

1) Employment is freely chosen
2) Freedom of Association and the Right to Collective Bargaining are respected
3) Working conditions are safe and hygienic
4) Child labour shall not be used
5) Living wages are paid
2) Working hours are not excessive
3) No discrimination is practised
4) Regular employment is provided
5) No harsh or inhumane treatment is allowed

Work on this code within the ETI has involved a lengthy process of dialogue between members in order to gain a consensus on the way forward. By the end of 2000, the initial three pilot schemes remained unfinished and two more schemes had been started. In the garment sector work on China is still underway, and a pilot has recently been proposed on garment production in Sri Lanka. Many issues have been raised, and the practical problems are enormous. No one is under the illusion that progress will be easy, and it remains to be seen what can be achieved. In the US, and more recently in Canada, similar multi-stakeholder initiatives have proved impossible to sustain (Maquila Solidarity Network 2000), with one or more of the stakeholders involved withdrawing. The ETI does have the advantage of a stronger and more clearly established consensus, but concedes in its report for 1999/2000 (2000:11) that only a "serious beginning" has made in terms of corporate progress in implementing the base code.

Meanwhile, debates over the validity of the codes-based approach have continued unabated, and have broadened from their initial participants of NGOs and trade unions to attracting some academic attention (Barrientos, McClenaghan and Orton 1999; Blowfield 1999; Picciotto and Mayne 1999; Seyfang 1999). Although there are already various competing analytical frameworks being developed for understanding codes, as yet there have been only a few studies on the actual general impact of codes and ethical trade initiatives within the garment industry

(Burns and Mather 1999; WWW 1998; WWW/CAWN 1999). However, some useful work on codes in the horticulture export sector has been done, and it continues to take place (Barrientos and Perrons 1999).

Increased attention to codes is also becoming apparent within the mainstream union movement, though primarily at the international level. The ILO has recently begun to devote resources to the codes issues, and many ILO documents on union strategies for the 21st century now make reference to codes as part of the wider series of debates on international labour (Taylor 2000).

The Changing Logic of the Garment Industry

The purpose of this chapter is to step back from these detailed debates and to revisit the issue of whether codes are an appropriate tool for tackling labour conditions in the garment industry. There are two aspects we intend to cover: first, whether codes can really challenge what has aptly been called "the logic of how the industry works" (Anner, quoted in Jeffcott and Yanz 2000:6), and second, whether they are an appropriate strategy for an industry in which the majority of the workforce are women.

In a globalised economy, the central driving force for most companies is the maintenance of profit levels in the face of intense competition. In labour-intensive industries such as garments, this is often translated into a need to cut back on labour costs. The key question is whether it is possible for such ethical trade policies to be implemented in the context of such strong downward pressures on labour in a weakly unionised and largely female workforce.

To answer this question we have to understand the specific nature of the garment industry. The garment industry has always been one of the most globalised industries, with shifting geographical and racial locations. Massive relocation has taken place over the past 30 years and shows no signs of stopping, as more countries are integrated into a global market and encouraged to compete for exports. It can also be argued that the international trading regime, specifically the Multi-Fibre Arrangement, has contributed to the extreme mobility of the industry. The introduction of the MFA in 1974 was designed to afford protection to the textiles and garment industry in developed countries by limiting the amount of imports to Northern markets from a specific country and industry sector under a quota system. Companies were encouraged to relocate production sites by the need to locate underutilised garment quotas to gain more access to Northern markets. Indeed, the phasing out of the MFA by January 2005 is set to bring a further round of relocation, with the biggest shift being from one poor country to another (Hale and Hurley 1999).

The garment industry has long been a focus of academic research, especially since garment production has remained fairly easy to enter for entrepreneurs with relatively low levels of investment, making it the classic "first stage" of industrial development for many countries. Work on the New International Division of Labour mapped the first wave of relocations in production sites in the 1960s and 1970s (Froebel, Heinrichs and Kreye 1980). Later research into global commodity chains mapped further rounds of relocation (Gereffi 1994), as production shifted from the newly industrialised Asian economies to neighbouring countries in South and Southeast Asia.

Attention has also been paid to the fact that one constant in this pattern of continual relocation, has been the continuing predominance of women. Globally, women typically make up 74% of the garment industry workforce; it is truly a women's industry (ILO 2000). Twenty years after a seminal paper by Diane Elson and Ruth Pearson addressed the question of why women workers are employed and the gender stereotyping that underlay the composition of the workforce, it is sobering to find the same stereotypes still in play (Elson and Pearson 1981). Describing the Guatemalan garment sector in a major garment trade journal, one scholar still ascribes the use of women workers to their innate "manual dexterity" and docility (De Coster 1999). Other work has looked at the phenomenon of the female workforce in countries such as Bangladesh (Kabeer 2000), and there have been extensive debates over waged labour and empowerment. It is clear that, whether or not women's work in the industry fed into their empowerment in the longer term, everyday working conditions for workers have remained grim even in Export Processing Zones (ILO 1998) and subject to the constant threat of relocation.

Thus far, most of the academic research on labour conditions in the garment industry has been linked to specific countries and/or production sites (see, for example, Kabeer 2000). Work on commodity chains can provide a useful context in which to analyse the global structures of the industry. It has been a focus for the Global Commodity Chains approach of Gereffi and colleagues (Gereffi and Korzeniewicz 1994), which has focused on issues of governance and power within the chains and the characterisation of garment chains as "Buyer-Driven". Others have argued that more complex models need to be developed, using the concept of a network and informed by the cultural contexts in which networks are embedded (for an overview, see Hughes 2000). For activists, however, the concept of linear chain has a particular resonance, since it draws attention to unequal power relations—important in helping to keep a focus on labour conditions and exploitation. Despite this, most academic chain analysis has involved substantive analysis neither of labour conditions nor of gender relations within this international context. Indeed, much of the research that has informed garment campaigns has originated within the organisations themselves, rather than from academia. For example, the research that promoted the establishment of the Clean Clothes Campaign in Europe was carried out by a Dutch NGO in the late 1980s (Smit 1989).

What is clear is that the garment industry is now controlled by marketing and retail companies that manage a global network of suppliers in low-wage countries. This includes newer brand name companies, such as NIKE and Liz Claiborne, which have never possessed a manufacturing base in the North but sourced from the beginning from Southern suppliers. Within the industry generally, including in the UK, retailers have become the dominant force and have maintained overall control within the industry whilst shifting their production sites from one location to another. For example, over half of the garments imported into Europe in 1994 were accounted for by retailers (Scheffer, quoted in Gereffi 1999). A considerable literature has emerged discussing these trends and emphasising that viability and profits in the garment supply chains increasingly come, not from economies of scale and mass production, but from the capacity to control complex networks of production. (Gereffi 1999). For example, one US retailer is estimated to have over 13,000 suppliers, who in turn source from up to 78,000 subcontractors (Kearney 1999).

These changing structures have been made possible by the development of information technology, which enables information, designs and orders to be communicated around the world 24 hours a day. Meanwhile, new technology at the point of sale has enabled retailers to closely monitor trends and to look for a quick response from manufacturers. The traditional two-season cycle has broken down, with design, fabric and colour changes being made more frequently. As a result, retailers are demanding shorter production runs and lead times, with manufacturers developing flexible production methods in order to survive in an increasingly volatile and competitive sector.

One consequence of the changing patterns of control and increase in international competition has been the massive growth of subcontracting. In this context, subcontracting can be defined as the manufacture of goods by one firm for another based on the specification of the lead firm (Unni, Bali and Vyas 1999). Often there can be several layers of firms or intermediaries mediating the relationship between the actual production workers and the end product market. The lead firms normally exercise considerable control over their sub-contractors in terms of price, quality and timing of the products they supply, but characteristically have had little concern for labour conditions.

The advantages to companies of subcontracting have been apparent in two main areas: production flexibility and the lessening of labour rights. Manufacturers are producing to order, and the demand can fluctuate enormously. There can also be production delays caused by late arrival of material or last minute changes in fabric or colour. By reducing the regular factory workforce and using subcontractors, employers can react to these changes but keep costs to a minimum. Subcontractors therefore act as buffers to seasonal fluctuations in demand. In some countries, such as the Philippines, up to 75% of output is contracted out (Green 1998). In the garment industry, it is common to further pass on the costs of irregular work to home-based workers. A recent ILO report estimates that a "great majority" of formal sector enterprises in Asia subcontracted a part of their prod-uction to homeworkers (ILO 2000:35). Current estimates of the garment industry workforce in Australia indicate that, for every factory-based garment worker, there are *15* outworkers (Homenet 1999). Thus it can be argued that, far from declining with the globalisation of the garment industry, homeworking is actually on the increase due to the spread of subcontracting (ILO 2000).

Downward Pressure on Labour Conditions

What has emerged in the garment industry is a network of inter-nationally competitive subcontracting systems. Many labour activists see a link between this and increased pressure on labour conditions. Of course, wages and conditions in the garment industry have always been low. Campaigners promoting ethical trade have drawn attention to low wages, compulsory overtime, hazardous conditions, frequent harassment and abuse of workers and lack of legal protection, especially for home-based workers (Green 1999). Revelations that wage rates can account for less than 5% of the final value of the product have been highly influential. In the oft-cited case of the sports shoe made in Indonesia and sold in the US for $100, wage costs make up a staggering 0.4% of the final price.[1]

Competitive international subcontracting has increased the threat to labour conditions through a process of downward pressure. In order to compete, companies at the top of supply chains put pressure on contractors, agents and trading companies for lower-cost goods. Meanwhile, with the increasing number of countries involved in export production, local manufacturers are locked into fierce competition for orders. Middlemen who have to meet the cost demands of the buying company maximise their own profits by squeezing manufacturers. Rather than turn down an order, local manufacturers accept unprofitable deals and make them work by increasing pressure on their own workforce through forced or unpaid overtime and by subcontracting to small workshops and to homeworkers, the lowest-paid workers at the end of the chain.

This growing pattern of international subcontracting means that the whole industry works on the basis of flexibility, short-termism, competition and insecurity. It is therefore no surprise that workers themselves are faced with these problems. Garment workers face daily insecurity as their employment is determined by fashion trends and market fluctuations. Even in larger factories, many employers have adopted ways of removing responsibility for their workforce when work is scarce. Workers may be employed on a casual, part-time, temporary basis, and there is increasing use of agencies that supply contract labour. At the same time, competition between local manufacturers to reduce costs and complete orders is resulting in an increase in work intensity. This is manifest in greater use of shifts, increased working hours and reductions in the numbers on production lines. Intensity is greatest when a particular production deadline has to be met, and workers are typically kept in the factory until the order is complete. Employers may even persuade workers that this is in their interest, since jobs will be lost if orders are not completed. Complaints against excessively long working hours are frequently made by both unions and NGOs (ILO 2000).

International subcontracting also undermines traditional forms of worker organising by not only creating huge gaps between workers and their ultimate employer, but also separating workers from each other. It is associated with divisiveness and the weakening of existing union power (Needleman 1998). In the US, the rise of subcontracting has made it difficult for garment workers to assert their labour rights under US law (Ho, Powell and Volpp 1996). At the same time the signing of NAFTA (the North Atlantic Free Trade Agreement) created a climate in which employers routinely threaten to relocate production in the face of unionisation attempts. (Bronfenbrunner, quoted in Campbell et al 1999) In Asia, several worker support groups report that subcontracting is sometimes directly used in response to workers' demands for improved wages and conditions (TIE 2000).

Competitive Subcontracting and Ethical Trade

The expansion of competitive international subcontracting presents a huge challenge to the promotion of ethical trade. The indications are that this competitive pressure is set to continue. One such indication was the announcement in May 2000 of the complete withdrawal of the major garment retailer C&A from the UK. Retailers are facing stagnant consumer demand and are seeking to sustain market position by price competition and lower prices from their suppliers (Anson 2000).

Ironically, it is the very companies promoting ethical trade that are demanding further reduction in the prices of garment imports. In fact, the retail companies at the top of the subcontracting chains are themselves creating the conditions that operate against attempts to implement their own codes of conduct. If competitive pressure is such that costs have to be cut, it may be impossible for local contractors to increase wage levels and bring health and safety measures up to international standards without going out of business. If the demand for flexibility in both price and production levels translates into insecurity and periods of intense overtime, it is unrealistic to expect standards on working hours and proper working contracts to be adequately implemented. In any case, if local manufacturers have no long-term stake in the business, their aim will be short-term profits, rather than investment in improved working conditions.

Any companies seriously seeking to overcome these dilemmas are also faced with practical problems associated with increasingly complex subcontracting chains. The first problem is actually knowing where their goods are produced. Most companies operate through agents, trading companies, or local contractors. These middlemen increase their power by providing as little information as possible. Often overseas companies do not know the names or locations of factories from which they are buying, and this information can change rapidly from one week to the next. Even if the factory itself is known, it is highly unlikely that local contractors will reveal the extent of outsourcing to smaller production units and homeworkers. Most companies buy from a range of local suppliers, so that even if they know where these are it will be impossible to monitor all of them.

As part of their commitment to ethical trade, some larger companies are insisting that their own representatives visit at least some of the factories from which they source. Some are also setting up their own buying operations and establishing more direct relationships with local manufacturers. There are indications, anecdotal at this stage, that this process is sometimes being accompanied by a significant reduction in the number of suppliers (ETI staff member 1999). This closer working relationship does provide greater opportunity for monitoring the implementation of company codes by those particular companies. However, what are its implications for workers in the production units that are no longer used, and for homeworkers at the end of subcontracting chains? And what about workers supplying less responsible companies?

Consulting Workers

A further major criticism of the codes initiatives is that, although they are fundamentally about workers rights, workers themselves have not been part of the process. Codes are not negotiated between employers and workers, but introduced in a top-down fashion by companies themselves. This has sometimes been done in consultation with NGOs and trade union officials, but these are typically in the country where the company is based, far removed from the actual workplace itself. In short, codes of conduct are being introduced on behalf of workers without their knowledge or consent. It is simply assumed that workers will see this initiative as being in their interest. This lack of consultation is often justified by the nonexistence of representative mechanisms. Existing trade unions may claim that it is their task alone to represent workers, but the reality is that effective and democratic unions are few and far between in the garment industry. The vast majority of women workers remain unorganised and beyond the reach of unions.

However, a number of other initiatives have developed around the world to support and represent the interests of women garment workers. There are a growing number of such women worker organisations seeking to improve conditions. Some define themselves as unions, others as women's groups, support centres and other forms of NGO.

For some years, the NGO Women Working Worldwide (WWW) has been part of and helped to promote a growing global network of such groups. Contacts and relationships have been built up as part of the work carried out by the authors as members of WWW. In this context, we carried out a small research and consultation exercise on codes awareness with our partners in six countries: Indonesia, the Philippines, Sri Lanka, Bangladesh, Pakistan and India. Their research with women production workers at the grassroots level clearly demonstrated that the women knew nothing about codes, even when their factories were supplying well-known companies that had codes, such as Nike and the Gap. Unsurprisingly, when the concept of codes was initially explained to them, workers showed a high level of scepticism, based on a distrust of anything introduced by management and on widespread experience of corruption. Many felt that even attempting to find out whether their companies had codes could lead to victimisation or dismissal. Nevertheless, they were curious to know more, and they welcomed WWW's suggestion of an educational programme on the issue of codes.

As a result of these responses, we developed an education programme and materials, which were then translated into local languages and used by local organisers. Workers' willingness to explore the potential of codes was demonstrated by their involvement in this education programme. We found that many women gave up their few hours of leisure time and also that many feared victimisation as a result of participation. Sessions were sometimes held in secret. At times, Indonesia was in a state of political turmoil and Bangladesh was under floodwater. Nevertheless, groups in all six countries reported that the programme had been positive and productive (WWW 1998). In part, this was because the discussion of codes opened up more general issues, such as the place of workers in international supply chains. Few workers had previously questioned where their products went after leaving the factory, and many became enthusiastic about using brand labels as a way of tracing supply chains. They began to see that codes of conduct could be a useful tool in confronting some of the problems of organising in the context of globalisation, as such codes provided a link between workers working for the same company in other countries and with consumer campaigns in Europe and North America. As Shirin Akther, one of the organisers in Bangladesh, reported, "Workers became aware that foreign consumers are trying to do something good for them. They have got the feeling that they are not alone. As a result their level of awareness and sense of their rights was raised" (WWW 1998).

However it also became apparent to us that workers did not see company codes as the solution to the struggle for workers rights, even in factories that were directly supplying the world market. There was a strong feeling that the impact of codes would be limited unless workers had proper work contracts and the right to organise. Although some codes might include these rights, there was no confidence that these would be implemented unless workers were in a position to act collectively. For codes to work, all groups saw it as crucial that worker representatives be involved in the implementation and monitoring of them. It was felt that this should ideally be done through trade unions. However, most workers had limited experience of trade unionism, except as remote and sometimes corrupt organisations; unions are banned in most Free Trade Zones and rarely operate in smaller subcontracted units. Everywhere, the struggle for genuine trade unionism was seen as more important than the promotion of company codes.

Gender Issues

The underlying question of whether codes can work effectively for women garment workers also needs to be raised. Gender perspectives can be lost in general debates over ethical trade, codes and the industry itself. Although there is no shortage of studies looking at the situation of women garment workers in a specific regions and factories, this does not mean that gender issues are raised. Yet it can be no coincidence that one of the most mobile and globalised industrial sectors is based on a predominantly female workforce. Similarly, although garment campaigns in Europe developed as strategies to specifically support women workers, in part because of the lack of an effective union presence for them, this original perspective has lost some of its emphasis on gender. At a recent conference in the Netherlands it was reported that, within the extensive European-based Clean Clothes Campaign, the visibility of women and the gender component of the campaign was getting sidetracked. Instead attention had been focussed increasingly on the actual process of monitoring and verification of codes.[2]

Commonly used codes such as the ETI Base Code do include generic antidiscrimination clauses, but it is hard to see them having much impact. More fundamentally, it can be argued that codes, in common with the labour standards they are based on, reflect the norms of an homogenised workforce in which union organisation is feasible (Barrientos and Blowfield 2000). In other words, they reflect a situation more characteristic of a male-dominated workforce than of the casualised and temporary women workers common to the garment industry, where in many countries informal sector workers can easily outnumber factory-based workers.

The specific position of women workers within the industry should be the starting point for entire codes, rather than simply a generic antidiscrimination clause. This is the case in Australia, where the

Textiles, Clothing and Footwear Union, together with its NGO partners, has developed a Homeworkers Code of Practice for the garment industry. This code contains provisions to ensure that homeworkers receive the minimum wages, benefits and working conditions to which they are entitled. The union itself monitors working conditions, and companies are required to disclose detailed information about the use of homeworkers in their supply chains (Fairwear).[3] The Australian example also provides the only current union approach to organising home-based and migrant garment workers that has met with any degree of success. In the current debates over the development of more effective forms of organising strategies for unions, it deserves a wider exposure.

Conclusion

Given the logic of an international industry characterised by ever more competitive subcontracting, it is difficult to see how ethical trade in the garment industry can move much beyond its "serious beginning". Furthermore, any attempt to improve labour conditions on a long-term basis has to be based on workers' own awareness and organisational ability. The problem is that the same processes operating against the implementation of codes of conduct are also operating against effective worker organisation. Traditional forms of trade union organising based on secure factory employment will not work in the context of a casualised and dispersed labour force.

This lies at the heart of the problem of improving labour conditions for women workers in the garment industry. There are substantive and valid criticisms of a codes-based approach, some of which we have outlined above. However, it would also be true to say that the limited union presence—well known in the context of Export Processing Zones, for example—also extends to other sectors in the industry, such as that of homeworkers (ILO 1998,1999).

Yet it is clear from the experiences of the WWW that the globalised garment industry can also provide opportunities for new alliances, both among workers themselves and between workers and those organisations that are campaigning on their behalf. The rise of ethical trade and the use of codes provide one arena in which some new alliances and coalitions are being developed. Whether they will be enough to mount an effective challenge to the "logic" of the industry and the pervasiveness of the system of international subcontracting remains doubtful at present. Ethical trade strategies need to take into account the realities of women workers' situation within global subcontracting chains. At the same time, they must recognise the potential for collaborative action at an international level. Only then can the movement for ethical trade begin to have a significant impact.

It is already apparent that codes and their implementation and monitoring will work best when workers are able to organise on the ground. However, it is also apparent that there is no single effective model of organising women garment workers. Rather, there is a diversity of types of worker organising, including "traditional" unions as well as less formal women worker associations and support centres at the grassroots. There is also more diversity internationally in the kinds of organisations working in support of labour rights, from the more traditional union structures to small NGOs such as Women Working Worldwide to larger ones such as Oxfam and Save the Children, as well as campaigning networks such as Clean Clothes and Labour Behind the Label.

This, if anything, may be the lasting legacy of the codes approach—the development of strategic alliances and coalitions among different labour interest groups. The development of garment campaigns throughout Europe provides a space for further work in this area. In the US, Sweatshop Watch is a Californian coalition of labour, union, community, women's and migrants' groups that has had some success at the level of state legislation (Homenet 1999). No doubt other examples of effective coalitions can be added to this short list.

As to the longer-term role and impact of the movement for ethical trade, this remains unclear. However, the findings of some recent research underline the fact that unions might also do well to add consumers to their agenda. In the UK, the Co-operative Bank commissioned research into ethical consumerism and found that there was the potential for as much as 30% of consumer spending to be ethically influenced. A third of consumers were "seriously concerned", and two thirds had looked for at least one ethical label (Cowe 2000). Strategies based on building connection and campaigns along commodity chains provide a space in which to bring producers and consumers closer together. It is crucial that labour rights and conditions remain at the heart of this new agenda.

Endnotes

[1] This example is given on the Clean Clothes Campaign website and has been used extensively as a campaigning tool. See Clean Clothes Campaign (nd).
[2] This was reported (speaker unknown) at the conference on women, development and labour organised by IRENE (Dutting 2000:34).
[3] For more information, visit the Fairwear website (Fairwear 2001).

References
Anson, R (2000) Clothing retailing in the UK: Forecasts to 2004. *Textile Outlook International* 86(March):82–102

Barrientos S and Blowfield, M (2000) Ethical trade and marginalised groups. Paper presented to workshop on Emerging Issues in Ethical Trade: The Position of Marginalised Groups, 22 March, Westminster Central Hall, London. Natural Resources Institute and University of Hertford Business School

Barrientos S, McClenaghan S and Orton L (1999) *Gender and Codes of Conduct: A Case Study from Horticulture in South Africa*. London: Christian Aid

Barrientos S and Perrons D (1999) Gender and the global food chain: A comparative study of Chile and the UK. In H Afshar and S Barrientos (eds) *Women, Globalisation and Fragmentation in the Developing World* (pp 150–174). Macmillan: Basingstoke

Blowfield M (1999) Ethical trade: A review of developments and issues. *Third World Quarterly* 20(4):753–770

Burns M and Mather C (1999) *UK Companies Operating in Indonesia: Responses to Ethical Trade Issues*. London: CIIR

Campbell B, Jackson A, Larudee M and Guttierez-Haces T (1999) *Labour Market Effects Under CUFTA/NAFTA*. Employment and Training Papers 27. Geneva: ILO

Clean Clothes Campaign (1999) *Made in Eastern Europe*. Amsterdam: CCC

Clean Clothes Campaign (nd) "Price Makeup of a $100 Sport Shoe Made in Indonesia". HTML file: <URL: http://www.cleanclothes.org/campaign/shoe.htm>, last accessed November 2000

Cowe R (2000) "Morality Is a Spending Force". *Guardian* 6 October. HTML file: <URL: http://www.guardian.co.uk/Archive/Article/0,4273,4072666,00.html>, last accessed March 2001

De Coster J (1999) Profile of the Guatemalan clothing export industry. *Textile Outlook International* September 84:84–113

Dicken, P (1998) *Global Shift*. 3rd ed. Liverpool: Paul Chapman

Diller J (1999) A social conscience in the global marketplace? Labour dimensions of codes of conduct, social labelling and investor initiatives. *International Labour Review* 138(2):99–129

Dutting G (2000) International Restructuring Education Network Europe (IRENE) Report: Women Treasure Boulevard—Report of the Expert Meeting on Women, Development and Labour. *News From IRENE* 29 & 30 (May):31–35

Elson D and Pearson R (1981) "Nimble fingers make cheap workers": An analysis of women's employment in third world export manufacturing. *Feminist Review* 7:87–107

Ethical Trading Initiative (ETI) staff member (1999) Personal communication with authors

Ethical Trading Initiative (ETI) (2000) *Annual Report 99/00*. London: ETI

Fairwear (2001) HTML file: <URL: http://www.awatw.org.au/fairwear/>, last accessed March 2001

Froebel F, Heinrichs J and Kreye O (1980) *The New International Division of Labour: Structural Unemployment in Industrialised Countries and Industrialisation in Developing Countries*. Cambridge, UK: Cambridge University Press

Gereffi G (1994) The organisation of buyer-driven commodity chains: How US retailers shape overseas production networks. In G Gereffi and Korzeniewicz M (eds) *Commodity Chains and Global Capitalism* (pp 95–123). Westport, CT: Praeger

Gereffi G (1999) International trade and industrial upgrading in the apparel commodity chain. *Journal of International Economics* 48:37–70

Gereffi G and Korzeniewicz M (eds) (1994) *Commodity Chains and Global Capitalism.* Westport, CT: Praeger

Gibbon S and Ladbury S (2000) *Core Labour Standards: Key Issues and Proposals for a Strategy.* London: DFID

Green D (1998) *Fashion Victims.* London: CAFOD

Hetherington P (2000a) "Women's Work". *Guardian* 20 April. HTML file: <URL: http://www.guardian.co.uk/Archive/Article/0,4273,4010000.00.html>, last accessed March 2001

Hale A and Hurley J (1999) What does the phaseout of the MFA quota system mean for garment workers? Focus on trade and development. *ICDA* 9(2):23–34

Ho L, Powell C and Volpp L (1996) (Dis)assembling rights of women workers along the global assembly line: Human rights and the garment industry. *Harvard Civil Rights-Civil Liberties Law Review* 31:383–414

Homenet (1999) *New Ways of Organising: Four Case Studies of Trade Union Activity.* Leeds: Homenet

Hughes A (2000) Retailers, knowledges and changing commodity networks: The case of the cut flower trade. *Geoforum* 31:175–190

ILO (1998) *Labour and Social Issues Relating to Export Processing Zones.* Geneva: ILO

ILO (1999) "Trade Unions and the Informal Sector: Towards a Comprehensive Strategy". HTML file: <URL: http://www.ilo.org/public/english/dialogue/actrav/publ/infsectr.htm>, last accessed March 2001

ILO (2000) *Labour Practices in the Footwear, Leather, Textiles and Clothing Industries.* ILO:Geneva

Jeffcott B and Yanz L (2000) *Codes of Conduct, Government Regulation and Worker Organising.* Discussion Paper no 1, Ethical Trading Action Group. Toronto: Maquila Solidarity Network

Kabeer, N (2000) *The Power to Choose.* London: Verso

Kearney N (1999) Corporate codes of conduct: The privatised application of labour standards. In S Picciotto and R Mayne (eds) *Regulating International Business Beyond Liberalisation* (pp 205–220). Basingstoke: Macmillan

Klein N (2000) *No Logo.* London: Flamingo

Maquila Solidarity Network (2000) "Resource Centre—Codes of Conduct". HTML file: <URL: http://www.maquilasolidarity.org/resources/codes/codes.htm#north%20downloaded%2028/2/01>, last accessed March 2001

Murray J (1998) Corporate codes of conduct and labour standards. In R Kyloh (ed) *Mastering the Challenge of Globalisation: Towards a Trade Union Agenda* (pp 45–104). Geneva: ILO

Needleman R (1998) Building relationships for the long haul: Unions and community-based groups working together to organize low-wage workers. In K Bronfenbrenner, S. Friedman, R W Hurd, R L Seeber and R A Oswals (eds) *Organizing to Win New Research on Union Strategies* (pp 71–86). Cornell: ILR Press

Picciotto S and Mayne R (1999) *Regulating International Business: Beyond Liberalisation.* Basingstoke: Macmillan

Ross A (ed) (1997) *No Sweat.* New York: Verso

Seyfang G (1999) *Private Sector Self-Regulation for Social Responsibility: Mapping Codes of Conduct.* Working Paper no 1, Overseas Development Group. Norwich, UK: University of East Anglia

Shaw L (1997) European Clean Clothes Campaigns. In A Ross (ed) *No Sweat* (pp 215–220). New York: Verso

Smit M (1989) *C&A: The Still Giant.* Amsterdam: SOMO

Taylor R (2000) "Trade Unions and Transnational Industrial Relations". HTML file: <URL: http://www.ilo.org/public/english/bureau/inst/papers/1999/dp99/>, last accessed March 2001

Transnationals Information Exchange (TIE) (2000) *Asia, Stories of Workers Struggles in Thailand.* Colombo: TIE

Unni J, Bali N and Vyas J (1999) *Subcontracted Women Workers in the Global Economy: Case of Garment Workers in India.* Ahmedabad: Gujarat Institute of Development Research /SEWA

UNDP (1995) *Human Development Report.* New York: Oxford University Press

Women Working Worldwide (WWW) (1998) *Women Workers and Codes of Conduct: Asia Workshop Report.* Manchester: WWW

Women Working Worldwide (WWW) and the Central America Women's Network (CAWN) (1999) *Women workers and codes of conduct: Central America Workshop Report.* Manchester: WWW

Yanz L, Jeffcott B, Ladd D and Atlin J (1999) "Policy Options to Improve Standards for Women Garment Workers in Canada and Internationally". Ottawa: Status of Women Canada. HTML file: <URL: http://www.swc-cfc.gc.ca/publish/research/yanz-e.html>, last accessed March 2001

Yeung H W (1998) The social-spatial constitution of business organisation. *Organisation* 5(1):101–128

Zadek S (1998) *Social Labels: Tools for Ethical Trade.* Luxembourg: Office for Official Publications of the European Communities

Women Working Worldwide is a small UK NGO working with an international network of women workers organisations that support workers in globalised industries, such as garments and electronics. WWW facilitates the exchange of information and the development of links between workers in different countries and between workers' organisations and those campaigning on their behalf in Europe. Its current work includes collaborating with Asian partners on the issue of codes of conduct and workers rights and on organising along subcontracting chains. WWW helps to coordinate Labour Behind the Label, a network of UK trade unions and NGOs, which mobilises consumer action in support of workers in the international garment industry.

Angela Hale is Project Director of Women Working Worldwide, a small NGO based at the Manchester Metropolitan University, where Angela used to teach. WWW works with an international network of women workers organisations to support the rights of women workers in the global economy. The focus is on industries supplying consumer goods to the world market, particularly the garment industry. WWW is currently participating in the UK Ethical Trading Initiative.

Linda Shaw is an active member of Women Working Worldwide and in this capacity has worked on the garment industry for several years. Linda works in adult and continuing education and is currently based in the Centre for Continuing Education at the University of Manchester. Trade union education, both in teaching and writing materials, has been a key aspect of her work, as, more recently, has a focus on gender and development issues.

12
Propositions on Trade Unions and Informal Employment in Times of Globalisation

Dan Gallin

The purpose of this contribution is to identify some of the issues which need to be addressed in order to advance the organisation of workers, and in particular women workers, in informal employment. The organisation of these workers, collectively described as the "informal sector", represents an existential challenge to the trade union movement: unless and until it puts itself in a position to effectively address this challenge, it cannot halt its decline, but in order to do so it has to undergo fundamental changes in its culture, its self-awareness and the way it relates to society. The issue of organising the informal sector is at the heart of the necessary transformations the trade union movement must undergo to recover its potential as a global social force.

Introduction: Why Organise the Informal Sector?[1]

Even now, the importance of organising informal sector workers is not recognised equally by all sections of the trade union movement. Part of the reason for this contribution is the confused and contradictory perception of the informal sector by trade unions. It is still a widely accepted assumption that the informal sector is a transitory phenomenon, and that it will be absorbed by the formal sector in time without the need for action by trade unions or the state. The experience of the last two decades, however, shows that this assumption of gradual formalization is unrealistic and only fosters dangerous complacency.

Unions, particularly those in the service sector, also face significant problems in trying to organize in the formal part of the economy and do not feel that they are in a position to use scarce resources for the informal sector. Admittedly, the heterogeneous nature of employment relations, the difficulties of locating and contacting workers in informal employment and—in some instances—obstacles created by legislation make organising difficult. However, unions also often underestimate the capacity of informal sector workers to organise themselves. Organising in the informal sector is not missionary work amongst an amorphous and passive mass of individuals. On the contrary, it depends on the ability to reach out to groups of workers who are survival experts and therefore, in many cases, extraordinarily dynamic and resourceful.

Organising workers in informal employment needs to be a priority of the trade union movement at both national and international levels, because: (1) it is here to stay; (2) it is growing, whilst the formal sector is declining in terms of organisational potential; (3) these two trends are linked and are irreversible in the short and medium term; and (4) consequently, the stabilisation of the formal sector organisations and building trade union strength internationally depend on the organisation of the informal sector. Organising the informal sector serves the interests of the majority of workers worldwide. Without wishing to belabour points which have been made elsewhere, we need to remind ourselves of some basic facts underlying the above statements.

It is impossible to conceive at the present time of organising a majority of workers at world scale without serious organising in the informal sector. The vast majority of the world's workers—including the poorest, who most need self-defence through organisation—are in the informal sector. In India, for example, the proportion of the active population in the informal sector (including agriculture) increased from 89% in 1978 to 92% in 1998. In Africa, Asia and Latin America the informal sector accounts for a share of employment ranging from significant to prevalent (ILO/TUIS 1999:3, 5, Tables 1 and 2; see also Table 1 in this chapter).[2] For Central and Eastern Europe data are generally not available, but anecdotal evidence indicates that the informal sector is rapidly growing as state enterprises close down or are privatised and unemployment increases (the same applies to China). Such statistical data as are available for OECD countries (the industrialised world) indicate that the informal sector also represents a significant part of the labour force: about 11% in Ireland and New Zealand, 19% in Germany and 20% in Italy (excluding agriculture).

It is no longer accurate today to describe the informal sector as "atypical". In most so-called developing countries, it is the formal sector—regular direct employment with a formal sector company— that is "atypical" in the literal sense. In many of the older industrialised countries, the informal sector, although it does not occupy a majority of the labour force, is becoming increasingly significant, particularly for women (ILO/TUIS 1999:Table 1). Equally, it is not appropriate to identify the formal sector as the "modern" sector, as opposed to the informal sector, which is supposed to be "nonmodern". What is

Table 1: Size of the Informal Sector

Informal Sector Share of	Latin America, Caribbean	Africa	Asia
Total employment excluding agriculture	15%	18%	15–30%
Total employment including agriculture	45%	75%	75–85%
Nonagricultural employment	57%	78%	45–85%
Urban employment	40%	61%	40–60%
Poor employment	50%	NA	NA
New jobs	84%	93%	NA

	Low-Income Countries	Middle-Income Countries	High-Income Countries
Total employment outside formal sector	80%	40%	15%

Table created by Jacques Charmes (Université de Versailles, Centre d'Economie et d'Ethique pour l'Environnement et le Développement).

"modernity"? Is factory work more "modern" than teleworking? As deplorable as it may be, it is a fact that sweatshops producing garments or components for the automobile industry or assembling printed circuit boards, in back alleys in Paris, New York or Macau, are more "modern" phenomena than a steelworks in Indonesia, Romania or South Chicago.

The growth of the informal sector since the 1980s has two main causes: the global economic crisis, and the way production is being organised by transnational capital. The world economic crisis is the result of political decisions. It is these that have led to the debt crisis in the developing countries, driven by the structural adjustment programmes of the International Monetary Fund and the World Bank (dismantling of the public sector, deregulation of the labour market) and led to the global crisis which started in Asia in 1997, continued in Russia in 1998 and hit Brazil in 1999. According to an ILO estimate (ILO 1998), this crisis has destroyed 24 million jobs in East Asia alone, mostly in the what the report terms the "modern industrial" sector.

To take Indonesia as an example, according to official figures, unemployment rose from 20 million in 1998 (when it represented 22% of the labour force) to 36 million at the beginning of 1999. The population living below the official poverty line (meaning a daily income of US$0.55 in urban areas and of US$0.40 in rural areas—about half internationally comparable rates) went from 37% of the total population in the middle of 1998 to 48% of it at the end of that year. Comparable trends have been reported in Korea and Thailand. In Russia and the other successor states of the USSR, in addition to the millions of unemployed, there are more millions of workers still in formal employment who do not get paid for several months at a time. For all of these, in the absence of serious social safety nets, the informal sector provides the only possibility of survival.

These are neither short-term trends nor trends that are reversible in the short term. Even if they are the results of policy decisions which are by their nature reversible, a reversal involving the adoption of different macroeconomic policies at a global scale depends on a fundamental shift in global power relations between labour and capital. Whether such a shift can be brought about depends in turn, at least partially, on the very question of whether the informal sector can be organised by unions. Even assuming that a shift of global economic policy can occur in the short term, its effects will be felt at the earliest in about a decade or two. Meanwhile, the labour movement cannot afford several decades of continuing decline.

The other factor that has contributed to the growth of the informal sector in the last 20 years or so has been the changing structure of transnational enterprise. The modern enterprise is essentially an organiser of production carried out on its behalf by others. Its core includes the management and employees at corporate headquarters and possibly a core labour force of highly skilled technicians. This core directs production and sales, controls subcontracting and decides at short notice what will be produced where, when, how and by whom and from where certain markets will be supplied. It may also perform key manufacturing processes. However, the company's real product is the label, design and marketing and its skills in organising production and distribution and quality control. Most of the production of the goods it sells and all labour-intensive operations will be subcontracted, also internationally. This type of company will coordinate cascading subcontracting operations which will not be part of its structure but will nevertheless be wholly dependent on it, with wages and conditions deteriorating as one moves from the centre of operations to its periphery.

For example, the footwear company Nike does not regard itself as a manufacturer, but as a "research, development and marketing company". In 1991, Toyota had 36,000 subcontractors. A significant part of the production of companies such as General Motors, General Electric, Kodak, Caterpillar, Bull, Olivetti and Siemens is carried out by others. United Brands has turned a large part of its banana plantation workforce into "independent farmers" who continue to produce for it and are wholly dependent on the company buying their product. Companies in the brewing, dairy and other sectors have turned their delivery drivers into "independent contractors".

By cutting down on the hard core of permanent full-time workers, by decentralising and subcontracting all but the indispensable core activities, and by relying wherever possible on unstable forms of labour (casual, part-time, seasonal, on call and so on), management deregulates the labour market, not only to reduce labour costs but to shift responsibility for income, benefits and conditions onto the individual worker. The outer circle of this system is the informal sector: the virtually invisible world of microenterprises and home-based workers. The informal sector is an integral part of global production and marketing chains. What is particular to the informal sector is the absence of rights and social protection of the workers involved in it. In every other respect, particularly from the economic point of view, the formal and informal sectors form an integral whole.

The deregulation of the labour market is also a strategy for eliminating the trade union movement. Subcontracting is a well-travelled road to evading legal responsibilities and obligations. The fragmentation and dispersion of the labour force, its constant destabilisation by the introduction of new components (women, youth and migrants of different origins) in sectors without trade union tradition (computerisation, services), the pressure for maximum profits (productivity) together with management intimidation—all these are obstacles to trade union organisation.

The decline of trade union density in most industrialised countries in the 1980s and 1990s is less due to transfers of production and relocations to the South and to the East than has been often assumed, although such transfers have of course played a significant part. More important has been the deconstruction of the formal sector and the deregulation of the labour market in the heartland of industrial trade unionism. For example, Japan and the US have lost half their trade union members over a period of 40 years; New Zealand and Portugal have lost half their trade union members in only 10 years; and Israel has lost three quarters of its trade union membership in the same 10 years. In Japan, union density declined from a high of 56% in 1950 to 28% in 1990, essentially due to subcontracting, and it continues to decline (eg by 16.7% between 1985 and 1995). In the

United States, union density peaked at 35.5% in 1945 and now stands at 13%. Some other examples of the decline of union density in the years between 1985 and 1995 include: in Argentina, union density declined by 42.6%, in Mexico by 28.2%, in the United States by 21.1%, in Venezuela by 42.6%, in Australia by 29.6%, in New Zealand by 55.1%, in Austria by 19.2%, in the Czech Republic by 44.3%, in France by 37.2%, in Germany by 17.6%, in Greece by 33.8%, in Hungary by 25.3%, in Israel by 77.0%, in Poland by 42.5%, in Portugal by 50.2%, and in the United Kingdom by 27.7%. The unions which have resisted this trend are in countries where most social regulation has been maintained (eg between 1985 and 1995 union density increased by 2% in Denmark, by 16.1% in Finland, by 3.6% in Norway, by 8.7% in Sweden and by 35.8% in Malta) or where unions have benefited from a favourable political situation (in the same decade, union density increased by 130.8% in South Africa, by 84.9% in the Philippines and by 62.1% in Spain). These are exceptional situations.

The deconstruction of the formal sector through outsourcing and subcontracting is a long-term trend that cannot be reversed unless we can change the cost/benefit calculations of companies when it comes to their employment policies. Together with the impact of the economic crises, this deconstruction has led to a decline of trade union organisation in most countries in all parts of the world, in leading industrialised countries as well as in developing countries and transition countries. This means that the stabilisation of what remains of the trade union movement in the formal sector now depends on the organisation of the informal sector. Only by organising the informal sector can the trade union movement maintain the critical mass in terms of membership and representativity it needs to be a credible social and political force. In practice, this means organising the global labour market to the extent that companies—and governments at their service—no longer have either the power or the incentive to create and maintain inequalities on the same scale.

It should be stressed again that any strategy based on the gradual absorption of the informal sector into the formal sector, let alone on the "elimination" of the informal sector (by decree? by extermination?) is programmed to fail (ILO/TUIS 1999:19, 30). In the current global economic and political context, no state or regional grouping of states has the ability or the political will to set in motion the macroeconomic changes that would create universal full employment under regulated conditions. On the contrary, for the foreseeable future we can expect more deregulation and a further growth of the informal sector. The issue is therefore not formalising the informal but protecting the unprotected.

What Is the Informal Sector?

The informal sector covers a multiplicity of activities and different types of relationship to work and to employment (ILO/TUIS 1999:chapter 1.3, 5–7). The working definition of the informal sector used by Women in Informal Employment Globalizing and Organizing (WIEGO)[3] includes: self-employed (in own account activities and family businesses), paid workers in informal enterprises, unpaid workers in family businesses, casual workers without fixed employer, subcontract workers linked to informal enterprises and subcontract workers linked to formal enterprises. However, it is possible to define the informal sector in several ways, and general statements that apply under one definition will cease to be valid under another.

In WIEGO's view, its definition and the general propositions that follow should be functional in terms of the intended purpose, which is organisation. The point of departure of this definition should be the situation of the worker as the worker perceives it. It should include not only self-employed workers but also all those who are not directly employed by a formal sector firm (even if the end product of their work is connected, three or four times removed at the end of a sub-contracting chain, to a formal sector firm). Informal sector work takes place in a rural as well as in an urban context, and is as important in agriculture as it is in certain industries (ILO/TUIS 1999:28). At the end of the day, everyone who works in a dependent situation is a worker; street vendors, home-based workers, tenant farmers, artisans, fishermen (or fisherwomen) and collectors of forest produce are workers. The traditional concept of a worker, reflected in the legislation of many countries, is based on a direct employee/employer relationship. As this relationship is being replaced by a variety of more diffuse and indirect but nonetheless dependent relationships in the process of production, trade union organising can no longer focus primarily on the employment relationship. Instead, it should focus on the worker and on his/her needs for protection and representation.

The most important general statement that can be made about informal sector workers, which is valid under any definition and crucial in terms of organising, is that the majority of them are women. Indeed, a majority of workers expelled from the formal sector by the global economic crisis are women. As the International Confederation of Free Trade Unions has reported, women are the principal victims

of the casualization of labour and the pauperisation created by the
crisis and have therefore massively entered the informal sector in
the last two years (ICFTU 1999). Even before the crisis women
constituted most of the informal labour force (child labour is also
strongly represented). The great majority of home-based workers are
women, and home-based work represents as much as 40% to 50% of
labour in certain key export sectors, such as garments and footwear, in
Latin America and Asia. Women also comprise the great majority of
street vendors in informal markets, who in certain African countries
represent up to 30% of the urban labour force.

Although workers in export processing zones (EPZs), or free trade
zones, are not in general regarded as part of the "informal sector",
inasmuch as they are wage workers in more or less regular employment, it is worth noting here that 90% of EPZ labourers are women
and that, in the majority of cases, workers' rights and social protection
are also nonexistent in EPZs. Like informal sector workers, EPZ
workers comprise mostly unprotected, largely unorganised female
labour. In Central America, organising women workers in the EPZs
has come about mainly as a result of work by women's nongovernmental organisations (NGOs), which have always supported unionisation
of women workers (see also ILO/TUIS 1999:50, Box 10).

How to Organise the Informal Sector

The obvious points of departure in seeking to organise informal sector
workers are successful existing examples of this kind of organisation.
What is true of workers in general is true of informal sector workers:
they will organize whenever they have a chance to do so, and they are
best organised by their own.

Two general paths of organisation exist. The first occurs when a
traditional union extends its field of activity to include informal sector
workers. For example, the Textile, Clothing and Footwear Union of
Australia (TCFUA) is organising home-based workers in its sector.
UNITE in Canada also organises home-based workers in the garment
industry. Other examples include the Timber and Woodworkers'
Union and the General Agricultural Workers' Union, both in Ghana.
A national trade union centre might create an organisation for informal
sector workers, as the UDTS did in Senegal (ILO/TUIS 1999:46).
In Hong Kong, the HKCTU assisted in the establishment of the Asian
Domestic Workers' Union, comprised mostly of Filipino and Thai
women. Although this union did not survive internal disputes, domestic
workers have organized elsewhere, for example in Britain, where their

union Kalayaan works closely with the Transport and General Workers' Union. Unions in Benin, Brazil (Força Sindical), Colombia, Germany (IG Metall), Italy (FILTEA-CGIL) and the Netherlands (FNV Vrouwenbond), among others, also organise and/or bargain for home-based workers. SIBTTA, the embroiderer's union in Madeira, has been organising home-based workers for 25 years and currently has about 8000 members; it may be the union with the longest history of organising home-based workers.

The second case is that of new trade unions created specifically to organise informal sector workers. An early case, and an example to many, is the Self Employed Women's Association (SEWA) in India, which started twenty-five years ago with a few hundred members and now numbers over 210,000 members in four Indian federal states. SEWA organises home-based workers, street vendors, paper pickers and refuse collectors and so on. It has created an infrastructure of flanking services: a bank providing microcredit, a vocational and trade union training programme at different levels, producers' cooperatives (artisans, agricultural producers) and service cooperatives (health, housing). SEWA is affiliated to three ITSs (ICEM, ITGLWF, IUF) and has joined with other unions to establish a national trade union centre in India concentrating on informal sector workers.

In addition to its ITS affiliations, SEWA is active in two international networks of informal sector workers. One is the International Alliance of Street Vendors, or StreetNet, which includes organisations or support groups in eleven countries. It was founded in 1995 and in the same year adopted the "Declaration of Bellagio" on the rights of street vendors. The second one is HomeNet, a network of unions, such as SEWA, SEWU, TCFUA and SIBTTA, which represent home-based workers, as well as other associations of home-based workers (in Bangladesh, the Philippines and Thailand). Together with SEWA, certain other unions and support groups at universities and in international organisations, HomeNet and StreetNet have formed WIEGO, another network. WIEGO seeks to work at different levels: research, policy proposals and coalition building.

In South Africa, the Self Employed Women's Union (SEWU) has been organised along the same lines. Recently, moves have been made to set up a similar organisation in Turkey. Women workers' organizations, including both formal and informal sector workers, have also formed in Hong Kong, Korea, Nepal, Pakistan and the Philippines.

Partnerships between unions and NGOs have helped organise informal sector workers. At the European Union level, the European Homeworking Group has brought together a coalition of those involved with home-based workers (unions, NGOs, church organisations, researchers and so on). The work of this group was one factor in influencing the majority of European governments to support the ILO Home Workers' Convention at the International Labour Conference in 1995 and to ensure its adoption in 1996.

In the UK, there are many local projects (NGOs or local authority schemes) and a national campaigning organisation, the National Group on Homeworking. This group has led the campaign for home-based workers to be included in the national minimum wage and has been a major influence on government policy, public awareness and trade union policy on home-based work. Other examples exist. At one stage in Greece, street committees were organised to represent home-based workers. In Portugal (mainland) work is being done through local rural organisations as well as trade unions. In the UK, a home-based workers' association was set up in one area.

In rural areas, and for obvious reasons in predominantly agricultural countries, there are a number of informal sector unions. SEWA organises rural informal sector workers such as gum collectors. Another example in India is the HKMP (ILO/TUIS 1999:59, Box 16). One example in Latin America is the landless workers movement of Brazil (Movimento Sim Terra–MST), which is currently facing repression in its struggles to occupy unused land belonging to large landowners. In the Brazilian federal state of Parana, the MST has established 82 encampments on unused land, with 7000 families involved, and has resisted police efforts to dislodge these encampments. Since 1980, over one thousand people have been killed in Brazil by hired assassins and police in the struggle over land, including many organisers of the MST and of other unions. Very few of these murders have been solved. On 19 August, a court in Rio de Janeiro acquitted three commanding officers of a military police commando which killed 19 MST members on 17 April 1996 at Carajas. The MST is a member of an international network of landless peasants and small holders called Via Campesina.

In summary: informal sector workers are already organising, partly within existing union structures originating in the formal sector, partly into new unions created by themselves, partly into associations which are sometimes described as NGOs but which are often in fact pro-tounions. International networks of informal sector workers already exist. The experience, activities and organisational structures created in this way are valuable resources and points of leverage for the entire trade union movement, at the national and international levels. Such organisations are either already a part of the trade union movement or its closest partners and allies. Any discussion and planning on organising the informal sector should include as a matter of course those who are already doing the job.

Notes on a Programme for the Informal Sector

A programme of organising the informal sector and at the same time defending the informal sector workers' interests has to have two aspects: *external* and *internal*. The external programme consists of the demands directed to workers' social counterparts: employers, public authorities, international organisations and so on. The internal programme focuses on what the labour movement itself has to do to improve its capacity to organise and represent informal sector workers.

External Programme

WIEGO proposes that the following points be included in a labour movement agenda of demands for the informal sector:

International labour standards. Several international labour standards relevant to the informal sector exist (ILO/TUIS 1999:15–18, 31). They should be used as organising and campaigning tools. For example: in 1996, the International Labour Conference adopted the Home Work Convention (No 177) and Recommendation No 184 thanks to vigorous and coordinated lobbying by three ITSs (ICEM, ITGLWF and IUF), the ICFTU Equality Department, the FNV, SEWA and HomeNet. WIEGO regrets that this coalition, which proved effective and powerful, did not remain in place as an action group after the adoption of the two international instruments, which have so far only been ratified by two countries (Finland and Ireland)—enough to take effect, but not nearly enough to get the attention of a majority of governments and international organisations. The ratification of Convention No 177 and Recommendation No 184 should be a continuing campaign theme for the international trade union movement and its allies.

The ILO Bureau for Workers' Activities points out that "the absence of a similar degree of coordination and cooperation was a factor in the failure to adopt an ILO instrument on contract labour in 1998" (ILO/TUIS 1999:32). It suggests that "the experience with Convention No 177 should be examined with a view to mobilising international support to bring contract labour rapidly back onto the agenda of the International Labour Conference and working towards the adoption of a strong Convention on this issue" (ILO/TUIS 1999:32).

Although ILO Conventions are not mandatory, they are influential in shaping national labour legislation and are a useful reference for union campaigns. In this sense, they offer opportunities that should be recognised and seized.

Social protection and services. The guiding principle of social protection should be that *all* workers need social protection (health, life and property insurance, old age security and safety nets) as well as social services (health, education and child care), regardless of their position in the process of production. This also applies to home-based workers who are own-account (self-employed) workers, ie they do not have an easily identifiable single employer, even though they may be a part of chains of production leading to big companies.

Microenterprise development has been seen by some as a first step to launch own-account home-based workers on a career as capitalist entrepreneurs. We regard these views as inspired by neoliberal doctrine without any relationship to what happens in the real world. As the BWA has pointed out, "for the vast majority of dependent and own-account workers the informal sector is not a stepping stone to improvement but a strategy for survival" (ILO/TUIS 1999:iii). Home-Net has stated that its experience has shown that collective organisation is essential not only for piece-rate home-based workers, who may have a more direct relation to an employer, but for the majority of own-account workers as well: "In today's international trading environment, a growing number of workers are outside legal regulations as 'workers' or 'employees' and collective organisation is becoming increasingly important". It follows that in the case of own-account workers, too, social protection schemes need to be discussed and negotiated with organisations.

SEWA's work shows that, in some instances, workers themselves can provide better social security systems than the state. The ILO's Strategies and Tools against Social Exclusion and Poverty (STEP) antipoverty programme is "based on the assumption that the extension of social protection to the informal sector is not feasible through national systems of social security" (ILO/TUIS 1999:36–37). Whether this is generally true, and to what extent, remains to be proven. In any event, however, the state remains responsible for the social protection of workers in informal employment.

The question, then, is this: how can the state strengthen and help develop alternative systems that may be developed by informal sector organisations, through funds, political and technical support, and make the employers accountable for them? Political support includes providing the legal space and framework for trade unions and informal sector organisations to provide social support services for all workers. In such cases, the state would remain responsible but would play an enabling rather than an implementing role.

At the same time, it remains "vital to ensure that formal sector employers do not see [voluntary grass roots schemes] as a cheap substitute for social security and thus as an encouragement to informalise more of their activities" (ILO/TUIS 1999:37). Extension of the state systems already in place must remain on the agenda of all workers' organisations. The ILO could serve as a forum for a discussion amongst trade union organisations, including informal sector workers' organisations, on the evolution of social protection systems to ensure social protection for all workers.

Internal Programme

Organising strategies. The ILO could also be the most appropriate facilitator for meetings involving all those involved in the issue—unions already organising informal sector workers (see above), other informal workers' associations, supportive NGOs, international trade union organisations and international networks of informal sector workers—for the purpose of developing coordinated organising strategies and practical cooperation in organising as well as building coalitions and alliances and developing a programme of common demands. There is a need for international meetings of this kind as well as regional meetings.

Coordination. International trade union organisations should have a contact person for the informal sector to whom all others involved in an issue can refer. Almost every ITS could have activities and membership in the informal sector. In the ICFTU, the Equality Department has already functioned in practice as a contact point. Such contact points are necessary to provide permanence and continuity to cooperation in organising and in pushing common demands.

Cooperatives. The creation of cooperatives can be an important flanking support measure for informal sector workers organisations, as it is already for unions in many countries (see also ILO/TUIS 1999:52). This role of cooperatives and their relevance to informal sector organisation could be discussed with information and advice from the International Cooperative Alliance and the ILO Cooperative Branch, among others. For example, the Friedrich Ebert Stiftung in Germany has a cooperatives department.

Education. Study circles have proved a successful didactic method in organising women workers in the informal sector (ILO/TUIS

1999:52–3). In this context, it should be noted that, beginning in 1997, the International Federation of Workers' Education Associations (IFWEA) has been developing an international study circle pro-gramme. These are local study circles, linked through the Internet, discussing the same issue simultaneously in different countries (IFWEA 1999). One of the current circles deals with "Women and the Global Food Industry". Others, conducted in partnership with ITSs, deal with transnational corporations. The IFWEA will work with any labour movement organisation and prolabour NGOs interested in organising informal sector workers and therefore—of necessity—conducting workers' education. It may be objected that informal sector workers are unlikely to own a computer or be able to access the Internet unless they are teleworkers, but this argument only strengthens the case for organisation: they can be members of local organisations that do have access to such technologies. In that respect, their situation is no different from that of formal sector workers in low-paid and low-skilled jobs. IFWEA's experience has shown that such obstacles can be overcome.

At the national level, a number of workers' education institutions and organisations have worked with informal sector workers in their own countries. For example, this year the Workers' Education Asso-ciation in Zambia has been instrumental in organising the Lusaka Street Traders' Association, which then affiliated to the Zambian Congress of Trade Unions.

On another educational front, HomeNet/StreetNet/WIEGO could produce an educational package to be used by ITSs, the IFWEA, national trade union centers or national unions in organising campaigns. Popular materials about existing organisations could be developed, people from these organisations could be identified who could talk about their experiences and—resources permitting—exchange pro-grammes and visits could be organised.

Representation. As we have seen, informal sector workers spon-taneously organise, sometimes with the help of unions or supportive NGOs. After the initial stages, they then face the difficulty of sustain-ing and developing their organisations. One of the main problems is that these organisations usually remain unrecognised by those with whom they need to bargain (public authorities, contractors, etc). For example, street vendors' organisations should be recognised by the police and municipal authorities and home-based workers' organisations by the labour department, the contractors and the employers. Their international networks should be recognised by the appropriate inter-national institutions. This is generally not the case today.

A related issue is that policies that affect informal sector workers are made without consultation with their organisations and therefore work against their interests. For example, urban planners never consult street vendors, and hence never plan for them. In some cases, collectors of forest produce have to sell to forest departments at prices determined by committees where the collectors have no representation and no role. Except for as yet rare instances where they have achieved genuine bargaining power and legal protection, home-based workers and domestic workers remain unprotected from employers who offer work on a take-it-or-leave-it basis. This lack of visibility and recognition has been an obstacle to the growth of informal sector organisations and in some cases a threat to their survival. A successful organising strategy therefore requires securing recognition and representation at the different levels required, first for organisations that already exist. The trade union movement is in the best position to help informal sector workers secure such recognition and representation.

The first step would be to make a start in the movement itself and in the institutions where it is represented. At the present time, informal sector workers are generally not represented in the institutions and organisations of the labour movement. Even though individual trade unions do organise informal sector workers in an number of cases (see above), national trade union federations make no provision for their representation within their structures. The same is true for the international trade union federations. Within the ILO structures, informal sector workers are not represented.

National trade union centers, the ITSs, the ICFTU and the ETUC should examine ways in which appropriate forms of representation of informal sector workers can be introduced in their structures, as well as ways in which formal cooperation with existing informal sector organisations can be established. The contact points suggested above could be a starting point. A working party could also be formed for that purpose, with a clear mandate to bring the organisations into the national and international trade union movement, not to keep them out.

Finally, the ILO should establish a special section to service informal sector workers, preferably within the Bureau for Workers Activities.

Conclusion

Organising in the informal sector takes place where the traditional labour movement intersects with the broader civil society. It is therefore intimately linked with the issue of engaging with civil society

Table 2: Acronyms Used in This Chapter

ACTRAV	Commonly used French acronym of Bureau for Workers' Affairs (ILO): Bureau des activités pour les travailleurs
BWA	Bureau for Workers Affairs (of the ILO)
COSATU	Congress of South African Trade Unions
EPZ	Export Processing Zones
ETUC	European Trade Union Confederation
FILTEA-CGIL	Federazione Italiana Lavoratori Tessili e Abbigliamento—Confederazione Generale Italiana del Lavoro
FNV	Federatie Nederlandse Vakbeweging (Federation of Netherlands Trade Unions)
FNV Vrouwenbond	FNV Women's Union
GLI	Global Labour Institute
HKCTU	Hong Kong Confederation of Trade Unions
HKMP	Hind Khet Mazdoor Panchayat (India)
ICEM	International Federation of Chemical, Energy, Mine and General Workers' Unions
ICFTU	International Confederation of Free Trade Unions
IFWEA	International Federation of Workers' Education Associations
ILO	International Labour Organisation/International Labour Office
IMF	International Metalworkers' Federation
ISC	International Study Circles (of IFWEA)
ITGLWF	International Textile, Garment and Leather Workers' Federation
ITS	International Trade Secretariat
IUF	International Union of Food, Agricultural, Hotel, Restaurant, Catering, Tobacco and Allied Workers' Associations
MST	Movimento Sim Terra/Landless Workers' Movement (Brazil)
NGO	Non-Governmental Organisation
OECD	Organisation for Economic Cooperation and Development
SEWA	Self-Employed Women's Association (India)
SEWU	Self-Employed Women's Union (South Africa)
SIBTTA	Sindicato dos Trabalhadores da Indústria Bordados, Tapeçarias, Texteis e Artesanato da Região Autónoma de Madeira (Portugal)
STEP	Strategies and Tools against Social Exclusion and Poverty (ILO Programme)
TCFUA	Textile, Clothing and Footwear Union of Australia
UDTS	Union Démocratique des Travailleurs Senegalais
UNITE	Union of Needletrades, Industrial and Textile Employees
WCL	World Confederation of Labour
WIEGO	Women in Informal Employment Globalising and Organising

and of forming broad alliances to advance a common agenda. A basic overarching principle in this common agenda is human rights: labour organizing is essentially a human rights issue. Workers, wherever they may be, organise to defend their rights as human beings. Ultimately, all union organisation is based on the defence of human dignity; everything else—wages, working conditions, benefits—follows from this basic issue. Every wage increase, every reduction in working time, every improvement in working conditions, every guarantee for job security opens up an additional space of freedom for the worker as an individual, a space of individual freedom and self-expression that can only be achieved by solidarity and by collective action. As important as any of these is the sense of being able to stand up to the boss.

If the rights of workers as workers are a human rights issue, workers' rights are a union rights issue because workers have no other way to express their collective interest, or to effectively defend their individual interest, except through independent and democratic trade unions. Nowhere is this more evident than in the case of workers in informal employment. These are the most exploited and most unprotected of all workers, whose dignity is constantly challenged by their conditions of survival. Here is where labour must join forces with the women's movement and human rights movements. Campaigning for the human rights of informal sector workers, and helping them organise into unions, is a crucial contribution to the social movement of tomorrow.

Endnotes

[1] An International Symposium on Trade Unions and the Informal Sector, organised by the Bureau for Workers' Activity of the ILO, was held in Geneva from 18 to 22 October 1999. The meeting was attended by 31 trade unionists from as many countries in Africa, Asia Pacific, Europe, Latin America, and North America, 16 observers from five ITSs, the ICFTU, and the WCL, moderators from the ILO, speakers from the ILO, ITSs, ICFTU, and WCL, and ILO officials. The following propositions have been edited from a contribution to this discussion by WIEGO (Women in Informal Employment Globalising and Organising). The previous version of this chapter was prepared by Dan Gallin (Global Labour Institute), with contributions from Martha Chen (Harvard University), Renana Jhabvala (Self Employed Women's Association, India) and Jane Tate (HomeNet, UK), as the WIEGO position paper for the October 1999 ILO meeting. Table 2 presents a list of the acronyms used in this chapter.

[2] This reference, which will recur frequently, is to the background paper of the ILO Bureau for Workers' Activities. For details, see References section.

[3] WIEGO (Women in Informal Employment Globalizing and Organizing), established in early 1997, is an international network of individuals from unions, academic institutions, and international development agencies concerned with improving the conditions and advancing the interests of women in the informal economy through better

statistics, research, programmes, and policies. It includes already existing women workers' organisations, some of which are themselves international networks (such as HomeNet [homeworkers] and StreetNet [street vendors]) or national unions (such as the Self-Employed Women's Association [India] and the Self-Employed Women's Union [South Africa]). Some of the unions participating in WIEGO are members of national trade union centers in their home countries, and some are affiliated to one or several ITSs and to the IFWEA. WIEGO organisations—particularly SEWA and HomeNet—have worked closely with the international trade union movement in securing the adoption of the ILO Home Work Convention, 1966 (No 177). One of the WIEGO programmes supports organising of women workers in informal employment at both the national and international levels.

References

International Confederation of Free Trade Unions (ICFTU) (1999) *From Asia to Russia to Brazil—The Cost of the Crisis.* Brussels: International Confederation of Free Trade Unions

International Federation of Workers' Education Associations (IFWEA) (1999) *Responding to Globalisation—International Study Circles.* Manchester: International Federation of Workers' Education Associations

International Labour Office (ILO) (1998) *The Asian Financial Crisis—The Challenge for Social Policy.* Geneva: International Labour Office

International Labour Office (ILO)/Trade Unions Internationals (TUIS) (1999) *Trade Unions and the Informal Sector: Towards a Comprehensive Strategy.* ILO reference BP/TUIS/99. Geneva: International Labour Organisation/Bureau for Workers' Affairs

Resources

Global Labour Institute. HTML file: <URL: http://www.global-labour.org>

HomeNet. Website. HTML file: <URL: http://www.homenetww.org.uk>

International Federation of Workers' Education Associations/International Study Circles. HTML file: <URL: http://www.ifwea.org/isc>

International Labour Organisation/Bureau for Workers' Activities. Route des Morillons 4, CH-1211 Geneva 22. Fax: +41 22-799 67 50. E-mail: actrav@ilo.org. HTML file: <URL: http://www.ilo.org/actrav>

WIEGO. HRML file: <URL: http://www.wiego.org/>

Dan Gallin is Chair of the Global Labour Institute (GLI), a foundation established in 1997 with a secretariat in Geneva. The GLI investigates the consequences of the globalisation of the world economy for workers and trade unions and develops international strategies for the labour movement. It works with WIEGO on the organisation of the informal sector. Gallin is coordinator of the WIEGO Organization and Representation Programme. From 1960 until 1997, Gallin worked for the IUF (the International Federation of Unions in Food, Agriculture and Catering), as General Secretary beginning in 1968. Since 1992, Gallin has also been the president of the International Federation of Workers' Education Associations (IFWEA), an organisation of labour educational institutions and labour service organisations.

13

A Manifesto against Femicide

Melissa W Wright

In Ciudad Juárez, a group of feminist activists has established the city's first sexual assault center, called Casa Amiga. They accomplished this feat after launching a social movement on several fronts against the notion that Juarense women are cheap, promiscuous, and not worth efforts to provide them a safe refuge from domestic violence, incest, and rape. The essay explores their efforts as a means for asserting the value of women in Ciudad Juárez, an assertion with reverberating effects in the *maquiladora* industry that has prospered based on this image of Juarense women. By combining a Marxist critique of value with post-structuralist analyses of the subject, the essay argues that projects such as Casa Amiga represent plausible sites for the organizing of alliances whose objective is to reverse the depreciation of laborers.

> The object before us, to begin with, [is] *material production.*
>
> (Marx 1993:84)

> That matter is always materialized has, I think, to be thought in relation to the productive and, indeed, materializing effects of regulatory power ...
>
> (Butler 1993:9)

Ciudad Juárez, Chihuahua has long been famous for women. By the middle of the last century, the city had become known for prostitutes and the brothels that were favorite haunts of American military men. It was a place many American teens would go to for their "first experience" or where fathers would take their sons for theirs (Nathan 1999). From the 1970s onwards, the female *maquila* worker joined the prostitute as the city's icon.[1] The transnational firms seeking "docile" and "cheap" labor sought such extensive supplies of female workers that women poured into the border city and transformed it from a predominantly agricultural city to one with a bustling nightlife. Downtown clubs and bars shocked many when they began catering to the young female maquila labor force that loves to dance. And the image of the maquila worker as "whore" was inaugurated.[2] Then, in the 1990s, Ciudad Juárez gained fame as the city of murdered women when almost 200 female corpses surfaced in the desert over a five-year period, many showing signs of rape and torture (Candia et al 1999). International news agencies ran headlines such as "Who is killing the women of Juárez?" Finally, Ciudad Juárez is the city that boasts Esther Chávez Cano, perhaps Mexico's currently most renowned feminist activist.

With an activist coalition she helped establish, Chávez is fighting against the famous spectre that now haunts Ciudad Juárez—the spectre of the worthless woman. This spectre is of the woman not worth protecting as she goes to work in the maquilas and then dances afterwards, the one who is not worth the cost of her own social reproduction, the one whose death is insignificant—the one, in short, who does not have value. Chávez has called the object of her struggle "*femenicidio,*" or "femicide." "When we say women are worthless," she explained, "this is *femenicidio.*" Femicide recreates the mythic worthless women who inhabit Ciudad Juárez. With the help of local and international activists, Chávez has launched a public war against femicide. "It is everywhere. In our homes, in our schools, in the maquila," she has said. "It is a crisis. When we look at women as if they were trash, then something is wrong" (author interview).[3]

Inspired by Chávez (and always by Marx), I say it is high time that people who oppose the notion of *worthless* women should openly, in the face of the whole world, publish their views, their aims, and their tendencies, and should meet this nursery tale of the spectre of worthless women with a manifesto. This manifesto would require international and national coalitions, and an alliance between labor groups in the US with resources and desires for cross-border organizing with those people waging a war against femicide in Ciudad Juárez. This essay is an attempt to think through such an alliance.

Introduction: Casa Amiga

In February 1999, Chávez, along with a group of Juarense women[4] and some international activists,[5] founded Casa Amiga: Centro de Crisis, Ciudad Juárez' first and only rape crisis and sexual assault center. To date, Chávez (who is the director), a paid staff of three, four volunteer psychologists, and several dozen volunteers have attended to hundreds of calls on rape, incest, and assault. Funds for the center have come from domestic and international sources. Chávez attributes her ability to organize the necessary resources for its founding to the international and national outrage over the women's murders. "When I started getting interviews (CNN, *The New York Times*, *People Magazine*, ABC's '20-20', to name a few), I knew we had an opportunity to do something," she said. She and the others involved in the project raised funds for modestly renovating a house near downtown that had been donated for the center. She received a grant from the Global Fund for Women for computers, obtained donations for staff training, and sought other equipment money from the maquila sector. "Our fridge and fax came from a maquila," she said. However, the center is struggling financially. "We have no operating budget," she explained. "It's easier to raise money for computers than for expenses. So we don't have enough for salaries or even to pay our phone bill." Indeed, the initial attention and funds that opened Casa Amiga's doors have not transformed into an ongoing basis of support for its maintenance. Therefore, Chávez and the others committed to the center's operation are not only providing a refuge from violence, therapy, legal counsel, and medical attention to assault victims; they are also having to write proposals and perform the public outreach necessary to generate financial support for the center's survival. "I hope we're here next year," said Chávez."If we're not, then what will women have in this city? It's a terrible thought. This place has saved women's lives."

The relationship between Casa Amiga and the survival of women in the city has been outlined by many. Ciudad Juárez is renowned for violence. The city has outpaced Mexico City as the country's murder capital (Nathan 1999), with the homicide rate for both men and women escalating over the last five years.[6] While the murder rate for women is far less than that for men, it is significantly higher than statistics reveal for female homicides per capita in any other major city in Mexico or in the United States. Still, Chávez frequently comes up against the notion that rape and even the murder of women are not problems warranting public discussion.

> We are fighting a battle against the people who always blame the victim. It's always her fault. How can it be a 15-year-old girl's fault when her uncle rapes her? Or the woman whose husband beats her everyday? Or the young woman who is kidnapped on the way to work in a maquila? This is what we're fighting against to save these women's lives.

That Casa Amiga is about saving women's lives by helping women regain their self-respect and self-confidence was reaffirmed by a staff member, who put it this way: "It is satisfying to see them return to their activities and recapture their self-confidence, to remember their ambitions and desires. When you see this then you realize that this group [Casa Amiga] is existing for a reason, because if it weren't here, many more lives would probably be lost" (Galindo 2000).[7]

This essay is a thought piece for linking the efforts behind Casa Amiga with organizing initiatives for workers in the maquilas. I attempt to dispel the notion that sexual assault centers and labor groups have explicitly distinct projects, even if we recognize their overlapping concern of human rights. My timing is strategic. This essay represents part of an ongoing dialogue among union members, community activists, and scholars on the left, who are figuring out how to build coalitions across different sorts of organizations (Craft 1990; Naples 1998; Johns and Vural 2000; Wills forthcoming). As part of this concerted effort, I am writing this essay now because a number of US labor groups, principal among them the AFL-CIO and the Teamsters, have launched initiatives for cross-border organizing with Mexican workers. While it seems most logical that unions would turn their efforts and resources toward the creation of independent[8] unions in Mexico and a class-based approach to capitalist exploitation, I urge us to consider moving beyond this approach if the goal is to enhance the value of working people in a cross-border alliance. I believe that workers' groups in the United States that want to make inroads into the maquiladora sector should support Casa Amiga and other such enterprises as part of an international organizing project.

My reasoning is this: We must take seriously the historical and geographic contingency of organizing, and, in Ciudad Juárez, union organizing—despite many attempts at it—has not proven popular among maquila workers. While there have been a number of efforts to organize independent unions in the maquilas, efforts which deserve international attention, there is no evidence to support the idea that these are the only or even the best options for enhancing the value of maquila workers in northern Mexico. Moreover, such efforts have typically been most successful among male workers and in factories employing a smaller percentage of women than is present in many maquilas. This is not an insignificant phenomenon in an industry that has historically relied upon the labor of women for its profit. That female Mexican workers have not joined unions en masse does not mean that these workers reject protest. In fact, female employees have, as I explain further below and elsewhere (Wright 1997), forced work stoppages and other disruptions over a number of issues. The challenge for those groups trying to form cross-border alliances is to strategize on how connections can be made between the diverse, local expressions of protest and US-based union efforts to organize workers

internationally. Closer attention must be paid to the many ways that
people challenge the different mechanisms aimed at their devaluation
and fight it out. Casa Amiga represents a site where women and men
are conscious of a conflict over the worthiness of the women of
Ciudad Juárez and are indeed fighting it out.

By using a Marxian critique of the labor theory of value, along with
a poststructuralist critique of the material subject, I shall try to
demonstrate how Casa Amiga's efforts to fight against the cheapening
of women are completely in line with union efforts to strengthen the
value of workers. Casa Amiga presents an opportunity for disrupting
the reproduction of a resource very valuable to the capitalist maquiladora enterprises in Ciudad Juárez: the disposable woman. Her
reproduction as a disposable human resource of labor is a linchpin of
maquiladora production and profit today. I hope to show how, in today's
Ciudad Juárez, Casa Amiga threatens the machinery dedicated to this
reproduction.

Background

The maquiladoras have been in business since the mid-1960s, when
they were called "twin plants" under the Border Industrialization
Program. They are export-processing facilities that do not pay tariffs
on the value-added during the manufacture process for exportable
goods; with recent NAFTA amendments, additional tariffs have also
been relaxed on nonexported products. There are more than 3000
maquilas, employing almost a million workers throughout the country,
with Ciudad Juárez claiming almost 400 facilities and about 250,000
maquila employees. While women dominated the employee base for
the industry's first 30 years (at 80% through the early 1980s), the
mixture of women and men is now about 50:50. Women still represent
the large majority of assembly workers, often above 70% in labor-
intensive operations, with men dominating the salaried supervisory
and technical positions.

Corporations with maquila facilities have fared well over the years,
and the number of maquilas is continually on the rise, especially since
the 1994 NAFTA agreement. If wages are any indication, workers
have done less well (Cravey 1998). Having withstood two devastating
currency devaluations, one in 1982 and the other in 1994, the average
paycheck has lost almost 50% of its buying power over the last 20
years. Maquila workers today earn about $4.00 a day.

Despite this blatant divorcing of productivity from wage increases,
independent worker organizations have not gained a solid foothold

in the maquila industry. This is not for lack of trying. Several valiant efforts to establish an independent union in a GE operation in Ciudad Juárez and in a Han Young facility in Tijuana led to protracted walk-outs, hunger strikes, and occasionally violent interactions between workers and the police-supported management. In both cases, contro-versies revolved around the workers' efforts to elect independent representation that would replace the government and company-friendly union, the CTM, or the labor federation, the CROC, institu-tional stalwarts since the 1930s. The workers at Han Young succeeded in enforcing their vote for the independent union, although they have had to protect this success several times over the last few years. More recently, a lengthy international campaign to support the replacement of the CTM by a local union at the Duro Bag Company in Rio Bravo, Taumalipas resulted in only four workers out of 498 voting for the independent union. These results have received international criticism, since the union election was not conducted by secret ballot and many who had publicly supported the independent union had already been fired (Naumann 2001).

Besides these organizing attempts, few others have made national news and fewer still international, and the organizing trend has not made much headway in Chihuahua. The most active independent labor group along the Chihuahua border, Frente Auténtico de Trabajo (FAT), has been trying since the early 1990s to gain a foothold in Ciudad Juárez. In 1996, with support from the Teamsters and the United Electrical Workers union (UE), FAT opened a worker center in Ciudad Juárez, with the aim of serving as a central location for organizing and educational activities. The center's educational programs have been very popular among the women workers; the organizing activities have been less so. While the efforts to organize independent unions deserve continued support, perhaps other strategies for enhancing worker value could be considered given the range of worker participation in different social organizations.

Non-union-linked protests have occasionally made the headlines and stifled production. For instance, after the December 1994 devalu-ations, several thousand workers walked off the line in a number of facilities. They demanded pay increases to offset the devaluation, which directly affected Juarense households in the form of higher rents and utilities and higher prices for just about every conceivable consumable good. The most notable among these walkouts was the 5600-worker walkout at the Ciudad Juárez Thompson-Electronic RCA television factory, which is still the country's largest maquila in terms of employee numbers, most of whom are women. However, despite this work stoppage, independent union representation was not achieved at RCA, although it was briefly attempted. Other protests— usually not covered in the newspapers and communicated only by word of mouth—have included work stoppages over cafeteria food poisonings, cut vacation time, and management refusals to respect certain key holidays, such as the Mother's Day celebration on 10 May. Workers have also refused to work when a favorite supervisor has been passed over for a promotion (Wright 1997). Such spontaneous expressions of protest belie claims that Mexican workers are culturally incapable of challenging authority and that Mexican women are too docile to stand up for themselves (cf Fernandez-Kelly 1983; Salzinger 1997). Still, for the most part, the call for unionization is not commonly heard among the maquila labor force.

However, the revelation in 1995 that over 50 women had been murdered and dumped in the desert since 1993 sparked a wave of protest that cut across the city. News of the murders was publicized in large part because Chávez had been compiling a list of names and murder dates from the back pages of the newspaper *El Diario de Ciudad Juárez* since 1993. Then a retired accountant, occasional activist, and member of the editorial board for *El Diario*, Chávez told me just after the news broke that she couldn't sleep anymore. She began to imagine what was happening in the city. "I realized something had changed here," she said, "This city had become a place for murdering and dumping women."

In 1995, Chávez and a fledgling feminist group called the Ocho de Marzo (after March 8th, International Women's Day), organized marches in which maquila workers, students, professionals, middle- and upper-class residents, labor activists, and artists blocked downtown streets. They painted utility polls pink and attached black ribbons to them. They blocked entrances to city buildings. They interrupted politicians' press conferences. Chávez's eloquence in such situations made her popular with the domestic and then the international press for quotes, and a movement to find the killers and stop the violence was suddenly launched. Chávez and the Ocho de Marzo pressured the federal government for a special prosecutor. They hounded the local police and mayor to dedicate more resources toward resolving the crimes and preventing new ones. They publicly criticized the police and mayor for ignoring the crimes and for ridiculing distraught families by claiming that their daughters, sisters, mothers, and cousins were whores. They met with the maquiladora association, known as the AMAC, to discuss the changing of shifts and security measures, though to little avail. They organized weekly searches for bodies through the desert areas where a number of the dead women and girls had been found. These efforts have met with some resistance: Chávez and others have been called "lesbians" by people hoping to humiliate them into silence, and Chávez has received threats.

As a result of such efforts, however, there has been an impressive outpouring of sympathy from national and international sources. "We knew," said Chávez, "that this was the time to act. If it hadn't been for the all of the attention to the murders, we wouldn't have Casa Amiga." In almost all of the international coverage on the murders, a connection has been made linking the crimes to the existence of the city's maquilas. By 1999, maquila workers accounted for about 30 of the victims. A suspect convicted for one murder had been a chemist in one factory. Other suspects still awaiting trial include five bus drivers for the companies contracted by the maquiladora industries to provide transportation service to specific neighborhoods. These men were discovered when a 13-year-old girl survived an assault and, having been left for dead in the desert, named her assailant as the driver of her company bus. She had been the last passenger on the route.

Yet despite this obvious overlap between maquiladora activity— given that a number of the victims were employees abducted on their daily commute, some apparently by company bus drivers—the maquiladora association has steadfastly refused to admit any connections tying the industry to the murders. Instead, along with a number of public officials, they implicate a Mexican culture that has been undermined by drugs, loose women, nefarious American influences, and weak family values (Tabuenca Córdoba 1995–1996). Their response has typically involved the following logic: factories have nothing to do with it; it's just a coincidence that the women in Juárez are being stalked on their way to and from work; therefore the maquilas owe nothing to efforts to stop the violence.

If we can make a connection linking the murders and sexual assault to the organization of production within the maquiladoras, could we not also make a connection between efforts to stop the violence and disruptions to these production systems?

In a previous article, I theorized the connections linking the production of value within the maquilas to the wasting of women inside and outside of them (Wright 1999). This connection becomes clear if we scrutinize a managerial discourse of turnover that is widely told within the maquiladora industry to explain why women are not trainable employees. It is a discourse, I maintain, for guiding an interpretation of women as imminently disposable due to their alleged intrinsic untrainability, which, in the world of manufacture, means that they are seen as lacking the ability to acquire skills. Consequently, according to this discourse, they do not gain valuable work experience over time; they simply get worn out. As their fingers stiffen, their eyes tire, their backs ache, and their migraines intensify—among other symptoms of repetitive stress syndrome—they become obsolete. Many leave of their own volition, as they can find work in a different maquila (still at the bottom of the pay scale) doing a different task that demands different muscles and forms of concentration. The maquila industry relies upon this constant mobility of female workers into and out of facilities, providing continual flexibility without diminishing the labor supply. I liken this pattern of women coming and going from one workplace to another to a form of corporate death. A woman's work experience in one maquila is completely erased when she assumes employment in another, as if her life in the previous company had never existed. Her past experience or work life completely disappears, and her future is full of such disappearances.

This pattern of coming and going reveals a cycle of consumption and discarding of women, as if they are always located in a cycle of waste. Eventually, since they are deemed to be untrainable, they will need to be discarded. I maintain that this maquila system, which revolves around the reproduction of disposable women, draws from many of the same discourses that are utilized to exculpate the maquila industry from the violence against women that continues to pervade Ciudad Juárez. It is in the overlapping of these discourses that I locate the complicity between maquiladora activity and the murdering and dumping of women throughout the city. This connection is also made by activists such as Chávez who, while not blaming the maquilas for the murders, maintain that they were exacerbated by a "social and economic violence against women in Ciudad Juárez" (author interview).

To make the connection between the turnover cycle and the violence against women in Ciudad Juárez, I combine Marx's critique of capital with Judith Butler's poststructuralist analyis of material production. This maneuver is not as complicated as one might expect given the vituperative exchanges cleaving poststructuralism from Marxism. A common thread fundamental to both theorists is the assumption that matter is always being produced; it has no terminus, only the appearance of such.[9] This theoretical discussion is central to my analysis of how turnover relates to the murders of women in Ciudad Juárez, and therefore central to my efforts to reveal how Casa Amiga challenges the organization of maquiladora production. In the next section I use Harvey's rendition of the circuits of capital detailed in Marx's critique to argue that working with Casa Amiga (as an example) should be considered as central to any project dedicated to disrupting the cheapening of human labor. Support of this group would be in direct support of a politics aimed at improving the standing of workers in relation to capital. It may take a bit of creativity to see the connections, but—in the spirit of Marx—it is a creativity the aim of which is to unveil the fluid relationships behind the apparently staid nature of subjects and their subjectivity.

Common Ground

The exploitation of value from human labor, says Marx, relies upon a dissociation of this value from the value of the laborer. The laborer is worth only the value of labor power, which is expressed through the payment of wages, whereas, the value of labor is realized through the exchange of useful goods. If the capitalist enterprise is to flourish, the value of the former must be less than the sum value of the latter. Otherwise, no profit is made and the venture fails. Key, then, is the recognition of the lesser value of labor power when compared to the value of abstract labor.

Technological innovation, says Marx, works toward this goal. Technology, or "the means of production," has the explicit purpose of cheapening labor power by enhancing the harvesting of relative surplus value. Harvey (1982) illustrates this relationship by detailing the circuits of capital and the important role of technology for the continual flow of capitalist value. He graphs the circuitry with the following formula: Money (M) is exchanged for commodities (C), which are put into the production process (P) and result in transformed commodities (C') which are then exchanged for money in the marketplace. The formula reads: M-C ... P ... C'-M'. The C consumed in production includes the means of production (MP), such as material inputs and technology, and the labor power (LP) necessary for production, so that C=MP+LP. The ratio of MP and LP must be such that a surplus is generated, as symbolized by C', which represents profit as realized for the exchange of M'. The technological component of MP represents an expense to capital that is justified by the costs it saves, or the value it mines, from labor by, for instance, increasing the average production output per worker—without increasing the cost of labor power—and thereby enhancing profit. Put another way, the energy of the worker (labor power) is cheapened, since technological aids mean more of it is dedicated to the labor process without an increase in the wages paid for this energy. Thus, concludes Marx (1988, 71) in *The Economic and Philosophical*

Manuscripts, "The worker becomes all the poorer the more wealth he produces" (Marx 1988, 71).

Over the last 50 years, labor unions in the United States have worked hard to link productivity to wages in an effort to curb the cheapening impact of technology on labor power. Obviously these efforts have resulted in substantial protections for workers across sectors, from industrial to administrative work. This strategy came under attack in the US during the 1980s, due in part to its effectiveness, and has been blamed for the flight of industries into the Mexico maquiladora program. After much soul-searching, as more industries have relocated to Mexico and during the NAFTA debates, many US labor groups are now poised to strategize over how to continue their project across national, cultural, linguistic, and class differences. This is a daunting task, but one that must be inaugurated for the gains made by labor groups in the US not to disappear completely.

How to do it? This question has been raised over the last several years by a number of labor and community activists in both the US and Mexico. As one activist who works with the Tennessee Industrial Renewal Network told me in the mid-1990s, "It's really hard to know where to begin when you've got some worker wanting a benefits package in terms of stock options and another wanting a food basket." Adding to the challenge of finding a common ground among workers in the US and Mexico is the difficulty of organizing independent unions in Mexico. Even the leader of FAT admitted to me in 1994, "It's very hard to organize a migrant and female population in Mexico," a sentiment shared a few years later by the director of the FAT worker center. So the question remains: how to stymie the continual cheapening of workers in Ciudad Juárez? How can we use Marx's insight into the intimate relationship binding technology to the cheapening of labor power to organize cross-border alliances in the contemporary context of Ciudad Juárez' maquiladora industries?

In considering this question, I have found the poststructuralist feminist critiques of Marxism to be helpful for expanding the possible conceptualizations of the relationship between technology and the cheapening of laboring subjects. First, there is the critique of experience (See Scott 1993), which shatters the assumption that the experience of class subsumes other life experiences. Life is just too complicated for a politics based on that assumption. Secondly, as feminist scholars and activists have urged, why not look at other forms of solidarity that bolster class positions by reaffirming the idea that different life experiences can contribute positively to coalition building across social groups (See Young 1990; Patel 1999)? I think a reading of Marx that emphasizes his view of materiality as in a constant state of production allows for an intersection with post-structuralist views of subjectivity to expand the concept of subversion to include the subversion of the discursive technologies so necessary to the devaluation of human beings.[10] This reading of Marx utilizes his critique of value without circumscribing a vision of subversive agency to a strict allegiance to class politics, especially when there is little empirical evidence to support this approach.

Judith Butler's work on the discursive production of the material provides a necessary theoretical dimension to a consideration of how discursive technologies in the maquilas contribute to the production of the Mexican woman as waste. Her attack on the sexual foundation of the subject also delves into the apparent stasis of material—in this case the materiality of the human body—to reveal the constant whir of processes behind the creation of bodies as stable material entities, which ground subjects distinguished by sex and sexuality. It is through the reification of such subjects, she maintains, that hierarchies of sex difference and sexuality are reproduced as if naturally foundational (Butler 1993).

Applying this insight regarding the fluid materiality of the grounded subject to Marx's critique of value, which is critical for exposing a specific materiality to what we call capitalism, I argue that the managerial discourse of turnover functions as a technology for shaping a homogenous subject, referred to as the Mexican woman, into the form of waste in the making. This subject represents human disposability.[11] Her body—hands, eyes, back, and womb, to name a few parts—surfaces in managerial explanations for why women maquila workers are not trainable and constantly turning over. "When you have female workers here in Juárez," one plant manager told me, "you can expect to have high turnover." According to the logic embedded within this turnover discourse, a worker who turns over—who does not return to work—is not worth training. The training or investment in her skill development would be wasted, because the chances of the worker turning that investment into further value by applying the skill to the labor process are not sufficiently high. Therefore, if a worker is seen to be the kind of subject who is likely to turn over, that worker is not viewed as a good candidate for skills training. In fact, that worker is intrinsically designed to be temporary, because the value that she brings to the workplace diminishes over time, rather than increasing.

The explanation of Mexican women as likely to turn over due to their cultural roles as wives and mothers and their lack of ambition ties into a discourse of turnover as indicative of worker disposability.

The assumption is that each individual instance of the Mexican female subject will turn over before she has acquired any skills. However, her labor is still desired in the maquiladora industry due to another related discourse that explains that Mexican women are, as a homogenous group, dexterous, attentive to detail, and docile. Such discourses only make sense when they are familiar both to those who tell them and to those who fight against them. References to female disposability resulting from lack of trainability abound in feminist studies of the workplace (Cockburn 1983; Elson and Pearson 1989; McDowell 1997).

And at this time in Ciudad Juárez, these discourses of female disposability, via the explanation of the female laborer's propensity to turn over, works into and supports other discourses of women in Mexico as already on the road to waste. We see this, for instance, as government and industry officials wonder if the women and girls killed on their way to work in the maquilas are worthy of our concern. The blaming of female victims of rape and even murder is all too familiar to those who try to problematize such events in contexts where we still scrutinize the victim's behavior for clues to her own traumatic ordeal. In Ciudad Juárez, these familiar choruses blaming women both for their own murders and for their disposability to the firm operate in tandem as exculpatory narratives for averting scrutiny of maquiladora accountability regarding worker safety, worker training, and infrastructural development. In addition, they deflect attention from the actual murderers. By locating the cause of female disposability within the bodies of the women themselves, the discourses ensure that victims materialize in the shape of their own undoing. We see it in their legs and breasts, exposed to view by short skirts and tight blouses, understood to be invitations for murder and evidence of women's lack of seriousness on the job (Wright 1999; Salzinger 1997). Such familiar notions as that that female sexuality, when perceived as overtly expressed, invites violence underscore the advice given by the Ciudad Juárez police department when they urged women who feared an attack to vomit on their aggressors as a way to make themselves less sexually inviting.

We also see the women's accountability for their own deaths in the physical location of their remains in the desert. This is seen as evidence of imprudent behavior; the question is asked: "What was she doing out there anyway?" We search a victim's body and life for answers to the questions that could be asked of maquila employees. Why was she so vulnerable when changing buses on her way home from the second shift? Why didn't anyone come to her assistance?

To which the resounding answer—by the police, public officials, and spokespeople for the maquiladora industry—has been: because of who she is. As Roberto Urrea, the former president of AMAC, said in an ABC "20-20" interview in 1999, "Where was she when she was last seen? In front of her plant or at a bar on Juárez avenida." Taken out of context, it is unclear why Urrea is referring to a woman's disappearance. Is she missing from work—or missing from life? What we do know is that, if she is in the wrong place, her disappearance is not worrisome, since there is nothing we can do to help a woman who is as likely to go to a bar as she is to go to work.[12]

Chávez and the others who founded Casa Amiga have challenged such discourses, which coalesce into a vision of female disposability, with a competing one. "We are fighting the idea that women aren't worth anything," Chávez has said. They say that the roots of femicide lie in a vision of Juárez women as worth less than what they offer to their families and to the workplace. Chávez said, "A woman goes to work so she can support her family. She works hard for the company, but when she is killed, people say she was a prostitute that isn't worth anything." The roots of this worthlessness, she says, are found in the home, on the street, and in the workplace. They are found in police apathy toward the crime. They surface in the refusal by maquiladora managers to enhance safety measures for their commuting workers. They can be seen in the blaming of women and girls for their own brutal murders. This is femicide: a climate for declaring women so unworthy that their deaths do not warrant concern.

Casa Amiga's competing discourse of femicide has been met with lukewarm and sometimes hostile responses by public officials and by the maquiladora managerial community. As the center's director, Chávez is continually fighting city officials for the support promised at its inauguration. Vandalism and robbery have hindered the center's efforts, and no arrests have been made for the destruction. While the maquila association made a public appearance at Casa Amiga's opening, a highly publicized event, it was initially wary of providing funds for the center's operation. Recently, a number of factories have made donations of about twenty thousand, and more facilities are allowing Chávez and other activists to hold seminars during the workday. Still, Chávez characterizes her relationship with the maquilas as a difficult alliance. "They know we have the publicity but they don't really trust what we're doing ... It's very hard to change the way people think about women here. We threaten them."

If this fight were to gain in popularity and the notion of female worthlessness was the point of the struggle, imagine what the impact might be on the current organization of the maquiladora labor process. What would happen to technologies for turning female workers into a resource of disposable labor power if stories of female worthlessness sounded preposterous? How would the circuits of capital flow as they are currently conceptualized in the specific context of Ciudad Juárez if the technology for cheapening this kind of laborer malfunctioned? What sort of movement would it take to sabotage this technology? What would happen if the response to the claim that Ciudad Juárez women are untrainable were met with an incredulous retort: How can you condemn someone's potential? How can you tell their future?

Conclusion

Casa Amiga has gotten off the ground because its organizers have formed an alliance among international and domestic activists, Mexican maquila workers, home workers and professionals, academics, and people working in the nonprofit sector. However, the center is struggling. Too few people are doing too many things, and the payment of salaries, utilities and other such expenses presents a monthly challenge. I am not arguing that Casa Amiga and other such organizations represent the only option for challenging capital's devaluation of laborers in the maquiladora sector. However, they could very easily represent one such option. Casa Amiga is actively waging a battle against a machinery dedicated to cheapening the very subjects that the maquilas need, today, in order to survive: the renewable source of temporary female labor. While independent unions face many obstacles in organizing in Ciudad Juárez maquilas, Casa Amiga has made some measurable gains toward raising public awareness, in both the national and international arena, regarding the exploitation and dehumanization of women in the city. This awareness, as expressed in media reports, typically makes a connection linking the violence against women to the maquiladora sector. If international labor organizers could make the same connection and could see how Casa Amiga's project for reversing a discourse of female disposability is in line with union efforts to preserve the value of the working classes, then perhaps some precious progress could be made toward the elusive endeavor of cross-border activism.

Endnotes

[1] "*Maquila*" is shorthand for "*maquiladora*," which refers to the export-processing facilities located in Mexico.

[2] For an example of the conflation of maquila worker and prostitute, see Bowden (1996), in which he bemoans the difficulty in telling these categories apart.
[3] Interviews were conducted for this chapter by the author in Ciudad Juárez between 1995 and 2000.
[4] A group called "La coordinadora pro-mujer" (The pro-woman coalition) was formed by women working in nonprofit organizations throughout Ciudad Juárez.
[5] Former CNN journalist Bryan Barger has been an important source of inspiration and funding for Casa Amiga. He has just founded a nonprofit organization in Washington, DC that supports efforts for opening sexual assault centers in third world countries.
[6] This statement is based on figures provided in an unpublished report by Cheryl Howard at the University of Texas at El Paso.
[7] Original text: "Es una satisfacción verlas que han recuperado sus actividades y su confianza y vuelven a ser un ser humano con aspiraciones y deseos; Cuando ves, eso te das cuenta que este grupo tiene su razón de existir, porque tal vez se perderían muchas más vidas si no existiera." Translation by author.
[8] Independent unions are those without official ties to any political party. The majority of union membership in Mexico is within party- (typically PRI-) affiliated unions, which, in the maquilas, have worked hand-in-glove with *maquiladora* management.
[9] My thesis is informed here by Miranda Joseph's (1998) insight into the possibilities for dialogue between a Marxian and a poststructuralist approach to production and systems of valorization.
[10] Traditional Marxist analyses view technology in fixed terms, as things with predetermined physical dimensions (cf Braverman 1974).
[11] My discussion here of disposability derives from a larger argument regarding the dialectical relationship linking the production of value to the production of its antithetical condition or, as Nancy Munn (1986), has put it, to its "negative condition." I refer to this negative condition as disposability.
[12] In fact, Urrea was answering a question from John Quinones regarding the murders.

References

American Broadcasting Company (1999) 20-20. January 20, 10 pm EST. Transcript # 99012002-j11
Bowden C (1996) While you were sleeping. *Harper's* 293(1759):44–53
Braverman H (1974) *Labor and Monopoly Capital: The Degradation of Work in the Twentieth Century.* London: Monthly Review Press
Butler J (1993) *Bodies That Matter.* New York: Routledge
Candia A, Bénitez R, Cabrera P, De la Mo G, Martinez J, Ortiz R and Velásquez I (1999) *El silencio que la voz de Todus Quiebra: mujeres y nótimas de Ciudad Juárez.* Chihuahua: AZAR.
Cockburn C (1983) *Brothers: Male Dominance and Technological Change.* London: Pluto Press
Craft J A (1990) The community as a source of union power. *Journal of Labor Research* 145:145–160
Cravey A J (1998) *Women and Work in Mexico's Maquiladoras.* Lanham: Rowman and Littlefield
Elson D and Pearson R (eds) (1989) *Women, Employment and Multinationals in Europe.* New York: MacMillan
Fernandez-Kelly P (1983) *For We Are Sold, I and My People.* Albany: State University of New York Press

Galindo A (2000) Cumple un año de servicio Casa Amiga. El Diario de Ciudad Juárez
    10 de febrero 3B
Harvey D (1982) *The Limits to Capital.* Oxford: Blackwell
Harvey D (2000) *Spaces of Hope.* Berkeley: University of California Press
Howard C (2000) Unpublished essay on homicide rates in Ciudad Juárez. University
    of Texas, El Paso
Johns R and Vural L (2000) Class, geography, and consumerist turn: UNITE and the
    stop sweatshops campaign. *Economic Geography* 74:252–271
Joseph M (1998) The performance of production and consumption. *Social Text*
    54:25–62
Marx K (1988) *Economic and Philosophic Manuscripts of 1844.* Buffalo, NY: Prometheus
    Books
Marx, K (1993) *Grundrisse.* London: Penguin Books
McDowell L (1997) *Capital Culture: Gender at Work in the City.* Oxford: Blackwell
Munn N (1986) *The Fame of Gawa: A Symbolic Study of Value Transformation in a
    Massim (Papau New Guinea) Society.* Cambridge, UK: Cambridge University Press
Naples N (1998) *Community Activism and Feminist Politics*: *Organizing Across Race,
    Class, and Gender.* London: Routledge
Nathan D (1999) Work, sex, and danger in Ciudad Juárez. *NACLA Report on the
    Americas* 33 (3):24–32
Patel P (1999) Difficult alliances: Treading the minefield of identity and solidarity
    politics. *Soundings* 12:115–126
Salzinger L (1997) From high heels to swathed bodies: Gendered meanings under
    production in Mexico's export-processing industry. *Feminist Studies* 23:549–574
Scott J (1993) Experience. In J Butler and J Scott (eds) *Feminists Theorize the Political*
    (pp 22–40) New York: Routledge
Tabuenca Córdoba M S (1995–1996) Viewing the border: Perspectives from the "open
    wound." *Discourse* 18:146–168
Wills J (forthcoming) Community unionism and trade union renewal in the UK: Moving
    beyond the fragments at last? Working Paper no. 1. Geographies of Organised
    Labour. *Transactions*
Wright M W (1997) Crossing the factory frontier. *Antipode* 29(3):278–302
Wright M W (1999) The dialectics of still life: Murder, women, and the maquiladoras.
    Public Culture 29:453–473
Young I M (1990) *Justice and the Politics of Difference.* Princeton, NJ: Princeton
    University Press

Melissa W Wright is currently an Assistant Professor in the Department of Geography and in the Program of Women's Studies at The
Penn State University. Her research has explored the role of gender,
nationality, and race in the organization of multinational production
in Ciudad Juárez and in southern China. Her current research examines how the negotiation of gender and nationality affects efforts
by multinational corporations to transform the human resources of
northern Mexico.

14

Union Responses to Mass Immigration: The Case of Miami, USA

Bruce Nissen and Guillermo Grenier

This chapter places the attitudes of US unions toward immigrants within the context of a "globalized" environment and a contested and problematic history of the US labor movement regarding its conflicting tendencies toward international solidarity and nationalism. Following a review of that history, the article examines the relationships of four unions in the heavily immigrant Miami, Florida area with immigrant workers in the past four decades. The evidence indicates that explanations for differing responses can be found in the union's structure, its external environment, its leadership's vision and ideology, and its internal "cultural" practices.

Introduction: Globalization and Labor Internationalism

The recent "globalization" of the economy in the United States has forced the US labor movement to reexamine its practices in relationship to workers and labor movements elsewhere in the world. The most immediate stimulant to a reexamination was the relocation of US manufacturing facilities into other countries, especially to low-wage nations. This was new for US unions long accustomed to the export of commodities, but not of jobs. Beginning with the textile, shoe, and garment industries in the 1960s and 1970s and later in other industries, US unions faced the erosion of their membership base as their industries fled abroad.

Globalization of capital is also leading to a smaller but still significant globalization of the workforce in the form of immigrants to the US, largely from Asia and Latin America (Stalker 2000). While there is no simple one-to-one relationship between mobility of capital and mobility of workers, globalization sets up a complex constellation of relationships that turn immigration into a labor supply mechanism in advanced industrial (or postindustrial) nations like the US. The new globalized form of capitalism uproots local economies and drives people in less-developed countries out of agricultural and/or formerly protected industries. It also creates opportunities for people to emigrate through the establishment of ties created by military and political policies aimed at promoting international capital mobility (Sassen 1988). And, on the receiving end, the growth of "global cities" with low-wage employment needs easily filled by immigrants from less-developed countries creates significant labor market forces pulling immigrants into those cities (Sassen 1994, 1998). Reduced costs and easier global transportation and communication also facilitate the process. Intercountry income differentials and poverty and slow growth in countries of origin do not explain modern migration, but more complex explanations based on the evolving world political economy do. This changed global environment is forcing US unions to reevaluate their international relationships, both with workers and labor movements abroad and with foreign-born workers within the confines of the US. This reevaluation follows a highly problematic history.

History: International Solidarity or Exclusionism and Chauvinism?

The US labor movement has always vacillated between impulses toward international solidarity and nativism or exclusionism. Aside from the Native American population (killed or put in reservations), the country was composed entirely of immigrants. Early immigrants, mostly German, Irish, and English, had traditions of socialist and union activism that inclined them toward a natural fraternity and solidarity with their brethren abroad. Mid to late nineteenth-century labor organizations and ethnic workingmen's associations favored unlimited European immigration, both because of ties to the old country and for ideological reasons tied to the skilled artisan "producerist" thinking of the time. Northern and Western European immigrants were especially welcomed due to their cultural and national similarities to the skilled workers comprising most labor organizations (Lane 1987:9–32).

The opposite tendency was shown by attitudes toward Chinese immigrants, particularly in California. The labor movement in that state led a vicious and racist attack upon Chinese immigrants, including murderous riots and successful pressure to end further Chinese immigration (Saxton 1971). Chinese—and later Japanese—were considered the "other," and hence were attacked rather than welcomed. Top labor leader Samuel Gompers led the lobbying for exclusion, despite his denials that he had any prejudice against "Asians." In fact, Gompers considered Chinese an unassimilable inferior race that would degrade labor standards and lower the conditions of working people.

The immigration question merged with the race question; the issue of who gets defined as a legitimate part of the nation—who is "us" rather than "them"—shifted uneasily along lines of racial and nationality classification. Socialist, anarchist, and other left-wing class-conscious ideologies existed within the workforce and the labor movement, but they were not dominant. Hence, in the second half of the 19th century national and racial solidarities often undercut class-based solidarity.

The shift from international solidarity and republican egalitarianism to exclusionism and nativism in the labor movement from 1880 to 1900 was prolonged and reluctant. Technological change weakened the position of skilled craftsmen, as did a shift in European immigration patterns from Northern and Western countries to those in the South and the East (Lane 1987:37–52). Convinced that the very survival of their unions depended on exclusion, craftsmen sacrificed lingering principles of worker solidarity. By 1900 the "official" labor movement was anti-immigration. (The "unofficial" Industrial Workers of the World—the IWW—carried on the internationalist tradition between 1900 and 1920.) The shift toward exclusion accompanied a trend toward business unionism within the American Federation of Labor (AFL) craft unions. Solidarities of all types narrowed; broad class interests were sacrificed to win increased wages and benefits for the fortunate few inside the unions. The AFL strongly supported the 1917 literacy test for immigrants and supported the draconian 1921 and 1924 laws freezing future immigration to small numbers based on formulas favoring Northern and Western Europeans (Lane 1987; Parmet 1981).

During World War I, Samuel Gompers—who had become the leader of the AFL—pushed the official US labor movement into all-out support for the war in a deal with US President Woodrow Wilson, who promised governmental support for the AFL's organizational interests (Larson 1975). The Bolshevik Revolution in Russia also stimulated AFL leaders to begin a long history of putting the US labor movement at the service of US Cold War objectives. Extensive worldwide labor movement activity, based not on worker solidarity but on anti-Communism and often carried out through clandestine ties with

US government agencies, became a very problematic "foreign face" of the US labor movement (Cantor and Schor 1987; Radosh 1969; Sims 1992).

The labor movement's attitude and role regarding immigrants and its broader attitude and role in foreign policy and international solidarity activities were not identical, but they have been logically and historically closely intertwined. Sometimes immigration issues were central and at other times military and foreign policy issues impinging on foreign workers were. In both cases the ideological dividing line was between policies and measures promoting unity and solidarity among workers regardless of nationality, race, or other characteristics and those promoting narrower or non-working-class identities and solidarities. Thus, labor movement attitudes toward immigrants tend to mirror more or less nationalistic attitudes in the broader arena of international affairs.

The immigrant issue played very little role in US union affairs between 1924 and the 1970s because immigration was so low. Following the trauma of the Great Depression in the 1930s and World War II in the 1940s, the AFL and its new industrial union counterpart, the Congress of Industrial Organizations (CIO), turned their international activities toward supporting US global dominance of other countries and fighting the "Communist menace." The merger of these two organizations into the AFL-CIO in 1955 solidified conservative dominance of the overall movement. During this period the US labor movement favored free trade, because worldwide US corporate dominance ensured that exports far exceeded imports. Free trade meant jobs. However, by 1970 imports were rapidly destroying jobs in the United States, especially in the apparel, auto, and steel industries. The AFL-CIO quickly changed its position and in 1971 it endorsed protectionism wholeheartedly (Frank 1999:133). "Us" became union workers and their domestic employers; "them" became foreign companies and workers alike.

Under withering attack for its protectionism, US labor became more sophisticated in the 1980s and 1990s, developing "fair trade" policies based on adherence to universal labor and environmental standards. The 1993 battle over passage of the North American Free Trade Agreement (NAFTA) was particularly significant in this regard (Nissen 1999). Equally significant was the overthrow of the old AFL-CIO leadership in 1995 by new leadership that removed the Cold War operatives from the federation's international affairs department.

The US Labor Movement in the Year 2000 and Beyond

By the year 2000 the US labor movement's main approach to international labor issues had turned toward solidarity with workers abroad (and, to a limited degree, with popular movements concerning environmental protection, women's rights, antiracist struggles, etc) (Brecher and Costello 1994; Cohen and Early 1999; Frundt 1998; Nissen 1999). The AFL-CIO had also changed its position on immigration. True to its business union character, in 1986 it supported the Immigration Reform and Control Act (IRCA), which attempted to halt illegal immigration by penalizing employers for knowingly hiring "illegal aliens," or undocumented workers. In reality few employers were ever penalized, yet workers without documents were routinely deported if they dared to assert their rights or to unionize. In late 1999 and early 2000, the AFL-CIO called for repeal of employer sanctions, a new amnesty for undocumented workers, and a massive program to educate immigrant workers about their legal rights (Bacon 2000a, b). In June 2000 the AFL-CIO cosponsored with community organizations in Los Angeles a massive rally of over 15,000 people calling for amnesty for undocumented workers (Candaele and Dreier 2000).

Overall, the second half of the 1990s brought a more progressive, internationalist, and proimmigrant turn within the national US labor movement than had previously been present. However, this change has been slow and partial. Statements may not reflect equivalent changes in policies and attitudes, and national policy may not mirror local practices where immigrant workers encounter unions.

Aside from some recent scholarship on unions and immigrants (Delgado 1993; Milkman 2000), little research has been done on the subject. This chapter partially fills the gap by examining the responses of four South Florida unions to mass immigration. Two are building trades craft unions, the Carpenters Union and the Ironworkers Union. Two are industrial unions, one in the service sector (Hotel Employees and Restaurant Employees—HERE) and one in apparel production (the Union of Needletrades, Industrial, and Textile Employees—UNITE).

Changing Workforce in South Florida

As Table 1 shows, the percentage of foreign-born in the Miami area grew from under 10% in 1940 to almost 60% of the total population

Table 1: Percentage of Foreign-Born Residents in the Miami Standard
Metropolitan Statistical Area, Selected Years

Year	1940	1950	1960	1970	1980	1990	1998
% Foreign-born	9.7%	12.1%	16.9%	41.8%	53.7%	59.7%	59.0%

Source: For 1940–1990 figures, US Census Bureau (1999b). For 1998 figures, US Census
Bureau (1999a). The adult civilian labor force is even more heavily immigrant: by 1998 it
was 65.5% foreign-born. Industry employment data in Table 2 also show increasing
percentages of immigrants.

in 1998. (Tables 2 and 3 provide supplementary information.) Thus,
unions in the area were operating in an increasingly immigrant workforce, mostly from South and Central American and Caribbean
nations. The following four sections relate the reaction of each
union.

Ironworkers Local 272

In the post-World War II period, Ironworkers Local 272 was a typical
US building trades union. It represented craft workers doing steel and
ironwork in building and construction projects by referring workers
to unionized construction projects. After completing a job, workers
returned to the union hiring hall for referral to another construction

Table 2: Percentage of Immigrant Labor in Various Industries, Miami-Dade
County, Selected Years

Year	1980	1990	1998
% immigrant labor in Construction	39.4%	60.2%	74.6%
% immigrant labor in Eating & Drinking trades	29.9%	51.3%	67.3%
% immigrant labor in Hotel/Motel	39.8%	65.7%	67.4%
% immigrant labor in Apparel	82.6%	85.7%	(Sample size too small to be usable)
% immigrant labor in Nursing Home	19.5%	54.0%	(Sample size too small to be usable)

Sources: For 1980, the 1980 Census, State of Florida, Table 227, pp. 941–942; for 1990,
the 1990 Census, analysis of PUMS data; for 1998, US Census Bureau (1999a).
The immigrants in Miami-Dade County came primarily from Cuba, followed by other
South and Central American and Caribbean nations. Table 3 shows country of origin.

Table 3: Country of Origin of Immigrant Workers in Miami-Dade County, 1998

Country of Origin	Cuba	South America (Colombia)	Central America (Nicaragua)	Haiti	Dominican Republic	Jamaica
% of all immigrants	54%	14% (7%)	12% (6%)	6.4%	4.3%	2.2%

Source: US Census Bureau (1999a).

job. A skilled workforce was maintained through a three-year union apprenticeship program. In times of labor shortage, the local would also refer nonunion workers to job sites, but only if all union workers were employed.

The local had only two basic categories of worker: apprentices, whose wages rose steadily toward full pay as they progressed through the program, and full-fledged journeymen. Journeymen and apprentice pay rates were specified in the union contract. Consistent with traditional US building trades union practice, entry into the apprenticeship program was often restricted to relatives of those already in the local. In the words of Dewey Tyler, the local's current business manager:

> Ironworkers Local 272 was a closed local in the 1960s … You couldn't get into the apprenticeship school—you had to be a relative … So when the Cubans came over and tried to get work with us, our union kept them out. They didn't let anyone in. So they had to work wherever they could. And we said, well, they can't do our work. We thought we were infallible. (Tyler interview)

At one time, according to Tyler, the local had 200 members, but 3000 people working out of the union hall. In 1971 the national union forced the local to take in 500 new members, but only a "token" number were minorities or immigrants (Tyler interview). Government efforts to get the union to open its ranks were mostly unsuccessful. The one leader who attempted to bring in Hispanics to the local was voted out of office after one term, at least partly due to backlash against the more open policy (Phillips interview). The numbers of immigrants and African Americans in the local crept up slightly in the 1980s, but the local was still overwhelmingly native and white. Prior to the 1990s, the union's immigrant membership percentages lagged

Table 4: Immigrant Percentage in Construction Industry, Ironwork, and Union Membership, Selected Years

	1960s	1970s	1980s	1999
% in construction industry	unavailable	unavailable	39%	75%
% doing ironwork (est.)	10%	15–30%	40–50%	60+%
% in Local 272 (est.)	1–2%	10–15%	20%	Over 50%

Sources: Construction industry percentages: US Census figures. Ironwork percentages: estimates from Dewey Tyler and Dave Gornewicz, Business Manager and President of Ironworkers Local 272. Union percentages: estimates from Dewey Tyler.

behind those of the industry as a whole. (Table 4 shows the percentages for the last four decades of the century.) Prior to the 1990s, according to the current president of the local, Dave Gornewicz, the attitude of both the leadership and the rank and file membership toward immigrants was "hostile." He describes attitudes as:

> ... typically prejudiced attitudes. Stereotyping people: "*Some* of them are all right. They don't have the same skills as we do. You can't trust them all." Every backward thing you can imagine ... completely racial—not anything to do with the skills. (Gornewicz interview)

Exclusionism shrank the local as Hispanic and other immigrant contractors and workers worked nonunion and took over an increasing percentage of all the work.

At the time of the 1992 union leadership election, there were only 73 union members working in the local's entire five-county jurisdiction (Tyler interview). The local was about to collapse. Reformer Dewey Tyler was elected business manager on a platform calling for change in the local's direction. Facing opposition to admitting immigrants, Tyler instituted an education program centered on the need to organize the relevant labor force if the union was to survive. Beginning with the leadership and eventually extending to much of the membership—by early 2000, almost 40% of the local's members had been through formal training—he eventually convinced the majority of the members of the need to end the "country club unionism" and to organize all workers, including immigrants. In 1996 the local began a formal organizing program, including special Hispanic and Haitian organizing committees. Membership has grown rapidly ever since, as can be seen in Table 5. Tyler estimates that the local's "market

Table 5: Membership of Ironworkers Local 272, Relevant Years

1996	1997	1998	1999	March 2000	Dec 2000
538	549	653	810	844	1,025

Source: Ironworkers Local 272 (2000).

share"—the percentage of the work that is done union—grew from under 1% in 1992 to 20% by early 2000.

The new leadership has appointed a staff more representative of the work force than had previously been the case. Gregorio Cisneros, a Peruvian immigrant, is the primary organizer of Hispanic workers. In a few short years, his skill, dedication, and impressive track record have catapulted him into the position of the third highest-ranking official in the local. In another example, Antonio Parker, a black immigrant from Jamaica, was elected Recording Secretary in 1998 (the first elected immigrant leader) and was later appointed Apprentice Director for the local (Parker interview).

Internal opposition to the change was eventually isolated and defeated; the opposing presidential candidate received only 15 votes in the 1998 election against Dave Gornewicz, a strong reform supporter. Gornewicz attributes success in overcoming backward attitudes to two factors: 1) an extensive education program, lasting years; and 2) a growing "interfacing" with immigrants within the union and on the job, leading to a recognition that they are capable of doing the work. Attendance at the monthly membership meetings (averaging 50–85 persons) has been approximately 40% immigrant (Gornewicz interview; Tyler interview). Despite lingering fears from long-term non-Hispanic white members, the new leadership is fully reconciled to the complete transformation of the union local, including that at leadership levels, as Dewey Tyler indicates:

> I've had people concerned, saying, "What's going to happen? Is this local going to be where the business manager and the business agents are black and Hispanic? And I say, "Well, I would certainly hope so! Because I would hope that the membership get to vote on who's going to be there." That's democracy. Greg Cisneros, at some point in time, will be the President or the Business Manager of this local. (Tyler interview)

Changes in the composition of the apprentice program guarantee that the changeover to a new membership base will be permanent.

Of the 124 apprentices in the Florida East Coast program, 50–60 are Hispanic, 40–50 are black (both African-American and African-Caribbean) and only 17 are non-Hispanic whites. The local would like to raise the number of non-Hispanic white apprentices to approach that of their nonwhite counterparts, but finds it difficult to recruit sufficient numbers to do so.

A newly flexible structure also helps insure permanence. Most nonunion workers in the building trades are less skilled than union journeymen, but too skilled (and too well paid) for apprenticeship, with its low pay scales. So the local now has categories between the full "J-I-W" (Journeyman Ironworker) and the mere apprentice. They issue a "structural steel" book to some new members, a "rodman" book to others, and they even have a "utility program" with three classifications for those with very low skill levels. Training and/or on-the-job experience helps members move up into the full journeyman status. The local can now recruit new workers at all skill levels.

The local has not fully changed to an immigrant-friendly union, which is only natural given its past history. Neither of the two secretaries at the union hall speaks Spanish or Creole, and only one of the two apprenticeship school secretaries speaks Spanish (but not Creole). The local's Web site is in English only, although some literature used for recruitment and education is written in English and Spanish. At the union hall, Gregorio Cisneros handles all communication with Spanish-only speaking members, by all accounts quite efficiently. In perhaps the greatest failure to fully change to a more representative structure, the local's five-person executive board is all white and native-born except for one Hispanic. Antonio Parker had to relinquish a board position upon becoming the Apprentice Director in 1999. He and Dave Gornewicz note that constitution and by-laws requirements imposed by the national union regarding meeting attendance and past dues payments make it difficult to further diversify the executive board, although they hope to do so in the future (Gornewicz interview; Parker interview).

United Brotherhood of Carpenters Regional Council

Like the ironworkers' union, the carpenters' union (the United Brotherhood of Carpenters—the UBC) was traditionally a virtually all-white, male craft union operating through a hiring hall. The UBC's South Florida Regional Council was large and powerful in the 1960s, when its membership reached almost 12,000, about 95% of the work

Table 6: Membership and Hispanic/Non-Hispanic Breakdown in the UBC, Selected Years

Year	Total Members*	Non-Hispanic	Hispanic
1973	7505 (100%)	6165 (82%)	1340 (18%)
1980	3303 (100%)	2520 (76%)	783 (24%)
1988	3834 (100%)	2740 (71%)	1094 (29%)
2000	3841 (100%)	2567 (67%)	1274 (33%)

* Total Member figures for 1973, 1980, and 1988 were derived from a count of Hispanic surnames on membership lists. The figure for 2000 was taken from the official records of the Council on March 15 2000.

in the craft at the time. It was the "only trade to open its doors" to Cuban immigrants, according to Ernie Taylor, Council President when interviewed in 1988 (Taylor interview). However, Taylor overstates the case: after initial progress, the union's membership immigrant percentages trailed those of the industry as a whole. Table 6 shows the union's membership trends. Relatively few Haitians have become carpenters in the United States, so we use Hispanic percentages as a rough proxy for immigrant penetration of the union. From 1980 to 1990 to 2000 the construction industry workforce went from 39% to 60% to 75% foreign-born, while the UBC's percentage of immigrants only increased from 24% in 1970 to 29% in 1988 to 33% in 2000.

Immigrants received some early acceptance, but they were mostly viewed by both members and leaders as threats to union jobs. Organizing them was a radical idea. This changed temporarily with the emergence from within of a talented and forceful immigrant Cuban leader. Jose "Pepe" Collado became a member of UBC Local 405 in 1969 after initially being refused membership. Collado states that union leadership at the time had a very backward attitude toward immigrants:

> They had no idea what they were doing. They thought they did. "Keep Cubans out because we don't need them." But they really didn't see how it was all going to change right from under them. Cubans came, building boomed, nonunion workers worked for nonunion contractors. But they didn't see how it would gut the union. (Collado interview)

In 1976 Collado was elected trustee of Local 405, and in 1979 he became the first Hispanic business representative on the Council. He mobilized his local's Hispanic workforce and used the growth of

Hispanic contractors as leverage to increase the presence of Hispanics in the appointed leadership ranks.

As the organizational attitude toward immigrants changed, the union also partially reversed a decline in membership from the early 1970s. By the mid-1980s, most of the "hard work" in the local was being done by immigrants, including not simply Cubans but other Hispanic workers, particularly Nicaraguans and Dominicans (Bittle interview; Jimenez interview).

Collado's influence made the Carpenters the most progressive South Florida construction union in the 1980s. In 1985 he was offered a staff job by the union's national president, who also placed the South Florida Regional Council under supervision and appointed a new president for it. In the late 1980s, the top leadership of the UBC attempted to impose institutional diversity in the ranks of the South Florida District Council leadership. At the time, this "top down" approach appeared to be succeeding. Two of six Business Agents and the state Organizing Director were Hispanics. Apprenticeship classes were offered in Spanish, and a new training level, journeyman training, was instituted to upgrade skills of workers, particularly Hispanics, who were already working or had experience. Collado moved up in the national union; today he is a member of the National Executive Board in charge of the entire southeastern United States, and is his union's highest ranking Hispanic. Yet most of his reforms died in the decade following his departure. Hispanic leaders he placed in staff jobs are gone; by 1998 contracts were no longer translated into Spanish, and often union representatives could not communicate with Spanish-speaking members.

In the late 1990s the union once again began trying to adjust to its multilingual membership. Contracts and tests are now again being translated. But they had not been for years. Current Executive Secretary-Treasurer Walter Seidel confirms the regression to previous backward practices:

> When we started doing the tests and contracts [in Spanish] I called Pepe and he said that all that had been done back when he was around. Nobody could remember ... nobody knew where the stuff was. (Seidel interview)

In 1995, the national union reorganized the District Council, once again to force more diversity and accountability in the council. The Executive Secretary of the Regional Council reports to Collado and is elected by the council's local unions. He is also structurally in charge of the organizing division, which the national union funds directly and in which five of the six organizers are Hispanics (two Cubans, one Colombian, one Salvadorean, and one Puerto Rican). Of the seven local unions—the regional council side of the organization—two have Hispanic Business Agents, one Cuban and one Puerto Rican. The Organizing Director is a first-generation Cuban-American raised in Boston. The organizing division is seen as a way of implementing the top union leadership's vision of a diverse and representative leadership structure within the council. Collado states, "Top leadership in our union has always wanted more immigrants in the ranks and in positions of power. Middle leadership has been the stumbling block" (Collado interview 2000).

This attempt to bypass the antipathy or indifference of local leadership through appointment from above of new organizing staff has brought mixed results. The Regional Council office has only one Spanish-speaking secretary, in the safety and health program. A newsletter is published in English only, very irregularly. Some "unofficial" local meetings are held entirely in Spanish (in the locals where Hispanics dominate membership rolls). Jorge García, the new Organizing Director, expresses the union's ambivalent attitude toward immigrants, and notes that old exclusionary attitudes are changing, albeit slowly:

> Immigrants are positive and negative for our unions ... the massive cheap labor they provide helps the nonunion shops, no question ... It's a double-edged sword. "They are out there, doing our job, we should organize them," but also, "we should exclude them, deport them ... because our trade is being diluted." But if we keep them out, like the union has been doing, they become a double negative ... If we go after them, it can revitalize us ... give us purpose ... we have 5% market share ... the attitude [of exclusion] has changed. (Garcia interview)

Angel Domínguez, recently appointed organizer and Business Agent, is less charitable:

> They [Regional Council leadership] are lost. They don't know what they are doing. They don't understand the people we need to organize and want to keep doing the same thing that hasn't worked for years. (Domínguez interview)

Domínguez has launched a series of community-based activities among Mexican workers in Homestead, a town just southwest of

Miami. Mexican immigrants now are a dominant force in the Homestead area "and to organize them, we have to go where they are and do what they do" (Domínguez interview). So he set up a booth at a flea market. The Regional Council leader could not understand why he was doing this, a symptom to Domínguez of the current leadership's lack of vision. Domínguez says business agents and leaders, uneducated about immigrants, do not recognize their significance as anything other than as a threat, so they do not use the union to defend immigrant worker rights. This restricts the union's ability to recruit and develop leadership from immigrant members (Domínguez interview).

The deterioration of the union's treatment of immigrant workers from the late 1980s until the late 1990s shows that dependence on one leader to advance the interests of immigrants is risky. When that leader moves up or on, reforms may disappear if changes have not been institutionalized and if the "cultural" practices of the union local are not systematically altered.

The contrast with the Ironworkers is striking. Ironworkers leadership systematically set up a plan, conducted education, and solidified majority leadership support for a major change in orientation toward immigrants. Only then did they implement their new organizing strategy. No such systematic process took place in the UBC, where change imposed from above has been more difficult to deepen than was the case with the Ironworkers' internal local insurgency. It remains to be seen if the UBC now has the necessary unified leadership, clarity of vision, strategic plan, and transformed internal "cultural" practices to make for a lasting change.

Hotel Employees and Restaurant Employees (HERE) Local 355

Known as Local 255 prior to a 1973 merger with two other locals, Hotel Employees and Restaurant Employees Local 355 is an industrial union local with jurisdiction over service workers in lodging and eating establishments. It organizes workers regardless of skill or craft, and has always represented relatively low-paid service workers in a sector with many immigrants. In the mid-1950s, a massive strike by both union and nonunion workers at hotels in Miami Beach included many immigrants from Cuba with a strong union consciousness. Following the 1959 Cuban revolution, more Cubans immigrated and took hotel and related jobs in the 1960s.

We lack data on union membership immigrant percentages in the decades following 1960, but minutes of Executive Board meetings show that seven of the 21 Executive Board members in the latter half of 1962 were Hispanic (6 August–3 December 1962 HERE Executive Board minutes). However, only one of the union's seven office staff in August 1963 was: the woman who answered the telephone (6 August 1963 HERE Executive Board minutes). As of 1965, four of the local's nine business agents had Hispanic surnames, although the president and business manager were white Anglos (August 1965 HERE Executive Board minutes). By 1967, the local's General Organizer was a Hispanic (4 December 1967 HERE Executive Board minutes).

In 1972, board member Ricardo Torres requested that local meetings be conducted in both English and Spanish, because a large percentage of the membership could not understand English. President Herbert "Pinky" Schiffman was unsympathetic: "Brother Schiffman explained that the By-Laws of our International Constitution clearly spell out that any meeting can be conducted only in English language. Therefore the constitution will supersede anything. A motion cannot be introduced in this respect" (6 March 1972 HERE Executive Board minutes). Despite Schiffman's refusal to accommodate immigrants' language needs, current leaders claim that he was well liked by members, including Hispanics. Partly this may have been due to the fact that his term corresponded with "good times" for the local, whose membership reached 7400 in 1965. However, in December of 1976 Schiffman was convicted of accepting gratuities from hotel owners, and in 1978 the local was put into trusteeship by the national union for financial irregularities (Vaira 1978). When the trusteeship ended in 1979, trustee Alvaro González was elected Secretary/Treasurer and Antonio Fernández became President and Business Manager. Twelve of the 15 officers and business agents of the local at the time had Hispanic surnames (23 April 1979 HERE Executive Board minutes). In 1980, bilingual meetings were again requested at the Executive Board, bringing about "lengthy discussion." The group decided that this would unduly prolong meetings, but provided for simultaneous translation for those needing it. Although the original motion was denied, more accommodation was provided than had earlier been the case (23 September 1980 HERE Executive Board minutes).

In the late 1970s and early 1980s, many Haitian immigrants entered the hotel industry. In 1981 the local hired its first Haitian organizer for a one-month trial period (27 October 1981 HERE Executive Board minutes). However, subsequent records do not indicate continued hiring of Haitians.

From 1980 to 1995, the local membership dropped and many unionized establishments went nonunion. González ran the local in an autocratic manner. In the early 1980s, a power struggle between González and local President Fernández led to accusations of inept organizing and squandered resources, financially shady relations with insurance companies, breakaway union attempts, and sensational accusations on local Cuban talk radio shows. The internal culture of the local was focused on these matters rather than on immigrant issues. Immigration only came up when González tried to remove an executive board opponent, Wilfredo Fariñas, for lack of US citizenship (25 September 1984 HERE Executive Board minutes). In late 1984, Fariñas was ejected from the meeting, despite his pleas that he had applied for citizenship and would be hearing back soon (4 December 1984 HERE Executive Board minutes). This behavior is consistent with current Business Manager Andy Balash's assessment of Gonzalez: "Al did not care about immigrants. Al did not care about anything but Al, as far as I heard" (Balash interview).

In 1990 Al González moved to a higher position in the national union, replaced at the local level by his son Robert González. In 1994 the local was put into trusteeship for financial irregularities: it owed the national union half a million dollars (Balash interview). When trusteeship ended in 1996, assistant to the trustee Andy Balash became the new Secretary-Treasurer and Business Manager. Balash developed a union leadership slate that includes the union's major immigrant groups. The Secretary-Treasurer/Business Manager is a non-Hispanic white (Balash); the President is a Cuban-American (Jorge Santiesteban); and the Vice President is a Haitian-American (Maria Angie Badio). The local's executive board also mirrors the national and ethnic composition of the membership, which is shown in Table 7. The local's 11-member Executive Board has among its members six Hispanics, three Haitians, one African American, and one Caribbean American (West Indies).

The local now runs its membership meetings in one, two, or three simultaneously translated languages, depending on the persons in attendance. Average attendance is 30–50 people, and 75–90% of attendees are estimated to be immigrants (Balash interview;

Table 7: Percentage of HERE Local 355 Membership by Nationality, March 2000

Cuban	Haitian	Non-Cuban Hispanic	Other
40%	30–35%	20%	5–10%

Source: Estimates by HERE Local 355 Business Manager Andy Balash and HERE Local 355 President Jorge Santiesteban.

Santiesteban interview). Of the eight office staff, including business agents and organizers, all speak English, six speak Spanish, and one speaks Creole. The local's quarterly newsletter is printed in English only because doing so in three languages is too expensive, and rather than offend the group left out if two languages were used, the "universal language" of English is used (Balash interview; Santiesteban interview).

The local's leadership attaches little significance to its immigrant membership base beyond requirements of representative leadership and staff. The local is not involved in Cuban, Haitian, or other immigrant community issues, and it does not consciously utilize national cultures or events to build the union. This statement by Balash regarding immigrants is representative:

> They're our members. They're reflective of our workforce. We have to represent them ... I, myself, running this union: I'm running it on behalf of *workers*. I really do not see Cuban, Haitian, or Nicaraguan. I see these are dues-paying members who happen to be immigrants. And we service them and try to take care of their needs as best we can. (Balash interview)

Thus, HERE Local 355 is neither strategic/innovative in its approach to immigrant workers nor backward and reactive. It is simply a union whose members happen to be mostly immigrant. It neither uses this fact to its advantage nor damages itself by attempts to discriminate against them.

Union of Needletrades, Industrial, and Textile Employees (UNITE)

The national Union of Needletrades, Industrial, and Textile Employees (UNITE) was formed in 1995 from the merger of the Amalgamated Clothing and Textile Workers Union (ACTWU) and the International Ladies Garment Workers Union (ILGWU). Both ACTWU and ILGWU operated in South Florida prior to this merger.

As is the case with HERE, the garment unions operated in workforces that had long been heavily immigrant. By 1980, the apparel workforce was 83% immigrant; by 1990, it was 86% foreign-born. When union staffer Anita Cofino transferred to the ILGWU office in Miami from New York in 1971, she found a membership that was predominantly Cuban:

> By the time I came down from New York with the ILG, the work force was practically all Cuban. Not Hispanic. Cuban. Some blacks

were in it but not many other immigrants. We had nearly 8000
members in 20-some factories ... It was our peak. (Cofino interview)

At that time, the entire garment industry in the Miami area employed
approximately 20,000 people, so the union had a healthy 40% of the
workforce under contract.

In the early 1970s, the union was an "immigrant union with an
immigrant staff," but Cofino reports that the two Anglo union regional managers during the 1970s had "no love" for Cubans. ILGWU
regional directors in the 1970s "tolerated but didn't want to see"
Cubans (Cofino interview). Over the course of that decade, the
ILGWU lost the majority of its organized plants to plant closings. It
failed to organize existing and newly opened nonunion shops, so
membership dropped precipitously. By 1981 it had only 806 members,
and by 1987 it was down to 231 workers, an insignificant 1.2% of the
19,000 still working in apparel manufacturing. At the same time, the
workforce increased in diversity. Hispanic immigrants still dominated,
but they came from Nicaragua, Colombia, the Dominican Republic,
and other Central and South American countries. Haitians also began
to work their way into the mix, the women in sewing and the men in
the pressing departments.

Since the production of suits and formal wear requires a more
skilled work force, the ACTWU plants survived the first wave of
ILGWU plant shutdowns. Cofino switched unions in the early 1980s
and found that ACTWU regional managers, who were from Alabama,
had a more positive attitude toward immigrants than their ILGWU
counterparts (Cofino interview). With their support, Cofino started
citizenship classes as well as a bilingual newspaper. By the early 1990s,
the newspaper was trilingual to serve both the Hispanics and the
growing numbers of Haitians in the shops.

Earlier, ACTWU had followed companies with union contracts as
they moved south, and had represented workers at large local subsidiaries of Hart, Schaffner, and Marx and other national companies.
Most plants had close to 100% membership, virtually all Cuban
women. In a right-to-work state, 100% membership demonstrates the
commitment of the workforce to the union. However, shifting demo-
graphics motivated a structural adjustment in the union. Traditionally
ACTWU amalgamates workplaces into one large local, as they did in
Miami until the early 1990s. Local 694 represented six worksites and
nearly 2800 workers with a 12-person Executive Board; nine were
Cuban, plus two white native-born and one Haitian man. This structure
had worked, but in the early 1990s it became unrepresentative of

the membership. Younger Central American and Haitian immigrants were not getting leadership representation. The board only met monthly, and membership meetings were not held at all. So the union deamalgamated, creating worksite locals under a South Florida Council (Russo interview; Russo 1993:39).

ACTWU was hit hard by a second wave of plant closings in the mid-1990s, which weakened the nonamalgamated model. By the time ILGWU Local 415–475 merged with the ACTWU South Florida Council to create UNITE Local 2000 in 1995, the need for another restructuring process was evident: "Our initial reason for deamalgamating was to involve the members, but with plant closings, board members losing their jobs and their base, constant elections, the model became problematic. Our base was going and we needed to find a new direction in organizing" (Russo interview). At the time of the merger, ACTWU was led by Florida District Manager Monica Russo. Today Russo is the UNITE Florida District Director.

Newly unemployed members from the closed garment plants led UNITE to new organizing opportunities. Retrained laid-off workers became Certified Nurse Assistants (CNAs) and went to work in nursing homes. UNITE followed them and established a nursing home organizing focus. A non-AFL-CIO union, Local 1115, had also been organizing nursing homes in the area. Local 1115 merged with the Service Employees International Union (SEIU) at exactly the time when UNITE and SEIU were drawing up plans to establish a joint nursing home organizing project named Unite for Dignity, with Russo as Executive Director. With the approximately 25 nursing homes under SEIU contract and the few already organized by UNITE, the new organization had a base. Unite for Dignity is not officially a labor organization, so the workers join either the UNITE Local 2000 or SEIU Local 1115. The Unite for Dignity Council combines members of both unions to devise strategies and plan activities. The attendance at these meetings is overwhelmingly immigrant. English is seldom spoken and the meetings are run in Creole and Spanish.

UNITE's structure continues to change to as a result of the organization's commitment to immigrant workers. The industrial division, including the remaining garment-cutting and distribution centers and industrial laundry shops, has two Haitian organizers, two Cuban organizers, another Hispanic staffer, and two African Americans. Unite for Dignity is led by five Haitians, including the organizing director, and an African American. Russo estimates that UNITE's current membership is 40% Haitian, 30% Hispanic, 20% African-American and 10% other, mostly immigrant, workers.

UNITE and Unite for Dignity have a more active presence in immigrant communities than any other South Florida union. They play a leading role in virtually any social movement involving immigrant and minority communities. Community groups, women's groups, church groups, solidarity movements, Haitian and other immigrant groups, and others frequently hold meetings in the building housing UNITE and Unite for Dignity. They are thought of as "community unions." This is in striking contrast with HERE and other local unions with a predominantly immigrant membership.

Explanations for the Unions' Differing Responses to Immigrants

The evidence shows that four factors explain the different patterns of local union response to immigration: union structure, environmental factors such as traditional employer and membership characteristics, leadership, and internal "cultural" practices.

Union Structure

Union structure influences likely responses to immigrants. The first structural factor is that the craft structure of building trades unions with apprenticeships and a hiring hall allowed "country club unionism" in the post-World War II decades. Qualified nonunion workers were kept out, and a traditionally all-white and all-native membership meant that African Americans and immigrants were excluded. Therefore, the two building trades unions in this study were the slowest to accept representative numbers of immigrants. In contrast, by the 1960s, both HERE and UNITE's predecessor unions, admitting anyone working in hotel and apparel industries, had admitted large numbers of (usually Cuban) immigrants, and both had immigrants on elected leadership bodies and staff.

A second structural factor is the degree of "flexibility." Here again, the traditional "apprentice-journeyman" structure of the construction unions made integrating immigrants more difficult. Ironworkers Local 272 created new categories of membership to solve the problem, and the Carpenters are struggling to do the same despite internal opposition over the alleged "dilution" of the craft.

UNITE displays two other types of helpful flexibility. First, it continuously realigns internal structures with external circumstances to remain representative of all cultures and nationalities. Both its deamalgamation and subsequent reamalgamation were done with this in mind. Second, it has even changed its jurisdiction to follow its immigrant workforce to their present place of employment. Nursing home membership, a jurisdiction far from its traditional apparel base, helps the union survive in a largely immigrant milieu.

National and regional union structures can also influence a union local's relationship with immigrants. Often influence on this issue from higher up takes the form of mere indifference (as with the Iron-workers and with HERE until very recently) or perhaps mild support for immigrant-friendly initiatives (UNITE). The attempt by the UBC national leadership to force "top down" change shows limited effectiveness. Local changes in leadership vision and cultural practices are also needed.

Traditional Employer and Membership Characteristics

The presence of a traditional labor force—and union membership—that has long been virtually immigrant-free makes racist and pre-judiced responses to immigrant workers as the "other" more likely than in unions with long histories working with immigrant laborers. Once again, the construction unions face the biggest obstacles on this account, and both construction unions discussed here were slow to deal with immigrants in a systematic way.

Sectoral shifts in the economy can either undermine or aid unions' survival in a heavily immigrant environment. Unions with little attach-ment to immigrants, such as the construction unions in earlier times, are hurt when the economy shifts from traditional employers or market segments because immigrants work for the newer, nonunion competitors and segments. However, unions so attached to their immigrant workforce that they will follow them, such as UNITE did in following ex-members into nursing homes, can use their immigrant ties to advantage. Immigrants then provide new organizing oppor-tunities and a loyal membership base.

Union Leadership, Vision, and Ideology

While structural characteristics and traditional employers/member-ships put limits and pressures on union leaders, it remains true that leadership vision and ideology play a role. The 1992 (and subsequent 1998) leadership turnover in the Ironworkers' union moved the local from a monopolistic "country club" business union ideology toward the broader interests of workers as a class. One new leader is class-conscious, envisioning a labor movement fighting for working class interests. The other is a "born-again" Christian with a strong moral vision of the "uplift" of the membership, of the trade, and of working people as a whole. Both have inclusive rather than exclusive views, opposing all forms of racism and exclusionary thinking. The leadership team also has a clear vision of how to deal with internal controversy sparked by their radical change in direction for the local: through educational classes and organizing for consensus within leadership bodies on the need to change.

The South Florida leadership of the UBC is not as clear, either in vision or in ideological commitment to immigrant organizing. It understands that it must organize immigrants to survive in South Florida, but displays ambivalence about that mandate and has fuzzy notions about how to accomplish it. The national union is running educational sessions with that leadership to instill greater clarity, but the final outcome is unclear. This example also shows that individual visionary leadership without a corresponding change in internal institutional and cultural practices is not sufficient. Collado's proimmigrant reforms died when he moved up in the union hierarchy. Systematic education and consolidation of a new understanding is needed, along with a conscious plan for integrating cultures within the union hall.

The leadership of HERE Local 355 traditionally lacked the vision or the ideology to see the immigrant influx as an opportunity, rather than an unimportant fact of life in the hotel industry. Present leadership appears more competent and fiscally responsible than its predecessors, but it does not involve the local in immigrant community issues, in striking contrast with the UNITE local.

Russo, UNITE's top leader in Miami, combines a class-conscious world view with a commitment to organizing immigrants—more so than any other union leader in the Miami area. Partially as a result, UNITE and Unite for Dignity have become the most successful "immigrant" unions in the region. The same views underlie efforts at structural flexibility and internal representation of all immigrant populations, as well as jurisdictional changes. Unlike building trades union leaders, Russo does not have membership with backward views on immigration, so progressive policies are easier to execute.

Internal Cultural Practices

Vision and leadership are not enough; the union must also be a comfortable location for immigrant workers. Members of different cultural and national backgrounds must easily intermingle and coexist in the day-to-day workings of the union. UNITE and Unite for Dignity are most successful, with frequent immigrant cultural, community, religious, and other activities, especially for the Haitian community.

This cross-cultural interaction within the confines of the union hall is consciously planned by the union's leadership, whose thinking is captured by this excerpt from an article by Russo (1993:49):

> In transforming one's attitudes—in transforming our unions—we don't do it by sitting around and talking about it. We have to get out there and roll up our sleeves. We have to live with each other, be with each other, and our human potential and our rich experiences start coming out. That's how we're building a multicultural organizing union in this world called Miami.

The UNITE union hall has a multicultural and immigrant "feel" to it unmatched by any other union in the Miami area.

Ironworkers Local 272 has not gone as far, but it has changed its internal cultural practices as much as any building trades union in the Miami area can. The local's leadership has made the union hall a comfortable place for all nationalities. The UBC is struggling to achieve the same goal. Although it is unclear if these efforts will diffuse throughout the organization, strides have been made. In August and October 2000, the UBC sponsored a "festival de amnistía" (Amnesty Festival) attended by hundreds of undocumented workers and their families, who celebrated native cultures and rallied for unconditional amnesty for all undocumented workers. Previously such an event would have been unthinkable.

Conclusion

A union's—or a broader labor movement's—practices toward immigrants are not identical to its relationship with workers in other countries, but the two are interrelated. The logic of "solidarity" or its absence is similar concerning people who may be seen as the "other" due to differences in culture, "race," or country of birth. The US labor movement has had a problematic history in all these respects.

In the 1990s the US labor movement shed most of its Cold War obstacles to international solidarity, and cross-border contacts are slowly spreading. With a slight time lag, attitudes toward immigrants have also changed: the US labor movement now "officially" welcomes and fights for the rights of all immigrant workers. Practice lags behind official theory, but a turn has been made.

Recent changes in official attitudes matter most at the local level, because it is here that the internal transformation of union cultures will have to take place. The decentralized American labor movement primarily operates at this level. Our study of four unions in Miami reveals that factors such as the structure of the union, traditional employer and member characteristics, the leadership's vision and ideology, and the union's internal cultural practices are critical. Obstacles to greater solidarity exist in all these dimensions, but they are surmountable if they are understood, exposed, and systematically attacked and undermined.

References

Asher R and Stephenson C (1990) American capitalism, labor organization, and the racial/ethnic factor: An exploration. In R Asher and C Stephenson (eds) *Labor Divided: Race and Ethnicity in United States Labor Struggles 1835–1960* (pp 3–27). Albany: State University of New York Press

Bacon D (2000a) Immigrant workers ask labor "which side are you on?" *Working USA* 3(5):7–18

Bacon D (2000b) Unions take on immigration-related firings. *Z Magazine* July-August:25–28

Brecher J and Costello T (1994) *Global Village or Global Pillage: Economic Reconstruction from the Bottom Up.* Boston: South End Press

Candaele K and Dreier P (2000) LA's progressive mosaic: Beginning to find its voice. *The Nation* 21–28 August:24–29

Cantor D and Schor J (1987) *Tunnel Vision: Labor, the World Economy, and Central America.* Boston: South End Press

Cohen L and Early S (1999) Defending workers' rights in the global economy: The CWA experience. In B Nissen (ed) *Which Direction for Organized Labor? Essays on Organizing, Outreach, and Internal Transformations* (pp 143–164). Detroit: Wayne State University Press

Delgado H L (1993) *New Immigrants, Old Unions: Organizing Undocumented Workers in Los Angeles.* Philadelphia: Temple University Press

Frank D (1999) *Buy American: the Untold Story of Economic Nationalism.* Boston: Beacon Press

Frundt H (1998) *Trade Conditions and Labor Rights: US Initiatives, Dominican and Central American Responses.* Gainesville: University Press of Florida

Grenier G (1990) Ethnic solidarity and the Cuban-American labor movement in Dade County. *Cuban Studies* 20:29–48

Haus L (1995) Openings in the wall: Transnational migrants, labor unions, and US immigration policy. *International Organization* 49(2):285–313

Ironworkers Local 272 (2000) "Local 272 Moves into a New Millennium: The Real Deal—Organizing." Slide show prepared by the union, 29 January

Lane A T (1987) *Solidarity or Survival? American Labor and European Immigrants, 1830–1924.* New York: Greenwood Press

Larson S (1975) *Labor and Foreign Policy: Gompers, the AFL, and the First World War, 1914–1918.* Cranbury, NJ: Associated University Presses

Milkman R (ed) (2000) *Organizing Immigrants: The Challenge for Unions in Contemporary California*. Ithaca, NY: Cornell University Press

Nissen B (1999) Alliances across the border: US labor in the era of globalization. *Working USA* 3(1):43–55

Parmet R (1981) *Labor and Immigration in Industrial America*. New York: G K Hall & Co

Radosh R (1969) *American Labor and United States Foreign Policy*. New York: Random House

Russo M (1993) This world called Miami. *Labor Research Review* 20 (Spring-Summer):37–49

Sassen S (1988) *The Mobility of Labor and Capital*. Cambridge, UK: Cambridge University Press

Sassen S (1994) *Cities in a World Economy*. Thousand Oaks, CA: Pine Forge Press

Sassen S (1998) *Globalization and Its Discontents*. New York: The New Press

Saxton A (1971) *The Indispensable Enemy: Labor and the Anti-Chinese Movement in California*. Berkeley: The University of California Press

Sims B (1992) *Workers of the World Undermined: American Labor's role in US Foreign Policy*. Boston: South End Press

Stalker P (2000) *Workers Without Frontiers: The Impact of Globalization on International Migration*. Washington, DC: International Labor Organization

US Census Bureau (1999a) *Current Population Survey, March.* Washington, DC: US Census Bureau

US Census Bureau (1999b) "Nativity of the Population for Urban Places Ever Among the 50 Largest Urban Places since 1870: 1850 to 1990." HTML file: <URL: http://www.census.gov/population/www/documentation/twps0029/tab22.html>, last accessed March 2001

Vaira P and Roller D (1978) "Organized Crime and the Labor Unions." Memo prepared for the White House by the Chicago Strike Force. HTML file: <URL: http://www.laborers.org/VAIRA_MEMO.html>, last accessed March 2001

Interviews with: Andy Balash, David Bittle, Anita Cofino, Jose "Pepe" Collado, Angel Domínguez, Jorge García, Dave Gornewicz, Paco Jiménez, Gloria Lewis, Antonio Parker, Kenny Peckel, George "Buddy" Phillips, Monica Russo, Jorge Santiesteban, Walter Seidel, Ernie Taylor, and Dewey Tyler. Bittle, Jiménez, Peckel, and Taylor interviews in 1988. Interviews with Collado in both 1988 and 2000. All other interviews in 2000.

Bruce Nissen is a Program Director at the Center for Labor Research and Studies at Florida International University. He is the author or editor of six books on labor issues, as well as a number of academic journal articles and book chapters. His two most recent volumes are *Which Direction for Organized Labor?* (1999, Wayne State University Press) and *Unions and Workplace Reorganization* (1997, Wayne State University Press). He is currently finishing work on an edited volume entitled *US Unions in a Globalized Environment: Shifting Borders, Organizational Boundaries and Social Roles.*

Guillermo J Grenier is Director of the Center for Labor Research and Studies and a member of the Sociology/Anthropology Department at Florida International University in Miami. He is the author of *Inhuman Relations: Quality Circles and Anti-Unionism in American Industry* (1988, Temple University Press), *Employee Participation and Labor Law in the American Workplace* (with Ray Hogler; 1993, Greenwood), and *This Land is Our Land: Newcomers and Established Residents in Miami* (with Alex Stepick; forthcoming, University of California Press), and the coeditor of *Miami Now: Immigration, Ethnicity and Social Change* (1992, University of Florida Press), and *Newcomers in the Workplace: Immigrants and the Restructuring of the US Economy* (1998, Temple University Press). He has also published broadly on ethnic relations and Cuban-Americans in Miami. His current work focuses on the impact of immigration and ethnic diversity on the labor movement in Miami.

Index

THE *Antipode* BOOK SERIES

Series Editors:
Noel Castree, Jamie Peck and Jane Wills

Antipode: A Radical Journal of Geography remains the only journal to offer a radical-Marxist/ socialist/ anarchist/ feminist/ sexual liberationist-analysis of geographical issues and whose intent is to contribute to the praxis of a new and better society.

As it enters its fourth decade, *Antipode* is a strong, vigorous and respected journal with a distinctive place in geography. Part of this distinctiveness lies in combining *Antipode's* long-held core objectives in progressive political change with initiatives designed to stretch the journal's boundaries and keep it abreast of new developments in radical geographical scholarship. This is not simply a question of identifying innovative or novel radical research and ensuring that *Antipode* becomes its natural home. More than this, the journal's strong reputation and the current vibrancy of Left scholarship in human geography means that it is an opportune moment to extend the reach and remit of *Antipode* with a book series. With a unique identity in the field of geography publishing, *the Antipode book series* will extend boundaries and visions of radical scholarship within geography.

For more information please contact Dr Noel Castree, Coordinating Editor, School of Geography, University of Manchester, Manchester, M13 9PL, UK, **email noel.castree@man.ac.uk**

108 Cowley Road, Oxford OX4 1JF, UK
350 Main Street, Malden, MA 02148, USA

 BLACKWELL *Publishers*

w w w . b l a c k w e l l p u b . c o m